THE HOME BOOK

P
by
re
Li
b

MURDOCH BOOKS

Contents

The green home

A green house is also a healthy house. When you decide to make your home 'green', you are making a decision that affects not only your household but also the environment. 'Going green' means making your house as energy efficient as possible, treating all resources as precious rather than something to be thoughtlessly squandered, thus reducing your impact on our fragile planet.

Saving energy makes sense

Many of the principles of an ecologically sound house also make economical sense. Building a house from scratch allows you to situate, orient and shelter the building to make the best of renewable sources of energy. Ideally, living spaces should face north in the southern hemisphere (and south in the northern hemisphere) to take greatest advantage of the sun for light and warmth in both summer and winter, so an energy-efficient house should also be a naturally comfortable one. If you are renovating or extending an existing house, consult an environmental architect to discuss your options for a low-energy design.

THE ENVIRONMENTALLY FRIENDLY GARDEN

Efforts to reduce your home's impact on the environment are particularly rewarding in the garden. There are many ways to reduce the amount of water you use, and kitchen scraps and other biodegradable household waste can be composted and returned to your soil. With a little extra care and observation you can grow an abundant, healthy garden without relying on pesticides and herbicides.

A carefully planned garden is an enticing haven for its inhabitants as well as environmentally friendly.

▶ Shrubs around the house will have a cooling effect on your home, as plants don't absorb and retain heat as much as concrete.

▶ Trees provide shade, act as a windbreak and filter noise and air.

▶ Deciduous trees near north-facing windows in the southern hemisphere, and south-facing windows in the northern hemisphere, allow the maximum amount of sun in winter when the branches are bare; in summer they provide shade.

▶ Pergolas and trellises covered in trailing deciduous vines provide shade in summer while allowing light through in winter.

▶ A hedge of native shrubs between the house and road absorb noise and pollution as well as attract native birds to the garden.

▶ A compost heap and a worm farm recycle biodegradable household waste and garden clippings into a natural fertiliser and mulch that can be put back into the garden.

▶ Mulch used on garden beds maximises water retention and suppresses weeds.

▶ A rainwater tank augments the local water supply.

In a hot climate
Paint the exterior of your house with light-coloured paint to help reflect unwanted radiant heat.

▶ Grey water is channelled onto the lawn rather than wasted.

▶ A fixed watering system delivers water directly to where it is needed without wasteful run-off.

▶ A small kitchen garden provides an abundant supply of fresh herbs, citrus and salad vegetables.

▶ Companion planting helps deter pests, avoiding the potentially harmful use of chemicals.

Saving water and energy

Conserving water not only takes the strain off your local supplier but also reduces pollution, as processing water requires energy, which in turn creates pollution. Saving water can also save you money as, increasingly, local suppliers are charging for the amount of water a household uses.

Solar energy

Install a solar or energy-efficient hot water heater. Since water heating accounts for up to 50 per cent of a home's energy use, installing a solar heater saves in energy bills as well as pollution.

Sun-powered electricity, harnessed by solar panels on the roof, can run all your house's appliances as well as heat water for the bathroom and kitchen. In a solar hot water heater, the sun directly heats up water in small pipes, which is stored in a tank for later use, usually in conjunction with a gas or electrical heater to boost the temperature of the water. Photovoltaic cells on the roof convert the sun's energy to electricity, which can be diverted to the fridge, sound system and washing machine. In some systems, surplus electricity is sent to the main electricity grid.

BATHROOM

The bathroom is the scene of many a water wastage crime — taps left on, long showers, deep baths, litres or gallons of water on its way to the sewage treatment plant every time you flush the toilet. Whether you think this matters or not may depend on the source of your water — when it just keeps on coming out of the tap, you may not give it a second thought until the water bill arrives, but when you rely on a rainwater tank, for instance, the inconvenience of running out may motivate you to be more careful about your water usage.

Water-efficient showers

The shower is the largest user of household hot water and accounts for roughly 20 per cent of the greenhouse pollution in the average home, but there are ways to cut your water consumption.

▶ *Fit a low-flow shower rose. These use 7–12 litres (1½–2½ gallons) a minute of water, compared with up to 20 litres (4½ gallons) a minute with a standard shower rose. Alternatively, fit your current shower rose with a flow restriction disc (a plastic insert).*

▶ *Take shorter showers. Cutting your shower time from 10 minutes to 5 could save as much as 27,000 litres (5939 gallons) of water a year. And if you cut down from a 5 minute daily shower to a 3 minute one, you could save as much as 40 litres (8¾ gallons) of water per shower.*

Turn it off
To save water, don't leave the tap running while you brush your teeth — turn it on and off as needed.

TOILET TRICKS

Up to one-third of water used in the home is flushed down the toilet — cisterns commonly contain 3–11 litres (½–2½ gallons) of water.

▶ Save water by fitting a dual flush to your toilet cistern. New models use 6 litres (1⅓ gallons) for a full flush, and 3 litres (½ gallons) for a half flush.

▶ For a single-flush toilet, reduce the flushing volume by placing an old juice container full of water, or even a brick, in the cistern.

Improve your ventilation

There are several measures you can take to improve the ventilation in your home.

▶ *Fit extractors, also called exhaust fans, in the bathroom and kitchen. Exhaust fans need to be discharged to the outside air and not to an enclosed garage, where they can cause condensation, mould and rot. They are useful in wet rooms such as bathrooms as well as in garages and workshops, where they can remove fumes.*

▶ *Install an overrun timer on the extractor fan in very steamy bathrooms.*

▶ *Fit air grilles, also known as trickle ventilators, into the window frames of living rooms and bedrooms.*

▶ *Maintain air-conditioning systems, especially filters.*

LAUNDRY

▶ Washing clothes and household linen in mainly cold water reduces both heating costs and energy consumption.

▶ Pre-soaking heavily soiled or stained garments minimises the need to use hot water and harsh chemicals.

▶ Full loads or half-load settings waste less water and detergent, and the fast spin setting reduces the drying time.

▶ Using concentrated detergents reduces the amount of chemicals released into the environment, and the correct dosage cuts out waste. Non-biological powder can be used if a household member has sensitive skin.

▶ Peg out the washing rather than using your dryer — the sun and wind are free.

▶ Using a range of natural stain removers keeps clothes looking good and cuts down on dry-cleaning costs.

Water from heaven

A sophisticated rainwater collecting system could work like this.

▶ *Rain falls on the roof and enters covered guttering, which keeps out leaves and other solid matter.*

▶ *Water flows from the downpipe through another type of mesh, which acts as a filter to keep out any leaves that somehow entered the gutter.*

▶ *The first 10 or so litres (2½ gallons) of collected rain wash straight to the garden, and only after the roof has had a good clean is water diverted to another filtering device, called a sump, and then to the rainwater tank.*

▶ *A pump attached to the rainwater tank allows you to use water from the tank for household appliances such as washing machines and dishwashers that require minimum water pressure in order to operate.*

▶ *Regular testing of the collected water indicates how suitable it is for drinking. Filters can also be fitted to taps to eliminate any lead in the water that may be present in the rainwater or leached from piping in the house.*

APPLIANCES

Choose energy-efficient appliances when buying new ones. Many countries have star ratings to make the choice easier. Top-rated fridges, freezers, dishwashers, washing machines, dryers and air-conditioners are much less polluting and also cheaper to run.

Use appliances only when you really need them — for example, use a broom rather than a motorised leaf blower in the garden.

FRIDGE AND FREEZER

▶ Locate the fridge in a cool spot — neither in the sun nor next to the oven.

▶ Ensure good air circulation around the coils and dust them regularly.

▶ Keep the fridge door seals clean and in good condition. (To test your seal, try closing the door on a sheet of paper. If you can pull it out easily, the seal is not working properly.)

▶ Don't leave the fridge door open unnecessarily. For every minute it's open, it takes 3 minutes to cool down again.

▶ Always turn off your fridge and leave the door ajar when you go on holiday.

▶ Defrost your freezer every 3 months to prolong its life and ensure it runs at maximum efficiency.

▶ Run the fridge between 3°C and 5°C (37.4°F and 41°F). Freezers should run at a temperature of between −15°C and −18°C (5°F and 0.4°F). Every degree lower costs 5 per cent more in running costs and greenhouse gas pollution.

▶ Cut down the chances of ice forming inside the fridge by covering all containers containing liquids.

DISHWASHER

▶ Choose a dishwasher that allows you to eliminate the heated drying cycle and dry by air instead, or turn your machine off before that phase.

▶ Save water by using the dishwasher's rinse and hold function instead of rinsing dishes before you load them into the machine.

▶ Wash only full loads in the dishwasher.

▶ Run the dishwasher at its lower temperature settings.

▶ Use a dishwasher detergent with low environmental impact. Alternatively, replace up to 50 per cent of a standard detergent with washing soda.

COOKTOP AND OVEN

▶ Match the size of pots to the size of a hot plate or burner — turn down the burner if flames are licking the side of the pan.

▶ When boiling or steaming, use the minimum amount of water.

▶ If possible, cook more than one item in the oven simultaneously.

▶ Leave the oven door shut. When you open the oven door, the temperature can drop by as much as 15°C (59°F). It takes more energy to restore the correct temperature.

Microwaves
Microwave ovens use less energy than conventional ovens. Fan-forced ovens use less than conventional ones, but more than microwave ovens.

LIGHTING

Choosing lighting is very much a personal decision, but bear in mind that for a living or family room, which serves many functons, you'll need to address lots of different lighting requirements.

▶ Natural light is best, whether it's from windows, skylights or light tubes (small, highly efficient skylights). Keeping these clean allows more light to enter your home.

▶ Make the most of reflected light — pale-coloured ceilings, walls and furnishings bounce light around rooms, making the best use of both daylight and artificial light. To spread light over large areas, use light-coloured shades, light tubes, skylights and diffusers over lights.

▶ Locate lights where you need them, and use spot lights for reading and sewing.

ENERGY-SAVING TIPS

▶ Switch off lights when they are not in use.

▶ A single, high-wattage bulb is much more efficient than a cluster of lower ones.

▶ Fluorescent lighting is the most efficient.

▶ Replace your most frequently used light bulbs with compact fluorescents — each bulb uses about a quarter of the electricity needed for a standard bulb and will prevent the emission of half a tonne or ton of greenhouse pollution over the life of the bulb. If you fit all your lamps and lights with energy-efficient bulbs, you could reduce your lighting costs by 80 per cent.

AIR-CONDITIONING

▶ In hot weather, shade all windows rather than turn on the air-conditioning. Windows are a main entry point for heat and light — highly desirable in winter, but uncomfortable and even oppressive in summer. Consider ways of shading windows in the summertime — for example, with awnings and deciduous trees.

▶ If you live in a hot climate, open up the house at night when the air is cooler.

HEATING

▶ To save on heating and cooling bills as well as the pollution these processes produce, insulate your home.

▶ Wear adequate clothing when the weather is cool — sometimes wearing a cardigan or jumper means you don't need to turn on the heater.

▶ Don't attempt to heat the entire house to the same temperature — keep one or two rooms cosy by shutting the doors to the rest of the house.

▶ Weatherproofing the house helps keep out cold draughts and rain. Apply weather strips to external doors; seal gaps under skirting boards, around the edge of window frames and under windowsills; check the ceiling for gaps where pipes leave roof spaces; and fill the cavity of outside walls with insulation in order to stop unwanted air leakage.

Turn it off!
Turn off microwaves, TVs, VCRs, DVD players, set-top boxes, computers and sound systems at the power point — they use power even when they are not operating.

▶ If you live in a climate with cool winters, consider ways of adding thermal mass to your home. Thermal mass describes heavy building materials such as brick, stone or thick ceramic tiles that are slow to heat and slow to cool. In the winter they warm up in the day and continue to radiate heat in the evening, while in summer they protect against excessive heat, especially when shaded. New brick, tile or concrete flooring is an obvious way of adapting an existing home to include greater thermal mass.

Recycling ideas

You can recycle a great deal of the packaging that comes home with the shopping.

▶ Use jars as airtight containers for spices and grains.

▶ Reuse plastic shopping bags for lining bins, especially bathroom ones, wrapping up disposable nappies, holding wet swimming gear — and shopping.

▶ Encourage young children to build a play supermarket with cereal packets, toothpaste and tea boxes, egg cartons and empty plastic bottles.

▶ Collect bottle corks to use as kindling, but take care not to use plastic ones.

▶ Use cardboard boxes for storage. Turn the flaps inside the box and fix them down with sticky tape for extra strength. Decorate the box by covering it in wrapping paper. They are also welcome — if temporary — toys for children, who can turn them into houses, boats and rockets.

▶ Convert egg cartons into seed-propagation trays. The whole cup can be planted in the garden at the appropriate time — just cut out the bottom.

Blanket stitch
When the edges of a blanket have frayed but the blanket itself still has life, trim any loose threads and use a thick woollen yarn to blanket stitch each side.

Bathroom recycling

▶ *Cut hand towels and face washers from old towels and spruce them up with cheerful borders.*

▶ *Use old toothbrushes for cleaning jobs as well as for hobbies such as ceramics.*

▶ *Recycle chipped but attractive mugs into tooth mugs but wash them regularly to avoid bacterial growth.*

▶ *Wash out a plastic bottle that has been used for softdrink or washing-up liquid and give it to the children to use as a bath toy — they'll have fun filling it up and pouring it out.*

Indoors

Housekeeping is about so much more than cleaning a house. Until the 15th century, cleaning was a peripheral activity to the central tasks of preparing food, gathering fuel, keeping the house warm and carrying water, but these days it's a much more complex business that involves caring for a diverse range of personal belongings, furniture, fittings, flooring and appliances.

Cleaning your home

In the quest for a clean and fragrant home, many of us regularly use a cocktail of expensive chemicals, but there's a small arsenal of safe, natural ingredients and techniques that are much cheaper and, more importantly, also safe for the environment.

Allergies and dust mites

Allergies can cause a range of symptoms from the irritating — a runny nose or mild rash — to the life-threatening, such as a severe asthma attack. Living with an allergy like asthma is an unfortunate reality for many children and adults. What's more, the incidence of these problems is rising sharply, and doctors cannot say why.

While some allergies, such as hay fever, tend to be more severe outside the house, your home can also harbour allergy triggers, or allergens. The main triggers around the house are dust mites, moulds, pollen spores and particles of skin and saliva from pets. These are all capable of triggering a range of allergy symptoms, especially ones involving the respiratory tract. All these triggers can also be found in household dust.

Microscopic in size, house dust mites proliferate in warm, humid, dusty conditions, eating the skin flakes that humans shed constantly. They love soft furnishings, such as mattresses, pillows and soft carpets. Good ventilation and moisture-reducing practices, such as fans in the bathroom and kitchen, help keep populations down.

DUST TRAPS

If family members suffer dust-related allergies, avoid these dust traps.

▶ Padded headboards and other types of upholstered furniture.

▶ Clutter and ornaments, unless they are behind glass.

▶ Books on open shelves.

▶ Heavy curtains — blinds, including roller blinds, are a better option, and vertical venetian blinds collect less dust than horizontal ones. If you do have curtains, keep them dust-free by regularly vacuuming them or, if possible, wash them every 3 months at 56°C (132.8°F) or above.

▶ Forced heating systems — vent coverings can help trap dust and prevent it from circulating in the house.

▶ Carpets — tightly woven short-pile carpets are less dusty than long, loose weaves, but hard flooring, such as timber or tile, is even better. If you choose carpet, vacuum it thoroughly every week.

▶ Cracks between floorboards — seal cracks to prevent dust blowing up from the space beneath.

▶ Cleaning the bedroom in the evening — clean earlier in the day, as cleaning can stir up dust in the air that takes a while to settle.

DECLARE WAR ON DUST

▶ Regularly vacuum under the bed, sofas and other pieces of furniture. To make cleaning easier, choose easy-to-move pieces with a minimum of detailing.

▶ Damp-dust furniture and ornaments, and keep the tops of tall furniture free of dust.

▶ Keep the doors and drawers of wardrobes and chests closed.

IN THE BEDROOM

Beds are breeding grounds for household dust mites. If someone in your household is sensitive to mites, you may find that respiratory problems or even eczema rashes worsen at night. These measures might help ease the symptoms.

BEDCLOTHES

▶ Wrap bedding stored in divan drawers in breathable plastic bags to prevent dust mite droppings falling on them.

▶ Launder bedding frequently to reduce dust and kill dust mites. Wash sheets, pillowcases and doona (duvet) covers weekly in hot water (56°C/132.8°F or above). If you prefer not to wash in hot water — perhaps for environmental reasons — or have bed linen that cannot be washed in hot water, add a mite-killing chemical such as benzyl benzoate to the wash and give the linen an extra rinse.

▶ In warm and hot climates, hang bedding in the sun for a few hours.

▶ Carry out steam treatments every 3 months or so. To be effective, the steam must be sufficiently hot for long enough not only to kill the dust mites but also to denature the allergen. Vacuum the dead mites and allergen afterwards.

▶ Doonas (duvets) are a better allergy option than blankets, as you can put them in an anti-mite cover.

Mighty numbers of mites
A double bed mattress can support a population of up to two million house dust mites. In the right conditions, a new mattress's mite population can reach this figure in 3 months!

Freeze out the mites
To kill mites, place bedclothes, soft toys and favourite blankets in a chest freezer for a few hours, or overnight. You can then wash them out in warm, hot or cold water (or vacuum them if they're not washable).

Specialised anti-mite bedding

Barrier covers, designed to prevent you coming into contact with the mite allergen, can be fitted over mattresses and pillows. The old-fashioned ones are made of plastic, which can make a night's sleep damp and uncomfortable. Modern covers, made from a soft, microporous material, allow water and air to penetrate.

Defeating damp

A damp house is not a healthy one — it's all too easy for moulds and other fungus, bacteria and mites (see page 18) to proliferate. The first step in fixing damp is to identify the source of the problem.

▶ Rising damp is water that rises up the walls from the ground. It is usually prevented by a damp course, which may need fixing or replacing after a number of years. In old houses they may be non-existent or disintegrated to the point where they are useless.

▶ Penetrating damp occurs when water comes through a wall after heavy rain, possibly because of a leaking downpipe or gutter, or an entry point above the damp course. Rust or blockages might be causing water to flood or leak into vulnerable areas.

▶ Condensation forms when water condenses from humid air and settles on cold surfaces such as windows or cold spots in poorly heated and badly ventilated rooms. Simple measures such as wiping away condensation and opening up windows can help.

▶ Improve insulation. This helps to eliminate cold spots, which in turn reduces condensation and associated mould growth.

▶ Look out for mould growth sites, such as old food and pot plants.

Mould

There are more mould spores in the air than any other biological particle — record counts are as high as 160,000 spores for every cubic metre (35 cubic inches) of air, compared to record counts of 2800 pollen particles per cubic metre (35 cubic inches).

Floors

Floors need to be tough and easy to clean, but the ideal choice really depends on your circumstances. A single person may find that taking out the vacuum cleaner once a week is enough to keep a carpet clean and looking good, while a mother of three young children may curse a carpet but find a timber floor that can be quickly wiped or swept clean a blessing. The question of comfort is also subjective, depending on climate and personal preference.

CLEANING TIMBER FLOORS

Sweep timber floors regularly, mop spills with a dry cloth or paper towel, and remove sticky patches with a damp cloth. The basic rule of thumb is sweep first, mop second. Water alone will remove light soiling and is fine for frequent cleaning.

For a tougher clean, consider the type of finish or sealer on your timber floor, as it will determine which treatment you use.

OIL-FINISHED TIMBER

Sweep, then clean an oil-finished timber floor with a damp mop. Wash with 1 part methylated spirits to 10 parts hot water. Mop spills with a dry, clean cloth and remove sticky foods with a warm damp cloth. To remove sticky food from an oil-finished timber floor, sprinkle an absorbent powder (talcum powder or flour) over it, then wipe with a warm, damp cloth.

If you wish to polish an oil-finished floor, use a liquid acrylic and spirit-based wax polish rather than an oil-impregnated mop.

POLYURETHANE FINISH

Mop sparingly with hot water alone or a mild soap or detergent solution, and don't let the wood become too wet. Once a month, mop with a mixture of 1 part methylated spirits to 10 parts water, then rinse with a clean, damp mop. Buff with a dry cloth tied to the end of a broom. A timber floor finished with polyurethane needs sanding and resurfacing every few years.

WAX POLISH FINISH

Brush off dust and debris regularly, and wipe over with a damp mop or cloth to remove sticky and oily stains. Polish and clean with liquid acrylic and spirit-based wax polish. To avoid a build-up of polish (which will eventually have to be removed), apply the polish sparingly only where it is needed, such as in heavy traffic areas, and don't apply too much.

REMOVING STAINS AND SCRATCHES

Stains on timber floors fall into two main categories — floors with hard finishes and those without. Hard finishes include polyurethane and other varnishes while the latter group includes natural finish, wax finish and penetrating stains.

RESTORING TIMBER FLOORS

DAMAGE	WITHOUT HARD FINISH	WITH HARD FINISH
Scratch	Wax	Touch-up kit (available from a flooring retailer)
Food	Clean up with a damp cloth, rub dry, then wax	Specialised cleaner
Chewing gum, crayon and candle wax	Apply ice, or iron over an ink blotter. Use a solvent-based wax to loosen	Ice or specialised cleaner
Oil and greasy stains	Saturate cotton with hydrogen peroxide and cover stain with cotton, then saturate second piece of cotton with ammonia and place over the first. Repeat. Dry and buff	Specialised cleaner
Cigarette burn	Shallow burn: rub with fine sandpaper or steel wool moistened with wax. Deep burn: remove charred parts, rub with fine sandpaper, stain, wax and buff	Shallow burn: touch-up kit comprising stain and refinish. Deep burn: replace individual planks
Water mark (and white spots)	Fine steel wool and wax, then fine sandpaper. Clean with fine wool and mineral spirits. Dry, stain, wax and buff	Not usually a problem
Mould on timber	Wood cleaner	Specialised cleaner and a scrub pad if stubborn
Heel marks	Rub wax in with fine steel wool and hand buff to return shine	Rub wax in with fine steel and hand buff to return shine

Check the finish

If you're not sure which finish you're dealing with, drop a little water on the flooring. A white mark indicates it doesn't have a hard finish. The mark will disappear when the water dries.

Removing stains from lino and vinyl floors

Quick action is always best — wipe, mop and scoop spills as soon as possible. Avoid using undiluted bleach, as it may cause yellowing, and abrasive cleaners, which can scratch or dull the surface. If you are left with stains, try the following.

▶ *Wipe the stain with an all-purpose cleaner.*

▶ *Try rubbing it with a pencil eraser.*

▶ *Use lemon and salt for rust stains — cut a lemon in half, sprinkle it with plenty of salt and rub it on the stain. Using a rag or sponge, rinse it with water.*

▶ *For thick grease or tar, try mineral spirits, but use it with caution, testing on a tiny portion first, as the spirits can take off the shine. Another way to remove tar is to cool it with an ice cube, and when it is brittle, pry it off with a spatula.*

▶ *Make up a bleach solution of 2 cups (16 fl oz) water and ¼ cup (2 fl oz) chlorine bleach and use it to remove many stains, including alcoholic drinks, coffee, tomato sauce and mustard. Remove organic stains such as blood, grass stains and pet accidents with this solution, or try lemon juice, or lemon and salt.*

CARPET

To protect your carpets, use doormats, preferably one inside and one outside each entrance. This removes a great deal of dirt that would otherwise get walked onto the carpet. Always wipe your feet and train others to do so. Some families habitually remove their shoes on entering their home, and this keeps floors cleaner as well as looking good for longer.

In a dirty carpet, the soil embedded at the base of the tufts grinds away at the fibre, gradually wearing it down, so vacuuming regularly prolongs its life. Carpet sweepers remove crumbs and other surface dirt, but vacuum cleaners pull out the dirt from deeper down. When tougher action is required, there are several options to choose from — spot treatments, carpet shampoos and cleaners, and carpet-cleaning machines.

To keep your carpet looking its best, manufacturers recommend regular care.

1. Vacuum at least once a week, more often in heavy traffic areas.
2. Get working on spills and stains immediately.
3. Wet clean every 1 to 2 years or as required.
4. Place castors and protectors under furniture legs to help prevent the pile from being crushed.

High heel damage on floors
The Hoover Book of Home Management, 1963, has the following advice about minimising damage wrought by the then fashionable stiletto-heeled shoe: 'A tactful way with visitors is to have a supply of tiny plastic heel guards at the ready for those sharp high heels...'. Consider this: a 57 kg (125 lb) woman in high heels exerts 900 kg per 6.5 cm² (2000 lb per 1 inch²) at each step.

Wipe your feet
When you come indoors, it takes a minimum of eight steps to remove dirt from the soles of your shoes.

VALUABLE OR DELICATE RUGS AND CARPETS

Delicate rugs and carpets, such as antique ones, need special treatment. Do not use valuable carpets in areas of high traffic or in doorways where they are likely to receive harsher, dirtier treatment.

▶ Vacuum delicate rugs with reduced suction, using the gentlest power on your cleaner. If you don't have a vacuum cleaner with adjustable power, adjust it yourself by placing a piece of clean plastic flyscreen on the nozzle.

▶ Vacuum slowly in the direction of the pile.

▶ Avoid wet cleaning.

▶ For serious spillages, blot and gently scrape as much as you can, then wrap the carpet tightly in plastic to avoid drying the stain. This helps prevent it setting. Whisk it off to a professional cleaner.

▶ When storing a valuable carpet or rug, line it with acid-free paper, then roll it up pile-side out to prevent wearing. Store it in an acid-free box.

ON THE SPOT

You can treat most stains on carpet in one of three ways, or a combination. Familiarise yourself with each of the following three methods, then use the list opposite to find and treat your particular problem.

▶ **Treatment A** Mild detergent (1 teaspoon neutral detergent — that is, no alkalis or bleaches — in 1 cup lukewarm water).

▶ **Treatment B** Vinegar solution (⅓ cup white vinegar in ⅔ cup water).

▶ **Treatment C** Ammonia solution (1 tablespoon household ammonia in ½ cup water).

STAIN REMOVAL

STAIN	REMOVAL METHOD
Ballpoint pen	Sponge with a dry cloth and methylated spirits (denatured alcohol), or a small amount of dry-cleaning solvent, before sponging with Treatment A. Finally sponge with clean water
Beer	Sponge with Treatment A, followed by Treatment B, before sponging with clean water
Blood	Blot with cloth or paper towel. Use cold water, working it into the pile. Blot again and repeat as necessary. Small amounts of blood should come out fairly easily. If this doesn't work, try the following steps: sponge with Treatment A, then Treatment C, then sponge rinse with cold water
Butter	Sponge with a small amount of dry-cleaning solvent, then sponge with Treatment A
Chewing gum	As for butter
Chocolate	Sponge with Treatment A, followed by Treatment C. Repeat with Treatment A before sponging with clean water
Coffee	As for beer
Cola drinks	As for beer
Crayons	Sponge sparingly with dry-cleaning solvent, followed by Treatment A. Finally, sponge with clean water
Dirt	As for chocolate
Egg (raw)	As for beer
Food	Remove excess then wipe with cloth wrung out with Treatment A
Food colouring	Professional carpet cleaner
Fruit juice and fruit	As for beer
Furniture polish	As for crayons
Glue (white craft)	Sponge with Treatment A, followed by Treatment B, then Treatment A again. Finally, sponge with clean water

STAIN	REMOVAL METHOD
Gravy	As for crayons
Ice cream	As for chocolate
Ink	Blot excess. Natural inks such as Indian ink are very difficult to remove
Iodine	Sponge with Treatment A, followed by Treatment C, then Treatment B and finally Treatment A again. Finish with clean water
Lily pollen	If dry, vacuum excess. If wet, soak up with dry cloths
Milk	As for chocolate
Mud	Let it dry completely first, then brush with a stiff brush to break it up. Finally, vacuum
Nail polish	Use non-oily polish remover on a cloth for small stains, then sponge with Treatment A. Finally, sponge with clean water
Paint	While still wet, emulsion can be rinsed off with water. If dry, break up the paint with the edge of a blunt knife and then vacuum. To remove gloss, use sparing amounts of mineral spirits but be warned — it can remove colour from carpet. When dry, for a superficial stain, try shaving off the paint with a sharp knife — only try it if you have a steady hand, otherwise you may risk holes
Pen (marker)	As for crayons
Red wine	Blot with paper towel or a dry cloth. Sprinkle with white wine, which is acidic, to neutralise the stain, or water, and blot again. Remove the remaining stain with a clean cloth and methylated spirits (denatured alcohol)
Rust	Put lemon juice on the mark, leave for 1 minute and rinse with water. Repeat if necessary
Shoe polish	As for crayons
Soft drinks	As for glue (white craft)
Soot	As soot is oily, do not attempt to remove it with water and detergents. Vacuum as much away as possible and tackle small stains with a solvent cleaner

STAIN	REMOVAL METHOD
Soy sauce	Sponge with Treatment A, followed by Treatment C, before sponging with clean water
Tar or oil	Remove with a spirit-based cleaner
Tea	Using a paper towel or dry absorbent cloth, blot as much as possible. Add a little water and soak up again until the colour is gone. You can also safely try Treatment A or methylated spirits (denatured alcohol) dabbed on the residue. Alternatively, try sponging with Treatment A, followed by Treatment B, before sponging with clean water
Urine (dried stain)	Sponge with Treatment A, followed by Treatment B, then Treatment C, then Treatment A again. To finish, sponge with clean water
Urine (wet stain)	Blot, then sponge with clean water. Sponge with Treatment C, followed by Treatment A. Finally sponge with clean water
Vomit	Scoop and blot as much as possible
Water stains	Seek professional help
Wax	As for crayons
White wine	As for glue (white craft)

Walls and ceilings

▶ Dust occasionally and remove cobwebs from the ceiling with a soft attachment on the vacuum cleaner, a soft cloth tied onto a broom brush or a dry cloth. Start at the ceiling and work down.

▶ Regularly spot clean all the hot spots — scuffs at door entrances, finger marks near light fittings and door handles, and sticky finger marks at child height on the wall. Try (in order of most gentle method first): a damp, clean, colourfast cloth; the same cloth dipped in a mild dishwashing detergent solution; or a clean cloth with a cream cleanser or bicarbonate of soda.

▶ Washing the ceiling is a messy job, involving buckets of water and drips, but a good clean can be almost as revitalising as painting, especially if the ceiling has been discoloured by cooking or mould.

WALLPAPER

Washable wallpapers are coated with a thin, transparent vinyl layer, which makes them easier to clean and more difficult to stain. Dust them regularly with a soft brush, and wipe over with a damp cloth dipped in mild detergent and warm water. Rinse with a damp cloth and a bucket of clean warm water.

Non-washable wallpaper requires gentler treatment. Dust regularly with a soft brush or cloth. Spot-clean by dabbing with powdered borax and brushing out. Another homemade remedy is to rub gently with a piece of bread rolled into a ball, or a soft rubber eraser.

The young artist

Artistic toddlers are usually eager to exhibit their talents on your floors and walls; some even like to sign their work with their initials! Swift action may save the day. Gentle rubbing with a little paste of bicarbonate of soda (baking soda) and water (see page 34) should remove crayon, pencil, ink and marker pen, but you may also need to try these methods.

Wax crayon

▶ *For hard, non-porous surfaces such as glass, use mineral spirits or powdered detergent on a soft cloth and rub gently, using small, circular strokes.*

▶ *For wooden furniture, use a strong all-purpose cleaner and soft cloth.*

▶ *For varnished and painted woodwork, brick and stone, brush with a nail brush dipped in dry-cleaning solution. Then mix the solution with powdered detergent and rub again. Rinse with clean water and dry.*

Paint

For varnished and painted woodwork and painted walls, try dabbing with a damp cloth. If this fails, try powdered detergent and a damp cloth, but be careful of glossy surfaces, as they may become scratched or dull. Finally, try nail polish remover.

Chalk

▶ *On wallpaper, use a damp cloth and household soap. If that doesn't work, rub the marks with an eraser.*

▶ *On brick or stone, brush with a stiff brush, then scrub with a paste cleaner or powdered detergent and water.*

▶ *On vinyl flooring or desk surfaces, use a liquid cleaner.*

Furniture

Your living room furniture is an investment. Treat it with care and respect, and it will remain in optimum condition for as long as possible.

CARING FOR WOODEN FURNITURE

▶ **Lacquered furniture** Lightly dampen a duster with a fine water mist spray, then dry with a second cloth. Buff with a soft cloth. While it is not necessary to polish lacquered furniture, an occasional application brings a shine to a dull surface.

▶ **Waxed furniture** Regular waxing, once or twice a year, helps protect it from heat and moisture. Although it's harder to apply, solid wax produces better results.

REMOVING STAINS AND MARKS

When your wooden furniture suffers the inevitable mishap, try the mildest methods first, and repeat gentle methods rather than use one harsh treatment. Before resorting to a commercial product, try some home remedies first, always working in a well-ventilated place.

▶ **Greasy finger marks** Dip the cloth in a mild solution of soap flakes, then wring so it is slightly damp. Wipe the marks with the cloth, and dry thoroughly.

▶ **Heat marks** White marks may indicate a damaged finish. Rub it briskly with a cream metal polish in the same direction as the grain, then follow with a wax polish. Do small sections at a time, wiping the polish away as you go.

▶ **Rough patch** Smooth it with very fine steel wool dipped in liquid wax polish. On veneered surfaces, proceed with great caution.

▶ **Water marks** Remove marks left by wet glasses as you would heat marks (see above).

▶ **Scratches** Mask light scratches with a similar coloured wax crayon or shoe polish. Leave it to be absorbed before buffing briskly.

▶ **Alcohol spots** Burnish with a cream metal finish, rubbing briskly in the direction of the grain. Follow with a light wax polish.

FABRIC UPHOLSTERY

All upholstery benefits from a regular vacuum to remove dust and other debris that finds its way into crevices. Preventative measures, some more fashionable than others, include the following.

▶ Soil and stain repellents work by making spills bead up rather than soak into the fabric.

▶ Antimacassars — typically small lacy circles or rectangles — protect the backs of sofas and chairs from hair grease.

▶ Throws are particularly handy for protecting upholstery from the rigours of pets and young children.

▶ Loose covers on sofas and lounge chairs can be laundered.

▶ Arm guards and back guards protect the most vulnerable spots on chairs and sofas.

Shampooing fabric upholstery

Like carpet fibres, upholstery fabric is generally worn away by dirt. Regular shampooing — perhaps once a year or even once every 2 years — helps to keep sofas and similar items of furniture clean.

Loose covers are usually designed to be washed, but check the care labels. If in doubt about shrinkage, wash the covers in cold water and replace them on the furniture when they are still slightly damp.

Hand-shampooing is good for delicate, dirty upholstery. Use a commercial shampoo and follow the manufacturer's instructions. In general, it's best to use a soft brush dipped in the foam made by a shampoo. Rinse by wiping the foam off with a well-wrung cloth dipped in clean water. Dry thoroughly, then vacuum.

For furniture with fixed upholstery, you might consider a home steam-extraction machine, which pumps liquid into the fabric and sucks it out again, eliminating the problem of wet seats, arms and cushions, which take forever to dry. Even so, good ventilation will help speed up the drying time.

LEATHER UPHOLSTERY

To spot-clean minor stains, wipe leather upholstery with a little water, taking care not to get the leather too damp. To clean leather upholstery more thoroughly, dust, then use saddle soap or a similar product. Let it dry thoroughly before using the furniture again. If the leather is beginning to crack or seems dry, use a leather conditioner but test in an inconspicuous spot for its effect on colour.

Window treatments

Curtains, blinds and shutters enhance your living area and also make it more energy-efficient, keeping excess heat and harsh light out during summer and helping to prevent heat loss during winter.

CURTAINS

Many types of curtains are washable, especially if you wash them by hand. First, take the curtains outside and shake them to get rid of as much dust as possible. If you're washing new curtains for the first time, soak them overnight in salty water to remove any fabric dressings (finishing treatments). (See also page 96.)

BLINDS

▶ Dust blinds regularly.

▶ To refresh the colour, wipe linen blinds with a cloth wrung out in methylated spirits (denatured alcohol) and vinegar, then wipe with a dry cloth.

▶ To remove stains, rub with a piece of bread.

▶ To wash a dirty roller blind, take it down but keep it rolled up around the roller. Wet the blind and leave it for a few minutes. Give it a bath in warm water and detergent by gradually unrolling the blind and sponging it as you draw it into the bath, but do not dip the spring part. Rinse in the same gradual fashion. Let it drip on the clothesline for a few minutes, then place on a towel on a table and dry from one end to the other with a second towel.

Reviving velvet curtains
Dust makes velvet and plush curtains dull as well as enticing for dust mites. Go over them with a brush of medium stiffness — against the pile for velvet and with the pile for plush — then hang them in the bathroom over a hot bath to revive the pile.

Lampshades

Which cleaning method you use will depend on the material.

▶ **Fabric** Use the vacuum cleaner with the dusting brush attachment, adjusted to low power suction, if possible. Attempt to clean spots with a mild detergent solution, but be careful — you risk making watermarks and/or dissolving the glue that holds the shade together.

▶ **Glass or plastic** Dust regularly. If necessary, wash with a clean cloth dipped in a detergent solution.

▶ **Paper and parchment** Brush often with a feather duster.

▶ **Raffia and straw** Vacuum with the brush attachment.

A clean sweep
An annual chimney sweep removes blockages, preventing poisonous gases from building up in the house. It also removes soot and creosote build-up — if it isn't cleared, it can fuel serious fires.

Fireplaces

If you burn real coal and log fires, make sure your chimneys are regularly swept by a professional who works to an authorised code of practice, otherwise soot will build up and may lead to a chimney fire. Smoky fires can be caused by the material you burn, such as damp logs, or by poor ventilation. Another reason can be the incorrect ratio of distances between the hearth, the chimney opening and the chimney top. This latter problem can only be remedied by a professional, who may raise the hearth, add extra height to the chimney or put a baffle or shield on the front of the hearth.

Cleaning fireplace surrounds

1   Vacuum all loose soot and ash.

2   Rub off as much remaining soot as you can with a dry brush or cloth.

3   Wash the surround with a strong all-purpose cleaner recommended for the surface, whether it is brick, stone or marble. Alternatively, apply a weak solution of ammonia in water with a stiff brush.

4   Wash glass doors as you would any glass, unless the manufacturer's instructions advise otherwise.

The kitchen

The kitchen is the hub of the house. It is also the room where you prepare, and possibly eat, your meals, so it needs to be scrupulously clean at all times.

CLEANING AND MAINTENANCE

Even if you don't care for cleaning any other part of the house, you should always keep the kitchen spotless and follow the rules of hygiene when storing and preparing food.

WORK SURFACES

The rule with cleaning the kitchen is to clean as you go — both before food and after preparation. Most surfaces — including Corian, laminate, marble, slate and tiles — can be cleaned with a cloth dipped in mild detergent and hot water. Some may be lightly scoured, while others may need oil.

> ▶ **Corian** It's a good idea to use a gentle scourer for stains on Corian, which is a blend of natural materials and pure acrylic polymer. Treat stubborn ones with very fine abrasive paper, then polish with a soft cloth.

Make cleaning easier
- *Reduce the likelihood of spills by covering food while cooking in the microwave.*
- *Use splatter guards on hot frying pans.*
- *Don't overfill saucepans.*

▶ **Granite** Wipe granite regularly with a hot cloth. Clean greasy marks with a few drops of household ammonia in water.

▶ **Laminate** Use a few drops of eucalyptus oil to disinfect laminate. For tough marks, use neat detergent, leave for a few minutes, then rinse. Do not scour. Take care with hot saucepans. Although laminate can take heat from pans and cooking utensils, it will become damaged if you leave them to stand.

▶ **Slate** To shine slate, wipe with a few drops of lemon oil, then polish with a soft, dry cloth.

▶ **Tiles** To remove stains from tiles, try rubbing on salt with a cut lemon.

▶ **Sealed wood** Place pots and pans on a tile or board to prevent burns to the bench surface.

▶ **Unsealed wood** Rub with boiled linseed oil and wipe excess off with a soft cloth. Try salt and lemon on stains and scorch marks.

CHOPPING BOARDS

▶ **Plastic** Scrub plastic boards with a small brush with hot water and detergent. Most are also fine in the dishwasher. To kill bacteria, wipe over with a mild solution of household bleach.

▶ **Wood** To protect wooden boards from splitting and warping, rub them with a little vegetable oil. To remove stains, scrub well with a stiff-bristled brush and hot water. Clear food odours by rubbing boards with salt — a natural disinfectant — and cut lemon. Store them where plenty of air can circulate.

Chopping
board hygiene
*The hygienic kitchen needs
two chopping boards —
one for vegetables, one
for meat. If chopping raw
meat, scrub the board
well afterwards.*

Natural cleaner recipes

Why use dangerous chemicals when almost everything you need to keep your kitchen clean — and much less toxic — is probably in your store cupboard?

THE RAW INGREDIENTS

Here's a list of basic ingredients for making all the cleaners you need.

- ▶ Ammonia
- ▶ Bicarbonate of soda (baking soda)
- ▶ Bleach
- ▶ Borax
- ▶ Laundry detergent
- ▶ Washing soda
- ▶ Washing up liquid
- ▶ White vinegar

All-purpose cleaner

> 2 heaped tablespoons bicarbonate of soda
> 1 tablespoon white vinegar

Mix the bicarbonate of soda and white vinegar together and store in an airtight container.

Strong all-purpose cleaner 1

This is a good all-round cleaner for many surfaces and materials, including kitchen appliances, glass and silver. It will also strip floor wax and dissolve resinous matter.

> 4 litres (140 fl oz/16 cups) hot water
> 100 ml (3½ fl oz) household ammonia
> 100 ml (3½ fl oz) white vinegar
> 200 g (7 oz) bicarbonate of soda

Mix the ingredients together and store in a tightly sealed bottle.

Strong all-purpose cleaner 2

This cleaner can be used in kitchens and bathrooms, on floors, tiles, cupboards, appliances, ovens and so on, but not on fibreglass or aluminium.

> 125 ml (4 fl oz/½ cup) washing soda
> 4.5 litres (156 fl oz/18 cups) warm water

Mix the ingredients together and store in a tightly sealed bottle.

Scouring cleaner

> 1 teaspoon borax
> 2 tablespoons white vinegar
> 500 ml (17 fl oz/2 cups) hot water

Combine the ingredients together and pour the mixture into a spray bottle.

Disinfectant

This disinfectant can be used in the kitchen, bathroom and around the house on various surfaces, including marble, plastic, fibreglass, fridges, nursery furniture such as cots and high chairs, plastic mattress covers and ceramic tiles (although you should test first on dark colours or coloured grout).

> 185 ml (6 fl oz/¾ cup) bleach
> 1.5 litres (52 fl oz/6 cups) warm water
> 1 tablespoon powdered laundry detergent

Mix the ingredients together.

Wash the surface and keep it wet for 5 minutes before rinsing and allowing it to dry.

THE KITCHEN SINK

Although these days many households have a dishwasher, the sink is still an essential part of the kitchen. Wipe the sink down each time you wash up, and scrub it at least weekly. If it needs a little more attention, check the following useful tips.

▶ **Acrylic** Remove water marks with white vinegar. Never use an abrasive cleaner such as an abrasive cleansing cream or a scourer on acrylic, as you will risk scratching the surface. Remove scratches with metal polish.

▶ **Corian** Clean as for a Corian work surface (see page 32). To restore colour to a stained sink, fill the sink with a solution of 1 part household bleach to 4 parts water. Leave for half an hour, then drain and rinse.

▶ **Enamel** Do not use bleach or scourers on enamel. Remove stains with borax and a cut lemon, or a paste of bicarbonate of soda and hydrogen peroxide (a gentle bleach). Start with bicarbonate of soda and add just enough hydrogen peroxide to make a paste. Rub, allow to dry, then rinse off.

▶ **Stainless steel** To avoid scratches, don't use abrasive cleaners or scourers. Use neat detergent on stains. For a shiny look, polish with methylated spirits (denatured alcohol) and a dry cloth.

TAPS

To remove caked dirt from kitchen taps, use a toothbrush dipped in detergent or bicarbonate of soda (baking soda). Most taps can be washed in a hot detergent solution or a solution of bicarbonate of soda.

▶ **Brass and copper** Wipe a lacquered finish on brass or copper taps with a damp cloth. Use metal polish on unlacquered surfaces. To remove verdigris or other tarnishes, rub gently with a paste of salt and lemon juice. Alternatively, wipe with household ammonia, rinse and dry with a soft cloth.

▶ **Chrome** Polish chrome taps with a cloth soaked in white vinegar or a weak solution of household ammonia in water.

Unblocking the drain — the natural way

When the water won't drain and you are faced with a sink full of water, try one of these natural drain cleaners, then use a plunger. Place the plunger tightly over the drain hole, push down then pull up rapidly, keeping the plunger over the hole. If your seal is tight, the air and water inside the pipe is forced back and forth, with any luck sloshing and sucking the blockage away. If you're unsuccessful, try a different drain cleaner and leave overnight.

Sodium bicarbonate and vinegar

½–1 cup sodium bicarbonate
250 ml (9 fl oz/1 cup) white vinegar

1   Pour the sodium bicarbonate down the drain, then slowly pour in the white vinegar. The sizzling sound is the reaction between the two.

2   Follow with water and repeat the whole process if necessary.

Ammonia in boiling water

2 teaspoons household ammonia
Kettle of boiling water

1   For moderate blocks, try household ammonia chased with a kettle of boiling water.

2   Use the plunger to loosen the blockage.

Washing soda and boiling water

2 cups washing soda crystals
Kettle of boiling water

Pile the washing soda at the opening of the drain then slowly pour on a kettle of boiling water.

Deodorising garbage bins

Regularly washing your bins with detergent helps to keep the smells at bay. Scrub off hardened dirt with a stiff-bristled brush and rinse with the garden hose. To deter flies, wipe around the top of each bin with citronella or tea-tree oil. Alternatively, soak strips of old sheet in a repellent solution made from 10 drops citronella oil and 3 drops peppermint oil mixed in 1 litre (34 fl oz/4 cups) water. Hang the strips inside the bin.

THE IDIOT'S GUIDE TO WASHING UP

The right tools will ease the daily drudgery of washing up. If you don't have a dishwasher, it's helpful to have a plate rack, draining board, bottle brush, hand mop, wire brush, plastic and metal scouring pads — and lots of clean tea towels.

▶ Before you start, stack dishes and pans in like piles — plates in one pile, glasses grouped together, pans and sticky utensils in another.

▶ Scrape all food scraps into the compost bin. Use a spatula on surfaces that might be damaged by scratching.

▶ Start with very hot water and a squeeze of washing up liquid or cleaning aid of your choice. A plastic bowl inside the sink means you can still tip liquids into the sink while washing up. It's also kinder on crockery and glass.

▶ Wash and rinse glasses first before resting them on a draining rack to dry. Rinse items in a second sink, if you have one, under a slow-running tap (turn it off when you tackle dirty saucepans or shift a new stack into the bowl) or a plastic bowl or bucket placed on a stool near the sink.

▶ Tackle the rest of the washing up in order of cleanliness — cleanest first, dirtiest last.

▶ Change the water when it gets dirtier than the next bowl of dishes!

Kitchen sponges
To freshen and revitalise kitchen sponges, dissolve a generous handful of salt plus 1 tablespoon of washing soda in 1 litre (32 fl oz/4 cups) of warm water. Dunk the cloths and sponges, leave for a couple of minutes, then rinse in cold water and allow to dry.

Basic dishwashing liquid

Use 1 teaspoon to 5 litres (175 fl oz/20 cups) water when washing up, or use 250 ml (9 fl oz/1 cup) per load in a dishwasher. (This won't remove coffee and tea stains.)

> 50 g (1¾ oz) pure soap
> 125 ml (4 fl oz/½ cup) washing soda crystals
> 125 ml (4 fl oz/½ cup) white vinegar
> 1½ teaspoons eucalyptus oil or tea-tree oil
> Few drops lemon or lavender pure essential oil for fragrance
> 5 litres (175 fl oz/20 cups) cold water
> 4.5 litres (158 fl oz/18 cups) hot water

1 Grate the soap into a saucepan and then cover with 1 litre (35 fl oz/ 4 cups) of cold water. Bring to the boil, then add the washing soda and stir until it has completely dissolved.

2 Stir in the eucalyptus oil, vinegar and essential oil.

3 Pour into a bucket, add the hot water, then stir in the remaining cold water.

4 When cool, transfer to smaller containers and label.

Crushing whitener

To whiten enamel-lined pans, finely crush egg shells and rub with a cloth dipped in salt.

POTS AND PANS

▶ Fill pots and pans with hot water as soon as they are emptied.

▶ Wipe out excess grease with newspaper, then wash with a solution of washing soda and hot water. Saucepans that have contained rice, potato and porridge (oatmeal) are better soaked in cold water.

▶ To clean a badly burnt saucepan, pour in a little olive oil, heat gently and leave to stand for 1–2 hours. Pour off the oil into a container, ready to use for the next burnt pan, and wash the pan as usual.

▶ To clean burnt food from a pie dish, dip it in very hot water, then quickly turn it upside down onto a flat surface. This traps steam, which loosens the residue.

▶ To restore a very burnt enamel baking dish, soak it in a mixture of water and strong soap powder. After a couple of hours, pour off the water and rub the dish with a soft cloth.

How you care for pots and pans depends on the material from which they are made.

▶ **Aluminium** To clean stained aluminium saucepans, boil 2 teaspoons of cream of tartar with 4 cups of water. Apple peelings or citrus skin will also clean aluminium saucepans. Simply boil them in the pan with a few cups of water.

▶ **Bakeware** Baking trays and cake pans need to be seasoned like cast iron to prevent them from rusting. Do not scour them, and check the manufacturer's instructions after purchase. After turning out biscuits (cookies) or cakes, fill bakeware with cold water, add a handful of washing soda and let it stand on a warm stove until the crust is loose and can be removed without scratching the surface.

▶ **Cast iron** Season new pans by brushing the bottom of the pan with vegetable oil. Gently heat over a low flame or in the oven for an hour. Remove from the heat and allow it to cool. Pour out the oil and discard, then wipe out the pan with paper towel. After using the pan, wash it in hot water and detergent, then dry. Brush on a little oil before storing.

▶ **Copper** Do not scour. Soak encrusted food in warm water. Clean off poisonous green stains. Clean the outside with a solution of 1 part salt and 2 parts white vinegar, rinse, then dry and polish.

▶ **Glazed earthenware** Soak in hot water and use a plastic scourer to remove food remains.

▶ **Unglazed earthenware** To season before first use, soak in water. Use hot water only, no detergent, to clean. Soak difficult stains but do not scour.

▶ **Enamel** Season as for cast iron. To clean, use a very gentle scouring pad. Bleach discoloured enamelware with a mixture of coarse salt and vinegar.

▶ **Glass** Heatproof glass baking ware and saucepans can go in the dishwasher. Use a plastic scourer when necessary.

▶ **Non-stick finishes** Soak to remove food; never use a scourer, as it will scratch and remove the surface.

▶ **Plastic** Do not scratch by scouring, as the scratches may harbour bacteria. Hand-hot water is fine, but dishwashers may get too hot.

▶ **Stainless steel** Scourers will scratch, but a patina of small scratches may not bother you. Stainless steel is usually dishwasher-safe. To remove calcium deposits, boil water and vinegar together.

GREASY GRILL (BROILER) PANS

When you've scraped off as much grease as you can with a spatula or newspaper, sprinkle with washing soda crystals and pour on boiling water. Leave it to soak for at least 10 minutes, then clean up. The grease and debris should lift off.

DELICATE CHINA

- ▶ When hand-washing heirloom china, place a towel at the bottom of the washing up bowl to help prevent chips and breakages.

- ▶ Check the manufacturer's instructions before placing bone china and porcelain in the dishwasher. The harsh detergents used in dishwashers can spoil some glazes, especially metallic ones.

GILT CHINA

Do not use washing soda or soap powder containing soda on gilt as it may damage it. Use a few drops of borax instead.

GLASS AND CRYSTAL

- ▶ Wash glass water bottles and flower vases with 1 tablespoon vinegar and 1 tablespoon salt in warm water. Stand for several hours, shaking occasionally.

- ▶ Wash very dirty cut glass in warm soapy water to which a few drops of ammonia have been added, and scrub gently with a small brush. (Do not use ammonia on glass decorated with gilt or enamel.)

- ▶ Dip crystal in a solution of 1 part vinegar to 3 parts water. Polish with a dry, lint-free cloth.

CUTLERY

- ▶ **Cutlery stains** Dissolve a little salt in lemon juice. Dip a soft cloth into the solution and rub the cutlery. Rinse in warm water and rub with a chamois.

- ▶ **Bone and wood handles** Stand the metal parts (never the bone) in a jar of hot washing up water, wipe the handles with a hot, damp cloth and dry.

- ▶ **Silver and silver plate** Wash silver cutlery as soon as possible — some foods leave stains that are hard to remove the longer you leave them.

- ▶ **Tarnished silver cutlery** Place a piece of aluminium foil in a plastic bucket and sprinkle over 3 tablespoons bicarbonate of soda. Lay the silver on top. Cover with hot water. Leave until bubbles stop, rinse and polish with a dry, soft cloth.

Tea and salt
To remove tea stains from china cups, rub it with a dish cloth dipped in crushed salt.

▶ **Stainless steel** Do not use steel wool. Rinse soon after using, as acidic or salty foods may cause pit marks.

▶ **Bronze** Treat Thai bronze cutlery like stainless steel. Remove green spots by rubbing with a soft cloth dipped in turpentine, then wash.

Kitchen knives

▶ **Blunt knives** *Sharpening stones are best. Wash individually by hand in cold or lukewarm water, as hot water can warp blades. Dry thoroughly and store in a wooden knife block.*

▶ **Rusty knives** *Soak in raw linseed oil for a few hours, then wipe off the rust. Polish the knife with emery paper.*

▶ **Stained blades** *Clean with emery paper rubbed with a slice of raw potato or salt and cut lemon. Alternatively, use a scouring pad.*

▶ **Stained knife handles** *Restore ivory handles by rubbing them with salt moistened lemon halves.*

COFFEE AND TEAPOTS

▶ Wash all coffee-making equipment thoroughly after use.

▶ To de-scale a drip coffee-maker, run a water and vinegar solution through the machine, or use a commercial product.

▶ To remove stains, fill the pot with 1 part bicarbonate of soda to 2 parts hot water and leave to stand overnight. Rinse thoroughly and dry.

▶ A patina of tea inside the pot may add depth of flavour to the brew, but it can look ugly on the spout tip. Wrap a piece of nylon stocking around a pipe cleaner and dampen it with salty water. Use it to clean the spout.

▶ To remove tannin stains inside pottery teapots, fill with 1 cup salt to 2 cups water, soak overnight, then rinse with hot water.

▶ To remove tannin stains from silver teapots, drop in 6 pieces of aluminium foil, add 1 tablespoon bicarbonate of soda and pour on boiling water. Leave to cool, then rinse out with hot water and dry with a soft cloth.

De-scale your kettle

- *Cover the element with vinegar, then top up with water. Bring to the boil and leave overnight, preferably for about 12 hours. Pour the liquid away.*

- *Fill the kettle with water and place it in the fridge overnight. The build-up comes loose in the cold. Next, boil the water; the lime in it will dissolve and can be poured away.*

Grease catcher

To make it easier to clean the grill (broiler) pan, line it with foil.

KITCHEN APPLIANCES

Most appliances can be wiped and washed with hot water and detergent or another general purpose cleanser of your choice, such as bicarbonate of soda (baking soda) mixed with water, which is mild, non-toxic and environmentally friendly (see page 34). Here are some specific tips.

STOVE

Cleaning a dirt-encrusted stove once in a while is a very time-consuming and labour-intensive job. It's certainly one of those jobs where a little prevention is much better than hours of unpleasant cure, so try to get in the habit of cleaning as you go and encourage anyone else who uses the stove to do the same.

▶ **The stove top** Every time you use the stove top, wipe it with hot water to prevent a build-up of spillages. Avoid abrasive cleaners on stainless steel and enamel tops. For encrusted stains, try a poultice made from a cloth soaked in a cleaning solution, leave for a few hours then wipe away. Alternatively, apply a caustic cleaner with a toothbrush, leave for a few hours, then scrub the mixture off with hot water.

▶ **The grill (broiler) pan** It's best to wash the grill pan in hot water and detergent after each use. But if your domestic routine slips up and you find yourself with a build-up of grease, scrape out the solids with a spatula, wipe the pan with balls of newspaper, then wash it.

▶ **The oven** Commercial oven cleaners contain highly caustic and unpleasant substances. To avoid having to use these, don't let the oven get too dirty before getting around to cleaning it. Wipe the surfaces with a hot, damp cloth after each use and clean up spills on the oven floor.

Clean alternatives

When you do have to clean the oven, try one of these alternatives to strong commercial cleaners.

▶ *Preheat the oven to warm, or proceed immediately after cooking in the oven. Place 125 ml (4 fl oz/½ cup) of cloudy ammonia inside, shut the door and switch off the oven. Leave overnight if possible, or for at least a few hours. Wipe thoroughly with hot water and detergent.*

▶ *Wet the surface and sprinkle it with bicarbonate of soda. Rub with fine steel wool, then wipe off the residue with a damp cloth. Repeat if necessary. Rinse well and dry.*

▶ *To clean very dirty shelves, soak them in a mixture of 1 part washing soda to 4 parts hot water. If the shelves are too large to be fully submerged in the sink, turn them around every 20 minutes, or use the bath or laundry sink.*

FRIDGE

▶ To wipe down the inside of the fridge, use a solution of 1 part bicarbonate of soda to 7 parts water. Wash any removable parts in hot water and detergent.

▶ To prevent mould from forming on the door seals, wipe over them with some white vinegar.

▶ If you can reach them, vacuum the coils behind the fridge, using your vacuum cleaner's brush attachment.

▶ To absorb odours, place a small, open bowl of bicarbonate of soda on one of the shelves. Change it regularly.

▶ To leave the fridge smelling fresh, wipe over the inside with a damp cloth and a few drops of vanilla essence.

Sweet and fresh
To wash and deodorise the fridge, kitchen bin or compost container, use a solution of 1 teaspoon lemon juice to 4 cups water.

DISHWASHER

Clean the filters and seals on your dishwasher regularly. To restore a dull interior, run the machine empty on a short cycle with 500 ml (17 fl oz/2 cups) vinegar in the detergent receptacle.

MICROWAVE

The microwave oven has been in our kitchens for many years now, but for most of us they are still simply a means to thaw chicken in an emergency or heat up a forgotten cup of coffee. But it can be used as a quick and fuss-free way to cook real family meals.

A microwave is a joy to clean. Simply put a large microwave-safe bowl or jug full of water into the oven, add a touch of lemon juice and a drop of ordinary dishwashing detergent and boil on High (100%) for 20 minutes. Do not cover or the water will boil over — also you want to produce lots of moisture. Remove the jug and wipe over the oven with a damp cloth — the dirt and grease will all have been loosened. Never use a commercial oven cleaner to clean the microwave oven.

You can cut down on the volume of messy washing up by taking a few precautionary measures, as follows.

▶ Put a sheet of paper towel on the turntable in the microwave. It will catch spills.

▶ Put foil inside the grill (broiler) pan.

▶ When reheating food, especially for solo diners, consider using a single bowl in the microwave rather than a saucepan and a bowl.

Small appliances

Here is some general advice on caring for and cleaning small kitchen appliances. Always remember to turn off the power and remove the plug from the socket before cleaning any electrical item, and also be sure to check the manufacturer's instructions on cleaning.

▶ *Always wipe over an appliance with a damp cloth immediately after using it.*

▶ *Wipe over chrome appliances with a paste made from bicarbonate of soda and water.*

▶ *Once washable parts, such as a food-processor bowl, are disassembled, rinse them in hot water, removing food debris with a soft brush.*

▶ *To clean your can opener, use a toothbrush and warm water with detergent in it. After drying, rub a little cooking oil over the teeth.*

▶ *Do not immerse electrical components in water unless advised to do so by the manufacturer. Dry each part carefully before storing.*

Caring for metal

As a general rule, metal can be dusted and, if necessary, wiped with a cloth dampened in water or a mixture of water and an all-purpose cleanser such as detergent. Rinse and dry it at once, especially if it's a metal that is prone to rust.

▶ Iron, silver, copper and brass are prone to tarnish — that's when the surface of the metal reacts with a substance in the surrounding air, forming a discolouring compound. The process is accelerated by humidity and warmer temperatures.

▶ Gold, platinum, pewter, bronze, aluminium, stainless steel and chrome do not tarnish, although they can stain.

▶ Metal polishes may be all-purpose or specific for a particular metal. They contain abrasives or solvents, sometimes both. The more valuable a piece of metal, the more care you need to take when cleaning it, and the less eager you should be to use all-purpose 'all metals' cleaners. If you use solvents and abrasives that are too strong, you run the risk of losing detail on raised designs and etching.

ALUMINIUM

▶ To brighten dull aluminium, boil 4 cups water with 4 tablespoons white vinegar.

▶ Harmful substances that will damage the metal include chlorine bleach, strong bicarbonate of soda solutions, and alkaline cleansers, including oven cleaners.

BRASS

A number of substances — including chlorine bleach, oven cleaners and some window cleaners — corrode and discolour brass.

▶ Rub briskly with a cotton wool pad wrung out in vinegar, then wash thoroughly in hot, soapy water. Rub dry with a soft towel.

▶ For mild tarnish, clean with a mixture of salt and lemon juice, then rinse. Use an old toothbrush to clean patterned areas.

▶ Try removing stubborn marks with Worcestershire sauce and salt — apply with a toothbrush, wash in warm water, dry well and rub with a clean cloth. If that doesn't work, try toothpaste on a toothbrush. Leave on for a while, rinse off with warm water and polish dry. Alternatively, try lemon juice and bicarbonate of soda or a paste of equal parts salt, white flour and vinegar. Rub on, leave for an hour and rinse off. Dry with a soft cloth then buff. Last of all, a simple piece without decoration can be boiled in a solution made from 1 tablespoon vinegar, 2 cups (16 fl oz) water and 1 tablespoon salt. Rinse and dry.

Removing wax from candlesticks

- **Hot method:**
  Melt wax with a hair dryer on the hot setting, and wipe the wax as it softens.

- **Cold method:**
  Place candlesticks in the freezer for about an hour. This makes it easy to peel off the wax.

To lacquer or not to lacquer?

Bronze, brass and copper readily tarnish and need regular polishing unless lacquered. Once thoroughly cleaned and lacquered they will stay bright and tarnish-free. However, if cracks begin to appear in the lacquer, they must be removed with acetone, the metal cleaned and lacquer reapplied. If you decide against lacquer, paste wax and mineral oil both inhibit tarnishing.

▶ To clean brass fireplace screens and tools, dust off the soot first, then wash in detergent and warm water. Rinse and dry with a soft cloth.

BRONZE

Do not wash bronze. Dust regularly with a soft cloth. Polish from time to time with a cloth dipped in boiled linseed oil, and buff with a soft dry cloth.

CAST IRON

▶ Protect items not used for cooking with paste wax. Oil hinges and locks with machine oil to prevent rust.

▶ Wash by hand and dry thoroughly after washing to prevent rusting — a few seconds on the stove top ensures all moisture evaporates.

▶ To remove rust, scour off and dry.

▶ To season cast iron pans, see page 39.

COPPER

▶ Rub in a mixture of 2 tablespoons vinegar to 1 tablespoon salt. Plunge into hot water and rinse. Dry thoroughly with a soft cloth.

▶ Never let copper stand in chlorine bleach for more than a few hours or the metal will become discoloured.

IRON

▶ Wrought iron merely needs dusting, but it can be washed if necessary. Rub stubborn marks with steel wool. Paste wax gives extra shine and protection against rust. Apply to a thoroughly clean iron with a cloth, allow wax to dry, then buff with a clean cloth.

▶ To remove rust, wipe with a solution of white vinegar and water.

PEWTER

▶ Wash in warm soapy water. To help keep pewter bright, add 2 tablespoons ammonia per 1 litre (32 fl oz/4 cups) water.

▶ For stubborn marks, try mixing finely powdered artist's whiting (sold in art supply stores) with a little oil and apply with a soft cloth. Rub in well, then polish with a clean cloth and finally a chamois. Rinse in warm water. Wipe dry with a clean towel.

▶ Remove grease marks by rubbing with a cloth moistened with methylated spirits.

▶ Pewter is vulnerable to damage by acids, including those in oak and unseasoned wood, and in some food. If necessary, polish it with silver polish.

SILVER

▶ Using silver is the best way to keep it looking bright; too much polishing can wear it out.

▶ Some foods tarnish silver, so wash silver or silver plate quickly after a meal. Items that contain sulphur tarnish silver. These include felt and chamois leather, as well as a number of foods.

▶ To wash silver, wash in very hot water and detergent. Rinse carefully (as soap residue can make it tarnish) and dry with a cloth rather than let it air dry, as water standing on silver causes tarnish.

▶ Rub egg stains on silver with wet salt.

▶ For other stains, use fine artist's whiting moistened with ammonia or alcohol, then wash and polish.

▶ Clean tarnished silver plate with starch mixed with methylated spirits (denatured alcohol) to form a paste. Let it dry on the silver, then rub off with a soft cloth.

▶ To prevent silver tarnishing after cleaning, smear lightly with petroleum jelly — but remember, this must be washed off before the silver is used with food again.

▶ To clean the old-fashioned way, cover the pieces with sour milk for half an hour, wash and rinse.

Remember to clean all silver thoroughly before polishing.

▶ To polish silver, use a commercial silver polish. Apply polish gently with a soft, clean cloth in a circular motion, polishing bit by bit for larger objects. Don't rub with a dirty cloth as the dirt can scratch — keep moving to a clean part of the cloth. Rinse polish off thoroughly with hot water, as it can sometimes corrode silver, then buff with a soft cloth. (Don't leave to air dry.)

▶ Don't polish silver plate too vigorously or you may rub it off.

▶ For valuable antiques, commercial silver polish may be too harsh. Instead, use a paste of distilled water and artist's whiting.

▶ Store silver in cloths, bags and drawer liners that have been treated with silver nitrate or other chemicals to retard tarnish. (It's unnecessary to clean tarnish before storing — polishing silver just before you use it will save time.)

Do not use soap to clean ceramic tiles as it may leave a thin film of scum, which will gradually build up over time and can be difficult to remove.

REMOVING STAINS FROM CERAMIC SURFACES

STAIN	METHOD
Mould and mildew	Mix 60 ml (2 fl oz/¼ cup) chlorine bleach in 2.5 litres (88 fl oz) of water. Scrub with a brush or toothbrush.
Limestone deposits	Scrub with a little white vinegar and water, and rinse.
Blood	Use hydrogen peroxide or household bleach.
Coffee, tea, food, fruit juice and lipstick	Wash with detergent in hot water then hydrogen peroxide or household bleach. Rinse and dry.
Nail polish	Wipe off with acetone, then, if necessary, use bleach.
Grease and oil	Use an all-purpose cleaner.
Inks and dyes	Steep the stain in household bleach until it disappears. Rinse and dry.
Chewing gum, wax and tar	Chill with an ice cube, then scrape away with a wooden spatula. Use paint stripper to remove any remaining trace.
Rust	Use lemon juice in conjunction with mild detergent to remove stains such as rust. Squeeze lemon juice into a glass and add a few drops of dishwashing detergent. Cut an absorbent cloth into pieces the size of the stain and saturate them with the mixture. Place the cloth pieces onto the stain, wiping off any excess solution. Leave for a few hours. Repeat if necessary, then rinse with water.

Fresh as a daisy

To freshen the air in the bathroom and remove odours, make sure it has adequate ventilation. If necessary, open the window and try one of the following non-toxic air fresheners.

▶ *Position 60 ml (2 fl oz/¼ cup) white vinegar in an open bowl on a high shelf.*

▶ *Do the same with a bowl of clay-type cat litter.*

▶ *Make a simple spray air freshener for the bathroom by combining 1 teaspoon bicarbonate of soda (baking soda) and 1 teaspoon lemon juice in 2 cups (16 fl oz) hot water.*

▶ *Scented candles can help to banish bathroom smells, even if they're lit for only a short while.*

▶ *Fragrant lemon essential oil kills germs. Add a couple of drops to the final rinsing water when cleaning the bathroom.*

▶ *For an antiseptic air freshener, dissolve 1.25–2.5 ml (¼–½ teaspoon) of any antiseptic essential oil (thyme, bergamot, juniper, clove, lavender, peppermint, rosemary or eucalyptus) in 5 ml (1 teaspoon) methylated spirits (denatured alcohol), then blend this with 500 ml (17 fl oz/2 cups) distilled water in a pump spray. Use your customised air freshener on the fine mist setting.*

THE HAND BASIN

Regularly wipe over the hand basin with or without a cleaner, and once a week give it a thorough clean. Be sure to rinse the plug hole well to avoid leaving bathroom cleaner on it, as this could damage the coating. To remove mould, scrub around taps and the plug hole with bicarbonate of soda.

TAPS

Regularly wipe taps with chrome, plastic, gold and brass finishes to remove traces of toothpaste and other toiletries. Clean with a solution of either washing-up liquid or bicarbonate of soda, using a toothbrush for crevices. To remove lime scale, wrap a cloth soaked in lime scale remover or vinegar around the tap and leave according to the manufacturer's instructions, or for up to half an hour.

THE BATH

Train members of your household to rinse the bath after they use it. Leave a cloth and light spray cleaner within easy reach so they can also wipe it over regularly to keep

Mould attack
The long-term solution is improving ventilation, by opening windows immediately after a steamy bath or shower, installing extractor fans, or fitting the room with wall vents so that steam and moisture can escape. Wiping away condensation will also help. Paint and grout is sometimes impregnated with fungicide.

soap and scum deposits at bay. An all-purpose bathroom cleaner will do the trick — use a commercial one or make your own, made up into a solution and poured into a spray bottle.

Once a week or so, you'll need to do a more thorough clean, scrubbing around the taps and plug hole and tackling any lime scale build-up. Bicarbonate of soda is ideal for scrubbing around taps and plug holes, while vinegar removes lime scale.

Warning

1   Do not use abrasive cleaners on acrylic baths, as they may scratch.

2   Products designed to remove lime scale may cause enamel to dull.
    Try using a plastic scourer, neat washing up liquid and elbow grease.

THE SPA BATH

Follow the manufacturer's instructions on maintaining and cleaning your spa bath. Perhaps once a week you will need to clean out scum left in the pipe work. You can do this by filling the bath with warm water and a disinfecting agent, such as sterilising tablets. Leave for 5 minutes. Empty the bath, then refill it. Turn on the spa and leave the water to circulate and rinse for another 5 minutes before emptying it.

THE SHOWER

Wipe over the floor of the shower recess with an all-purpose cleaner and use a lime scale remover as needed, perhaps once a week. Shower screens can be cleaned with a solution of washing-up liquid.

MOULDY SHOWER CURTAIN

▶ If you have a problem with mould on your shower curtain, dry the curtain soon after showering. This will at least cut down on the amount of mould.

▶ To clean mould from the curtain, you can use commercial mould removers but these often contain thickened chlorine bleach. Scrubbing with bicarbonate of soda is a less toxic alternative. Another method is to rub the curtain with a paste of vinegar or lemon juice mixed with borax. Rinse well.

▶ Black stains are difficult to remove, but leaving the curtain to soak overnight in a weak bleach solution may help.

▶ Some shower curtains, especially nylon ones, are machine-washable, but the plastic curtains are vulnerable to cracking, so proceed with caution. Some shower curtains are impregnated with fungicides.

DIRTY GROUT

You can buy products that whiten and kill moulds with fungicides. Alternatively, scrub with a solution of household bleach (1 part bleach to 4 parts water).

SEALANT

To remove mould from sealant, wipe it with neat vinegar, or rub over with a paste of bicarbonate of soda. As a last resort, spray on a bleach solution (1 part bleach to 4 parts water) and leave it for 30 minutes. Scrub, then rinse clean with warm water.

THE TOILET

Toilet cleaners are at the harsh end of the cleaning scale in both environmental and health terms. Most are based on strong acids, such as sodium hydrogen sulphate. Other ingredients may include paradichlorobenzene (PDB), fragrance, detergent and bleach. Use these chemicals with caution, as they can damage the skin and eyes; in addition, they do not readily break down. Never use more than one toilet cleaner, including bleach, at a time, as toxic gases may result.

Clean all the outer surfaces of the toilet — rim of the bowl, seat, outside of the bowl — by wiping over with a solution of detergent or a cleaner of your choice (see the box below). Clean the bowl with a toilet brush and disinfectant — either a commercial toilet cleaner or the gentler alternative above. To clean a toilet brush, hold it under the flushing water and rinse it in bleach.

Natural toilet cleaners

Take 250 ml (8 fl oz/1 cup) borax and 60 ml (2 fl oz/¼ cup) white vinegar or lemon juice. Mix the ingredients together and pour into the toilet bowl. Leave at least a few hours — overnight if possible — then scrub the bowl with a toilet brush. Add a few drops of pine oil to this recipe for extra disinfectant power.

To make disinfectant from essential oils, dissolve 20–30 drops of any oil with disinfectant properties — for example, cinnamon, clove, tea-tree, thyme, peppermint, rosemary or pine — in 1 teaspoon methylated spirits (denatured alcohol). Mix with 1 litre (32 fl oz/ 4 cups) distilled water and store in an airtight plastic or glass bottle.

Antistatic cloth
Soak a lint-free cloth in fabric softener and water. Squeeze out the excess and dry the cloth before using it. Use this cloth for cleaning.

The living room

The living area of your home is where you relax, socialise and probably watch television and listen to music, so it needs to be a place of comfort as well as order and beauty.

HOME ENTERTAINMENT EQUIPMENT

Some of this equipment — notably record players — have become redundant, but collectors will still want to play their vinyl records. Remember to switch off and unplug all appliances before cleaning them.

▶ To remove greasy marks and other spots, use a cloth dampened with methylated spirits (denatured alcohol).

▶ To clean disc and tape compartments, wipe them out with a cloth. To reach the corners, use a cloth dampened with methylated spirits over a cotton bud.

▶ Clean the stylus of a record player by brushing off dust with a paintbrush. Dip the brush in methylated spirits (denatured alcohol) and brush gently again.

▶ To clean a TV screen, remove dust with a soft cloth, then wipe with a cloth dampened in either a glass-cleaning solution or warm water. Never spray directly onto the screen as this can cause damage. If you have a TV with a plasma screen, check the manufacturer's instructions.

▶ Clean VCR heads with a cleaning cassette (available from your local video hire store). A bad case may need professional cleaning. Regularly clean the VCR, as dirty equipment damages tapes.

▶ Store your VCR in a cool, dry place, and try to avoid any sudden changes of temperature.

▶ Play and rewind VCR tapes at least once a year to redistribute tension evenly along the tape.

▶ Store CDs and DVDs in the cases provided, away from sunlight and direct heat.

▶ Hold each CD or DVD by the edge.

▶ Dust CDs and DVDs with a soft clean cloth, always wiping from the centre outwards. Do not wipe in a circular motion following the lines.

▶ To remove finger marks from CDs and DVDs, use a cloth dampened in mild detergent. If this does not restore the disc to full quality, try a little isopropyl alcohol (rubbing alcohol, available from chemists and some supermarkets).

PICTURES

Calculated neglect is the best treatment for paintings. They need a little of the right attention but nothing too harsh. Keep paintings away from humid places or rooms that may vary abruptly in temperature, so bathrooms and kitchens, attics and basements are usually out of bounds. Also, don't hang pictures near windows, where rain or sun could damage them, or near smoky candles.

Seek specialist attention for very valuable artwork, which should be listed separately in your home contents insurance policy. For other less expensive or cherished pieces, you can apply some home treatment.

- ▶ To clean unpainted wooden frames, use a soft cloth dipped in linseed oil.

- ▶ Clean painted frames with a cloth that has been dampened with a mild soap solution.

- ▶ To remove discolouration from gilt frames, rub with a piece of lemon, sponge with a solution of 1 teaspoon of bicarbonate of soda in 500 ml (16 fl oz/2 cups) of warm water, then polish with chamois leather.

- ▶ Dust picture glass with a soft cloth. To remove marks, use a little methylated spirits (denatured alcohol) or other glass cleaner — just enough to make the cloth damp — on a soft cloth. Never spray the glass with a liquid, as some may seep behind the glass and come into contact with the painting.

- ▶ Never touch paintings that are not behind glass, as skin oils can cause damage over time. Just gently dust these paintings with extreme care once a year. Use a fine soft brush and work from top to bottom.

BOOKS

The best way to keep books at their best is to read them, but there are also several other things you can do to ensure they remain in good condition.

- ▶ Regularly open books to help reduce dampness as well as prevent dust from settling too deep.

- ▶ Store books in adequately ventilated, glass-fronted cabinets to protect them from dust and sunlight, ideally at a temperature of about 15°C (59°F).

- ▶ Store heavy books flat to prevent the pages tearing away from the spine, and use book ends to stop books slumping against each other and becoming damaged.

- ▶ Dust books once a year by brushing the page edges with a thick make-up brush while the book is closed.

PHOTOGRAPHS

Your photographs will last much longer if you look after them properly. You might also like to scan them and make a digital photo album that you can store on your computer, or post on the internet for friends and family to enjoy; in this way, your original photos, if you have stored them correctly, will remain in good condition and last much longer.

▶ Store treasured photographs in good-quality paper albums interleaved with acid-free paper.

▶ Store all photographs in a cool, dark, dry place, such as under the bed.

▶ Use photo corners rather than glue to secure photos in place.

▶ Store negatives and old prints out of sunlight, at an even temperature. Place them in polyester covers to prevent the surfaces sticking together and to avoid bleaching of colours.

The home office

Whether your home office is a separate room or just a designated area in a corner of the living room, you'll need to keep your paper work organised and also care for your computer equipment.

THE PAPER CHASE

We may live in the computer age, but it's easier than ever to become overwhelmed by paper clutter, such as letters from school, invitations, newspaper clippings, bills and junk mail. Here's how to get sorted.

First, create an 'in' box that you go through once or twice a week. As you go, bin the items you don't need to keep. Then sort the papers into the following categories. You may need to set up a filing cabinet with suitably labelled suspension files.

▶ **Urgent** Unpaid bills. Go through this file regularly.

▶ **Personal** Letters, anniversary cards, and so on.

▶ **Banking** Statements, letters from the bank, spare cheque book.

▶ **House maintenance** Guarantees and instructions for the air-conditioning, water heater and other household appliances.

▶ **Tax** Anything that will be relevant at tax time, such as dockets and invoices.

▶ **School** Sports dates, school calendars, permission notes and timetables.

THE COMPUTER

▶ Place your computer where air can circulate around it.

▶ Do not expose it to long bursts of sunlight or direct heat.

▶ Do not store a computer in a dusty or damp environment.

▶ Make sure the cables are not laid next to a heater, or where they are likely to be tripped over.

▶ Do not move the computer when it is running, as the hard disc is vulnerable to damage by jarring.

▶ Dust the screen and body of the computer with a damp, lint-free, soft cloth. Do not allow moisture to seep into any openings.

▶ When cleaning the computer, do not use alcohol or other solvents, abrasives or sprays of any kind.

THE KEYBOARD

▶ To shift crumbs and dust, turn the keyboard upside down. If you leave these particles to settle deeply, they may cause intermittent faults.

▶ Turn the keyboard back the right way up and dust the keys with a small, soft paintbrush.

▶ If the keyboard is very dusty, use canned air to clear dust from around the keys.

THE MOUSE

▶ Remove the track ball cover.

▶ Remove the track ball.

▶ Clean inside the mouse with a cotton swab dampened with alcohol.

▶ Replace the track ball and cover.

Living with pets

Medical studies demonstrate that pets have a comforting and calming effect on us, which helps to keep us healthy. They can, however, bring dirt and fleas into your home, and if a member of your household suffers from allergies, you may need to take extra care looking after a pet and its belongings. Keeping pets out of bedrooms and off beds, ensuring good ventilation and cleaning regularly can all minimise the effect of pet allergens.

COMMON PET ALLERGIES

While you can, in theory, be allergic to any animal, there are some pets that are more likely to cause problems.

- ▶ **Cats** These animals are known for their meticulous grooming, which usually consists of much licking from head to tail. When the saliva dries, it flakes and floats off, landing on surfaces around the home. It is this dried saliva that contains the allergen protein that can trigger allergy symptoms such as asthma and a runny nose in sufferers. The particles are so light and small they spread easily, and even a tiny amount can be enough to cause problems. Cat saliva flakes are also highly persistent, and unless a place is washed thoroughly after a cat leaves, they can remain for years.

- ▶ **Dogs** Allergens are present in dog's saliva and skin particles. These may be carried by fur, but the hairs themselves do not trigger allergic reactions.

- ▶ **Mice** The urine of small creatures such as mice and hamsters is a common allergic trigger.

Pet etiquette

Minimise the transfer of bacteria and other disease-causing organisms from pets to humans.

- ▶ *Wash your hands after handling a pet, especially before eating.*
- ▶ *Keep cats and other mobile pets off food preparation surfaces.*
- ▶ *Give pets their own plates and bowls — do not share family ones with pets — and wash them every day.*
- ▶ *Do not encourage begging at the table.*

KEEPING PETS CLEAN AND FLEA-FREE

Homes with pets often smell of the pets themselves, but regular attention will minimise odours and keep the pets comfortable and free of fleas and lice.

There are many species of flea, but the main ones to worry about in the home are the ones that prefer humans, cats and dogs (*Siphonaptera* sp.). If you have a cat or a dog, tackling its flea infestation — or even better, making sure one doesn't happen in the first place — is the priority.

VACUUMING

This is the number one defence against fleas. It not only removes the fleas themselves but also their eggs and larvae. But vacuuming fleas does not kill them, so you'll need to replace the vacuum bag after each session (and seal the full bag in a plastic bag and leave it in the sun to kill the fleas, before disposing of it). If you have a non-disposable bag, place a little pyrethrin insecticide inside the bag before you begin.

Use bicarbonate of soda between shampoos on carpets and upholstery — sprinkle generously, leave for 15 minutes then vacuum. Consider steam-cleaning rugs and upholstery seasonally.

Bathing a pet

▶ *Use a non-slip mat in a tub to ease your pet's fears of slipping.*

▶ *Cover the drain with an inverted tea strainer to prevent hairs sliding down the drain and blocking the pipes.*

WASHING

▶ Regularly groom your pet dog or cat with a flea comb, and wash him or her weekly. Use shampoos with essential oils such as pennyroyal, eucalyptus and tea-tree or add 1 drop of lemongrass or citronella oil to your pet's regular shampoo.

▶ Wash your pet's bedding frequently in hot, soapy water, and dry it in the sun. In a high infestation period, such as midsummer, it's a good idea to do this at least weekly.

▶ To repel fleas and deodorise, wipe over pet belongings with water to which a few drops of tea-tree oil have been added. Use it also as a final rinse for a kennel floor and litter trays. (Do not use tea-tree oil undiluted, as it is poisonous when concentrated.)

▶ For a bad infestation, use a pyrethrin treatment in cracks, crevices, carpets and your pet's bedding or sleeping places. This paralyses the fleas, allowing them to be vacuumed up.

▶ Flea powders containing dust of rotenone and pyrethrins are not highly toxic but do not last long and need to be reapplied often.

▶ As a last resort, use a permethrin/methropene flea bomb. The former chemical kills adult fleas while the latter stops new hatchlings reaching maturity.

On the nose
The smell of pet urine on concrete is difficult to remove. To deodorise it, scrub the surface with a solution of 1 part white vinegar to 1 part water, or spray with straight methylated spirits (denatured alcohol).

Fresh litter
Place the litter tray in an area where there is good ventilation but away from where food is prepared or eaten. Regularly remove droppings — more than daily if necessary — and wash the tray frequently in hot, sudsy water, rinse in salt water then in white vinegar and hot water, and dry in the sun.

▶ Your vet may recommend monthly skin treatments and quarterly injections that also break the flea life cycle. It may be necessary to use other control methods, however, as these only take effect once a flea has bitten its host.

Essential oils in the home

Essential oils have a variety of uses in the home — not just in the laundry, but also as disinfectants, fragrances, stain removers and insect repellents. Check the table below to see how you can put eucalyptus and lavender essential oils to good use in your home.

HOUSEHOLD USES FOR ESSENTIAL OILS

ESSENTIAL OIL	PROBLEM	METHOD
Eucalyptus	Stains on clothing (e.g. perspiration marks, oil and soluble grease)	Add 2 teaspoons eucalyptus oil to a wash load or place an absorbent cloth under the stain. Moisten a clean rag with eucalyptus oil and gently but firmly brush the stain from its edge into the middle
	Stains on carpet	Put eucalyptus oil in a small spray atomiser and spray generously. Wipe with a clean absorbent cloth
	Ink on plastic or vinyl	Dip a cloth in eucalyptus oil. Test on a hidden patch first
	Glue, tar, chewing gum on fabric and other surfaces; adhesive tape on vinyl	Place a few drops on the stain, leave for 2 minutes and wash. Repeat a few times if necessary. Finish with a wipe of methylated spirits (denatured alcohol) and eucalyptus oil
Lavender	Washing bathroom	Kill germs by adding a couple of drops of lavender oil to the final rinsing water
	Washing clothes	Add fragrance to a washing load by adding a few drops of lavender oil to a face cloth and dropping it into the machine
	Mosquito bite	Apply undiluted to the bite

The pantry

A well stocked pantry and freezer can not only help you cater for last-minute guests but also minimise waste and reduce your shopping bill. For an efficient, healthy kitchen, follow these clever tips for shopping, storing and freezing as well as dealing with kitchen pests the natural way.

Pantry staples

Although it is best to shop regularly for meat, seafood and seasonal vegetables, there are certain staples that are handy to keep in stock. Here are some suggestions.

- ▶ Baking powder
- ▶ Beans, canned and dried
- ▶ Breadcrumbs, dry
- ▶ Capers
- ▶ Cocoa powder
- ▶ Coconut milk (cream)
- ▶ Cornflour (cornstarch)
- ▶ Couscous
- ▶ Dried fruits, such as raisins, currants and apricots
- ▶ Flour (plain and self-raising)
- ▶ Gelatine
- ▶ Honey
- ▶ Mustards
- ▶ Noodles
- ▶ Nuts
- ▶ Oils (olive, sesame, vegetable)
- ▶ Olives (in a jar)
- ▶ Pasta
- ▶ Polenta
- ▶ Rice, long-grain, short-grain and arborio (risotto)
- ▶ Soy sauce
- ▶ Stocks
- ▶ Sugars (raw, caster, white, brown, icing)
- ▶ Tabasco
- ▶ Tomato paste
- ▶ Tomatoes, canned
- ▶ Vinegars (white wine, red wine, brown, balsamic)
- ▶ Worcestershire sauce
- ▶ Yeast

The clever shopping basket

▶ *If chilled fruit juices, yoghurts and unprocessed cheese are in swollen food packages, it's a sign that the food is overpopulated with gas-producing micro-organisms — in other words, it's going off.*

▶ *Swollen cans indicate a fault in the original processing, which has allowed bacteria to multiply. Badly damaged cans could indicate that the can is no longer properly sealed.*

▶ *Dairy produce or delicatessen items not kept under refrigeration should always be cold when you buy them.*

▶ *Refrigerated foods past their use-by date presents a risk of food poisoning.*

▶ *Frozen and refrigerated foods stored outside the load line of the display cabinet, usually about 5 cm (2 in) below the rim, should be avoided.*

▶ *Frozen food packs with ice crystals, or clumps of ice between them, indicate refreezing, which usually means loss of quality.*

▶ *Torn packaging or imperfect seals usually indicate the food has deteriorated in quality.*

DRIED GOODS

Dehydration slows down the deterioration of food, but once the foods are exposed to water again — even when packets are open to the air — the microbes present in the food become active again. Store dried goods in a cool place away from sources of heat or direct sunlight, and inspect them regularly for contamination.

▶ Dried food keeps in an unopened container for about 6 months when stored at 21–24°C (69.8–75.2°F).

▶ Opened packages of dried fruit will keep longer if stored in the fridge.

▶ Once dehydrated foods, such as dips, are reconstituted, treat them as fresh food and refrigerate them.

CANS

Most canned food can be safely kept for at last 12 months. The exceptions are fruit juices, rhubarb, softdrinks and some baby foods, which have a maximum storage life of 6 months. Keep an eye on the use-by dates and use the oldest pantry items first.

The fridge and freezer

These are vital kitchen appliances, but how many of us know the rules for refrigerating and freezing correctly?

Refrigerating food inhibits the growth of spoiling micro-organisms and chemical changes in food. Most care is needed with foods of the flesh — meat, especially minced (ground) meat, liver, kidney, poultry and seafood — as these foods contain large numbers of micro-organisms that can cause spoilage and food poisoning.

When buying chilled (or frozen) foods, wrap them in newspaper to keep temperature changes to a minimum while you're on your way home. If putting them away is likely to be delayed, pack them in an insulated container. Put chilled foods away as soon as you get home.

Danger zone

Maintaining good hygiene in the kitchen is vital, as raw and cooked food may contain organisms that will multiply and become dangerous if the food is not treated correctly. Always bear this in mind when cooking and storing foods. Keep your hands, utensils and surfaces scrupulously clean, store food in its appropriate place (such as the fridge) and wash fruit and vegetables before you put them away.

An omnipresent fact of life, bacteria are present in most foods at harmless levels, and on your hands, arms, face and even inside your body, growing in temperatures between 4°C and 60°C (39.2°F and 140°F). Many are harmless, but high levels of harmful bacteria can make you ill, and may even kill you. The danger comes when harmful bacteria are transferred to foods, where they can multiply quickly and reach a dangerously high concentration. The transfer of bacteria from uncooked to cooked foods is particularly dangerous, as the cooked foods may not be heated again to destroy bacteria.

The most important principles of food hygiene are aimed at minimising the time food spends in the danger zone.

▶ If food is to be served hot, keep it above 60°C (140°F).

▶ When reheating, ensure the centre of the food reaches 75°C (167°F) to kill any bacteria present.

▶ If food is not going to be eaten immediately, refrigerate it after cooking.

Putting hot food straight into the fridge
Modern fridges can cope with large quantities of hot food without heating up other items. Cover the container, and if you're concerned the food will not cool quickly enough, divide a large quantity into smaller amounts in shallow dishes.

CRITICAL TEMPERATURES

TEMPERATURE	COMMENT
100°C (212°F)	Boiling-point cooking temperatures destroy most bacteria
60–74°C (140–165.2°F)	Warming temperatures prevent growth but allow survival of some bacteria
4–60°C (39.2–140°F)	Danger zone: temperatures in this zone allow rapid growth of bacteria, including food-poisoning bacteria
0–4°C (32–39.2°F)	Chilling temperatures restrict growth. Some food-poisoning bacteria may grow very slowly
0°C (32°F)	Freezing point
–12°C (10.4°F)	Freezing temperatures stop the growth of bacteria

RECOMMENDED STORAGE TIMES FOR REFRIGERATED FOODS

FOOD	KEEP FOR
Butter	8 weeks
Chilled meats and meals	Up to use-by date
Cream	5–7 days
Crustaceans and mollusks	2 days
Cured meat	2–3 weeks
Fruit juices	1–2 weeks
Leftovers	3–5 days
Meat	3–5 days
Milk	5–7 days
Minced (ground) meat and offal	2–3 days (variety meats)
Oil and fat	Approx. 6 months
Poultry	3 days
Seafood	3 days

Fridge hygiene

▶ *Store food you want to keep for a long time and foods such as seafood in the coldest part of the fridge.*

▶ *Store cooked foods above uncooked ones. This minimises the risk of food poisoning by drips from the uncooked foods.*

▶ *Wrap foods with strong odours, such as seafood and cheese, and avoid storing them close to milk and cream, which are susceptible to tainting.*

▶ *Throw out food that's going off — the slimy lettuce at the back of the fridge can taint other food.*

Fast thaw

If you don't have time to thaw meat in the fridge, the next safest method is under cool running water or in the microwave oven. If you're not sure that all portions of the meat have thawed, use a meat thermometer when cooking to check that the interior reaches 75°C (167°F).

FREEZING RULES

Freezers run at about −18°C (0.4°F), a temperature that almost, but not quite, prevents foods from deteriorating.

▶ Put frozen foods away as soon as you get home from the shops.

▶ You can cook vegetables from the frozen state. Many have been blanched before freezing and need only light cooking. Always completely thaw meat and poultry to avoid the possibility of starting cooking with a frozen patch, which then does not reach a bacteria-killing temperature.

▶ Food hygiene experts advise never to thaw meat out of the fridge because it may reach 4°C (39.2°F) — the temperature at which bacteria starts to breed, potentially causing spoilage and food poisoning. Allow 24–48 hours for a large piece of meat, or a whole chicken, to thaw in the fridge.

▶ If you thaw meat out of the fridge, don't be tempted to put it in the fridge once you have thawed it — to avoid food poisoning, you must cook it immediately.

▶ If thawed correctly in the fridge, food can be kept another 48 hours in the fridge, but it should never be refrozen.

FREEZING CHART

1–2 MONTHS	Biscuits (cookies) (unbaked)
	Bread (sliced)
	Cakes (unbaked)
	Milk
	Pancakes, pikelets and waffles
	Sandwiches (2 weeks to a month, depending on the filling)
	Sausages
	Scones (biscuits) (unbaked)
	Shellfish (raw and cooked)
	Soups
	Stews
2–3 MONTHS	Bread (unbaked)
	Cakes
	Cottage cheese
	Cream
	Filled pies (unbaked)
	Ice cream
	Leftover dishes
	Minced (ground) meats (except beef)
	Offal (variety meats) and bacon
	Oily fish (sardines, trout, mullet)
	Pastry (baked and unbaked)
	Poultry giblets
	Scones (biscuits)

Hoarding in the freezer

While a well-stocked freezer may be highly convenient, long-term hoarding of packaged frozen goods is not a good idea. It's better to stock less and buy more often, as a shop's freezing cabinets hold food at a lower temperature than home freezers.

FREEZING CHART continued

3–4 MONTHS	Butter (salted)
	Cheddar cheese, grated
	Fruit cake (unbaked)
	Ham
	Lamb
	White-fleshed fish
4–6 MONTHS	Butter (unsalted)
	Game
	Minced (ground) beef
	Pork
	Veal
6–8 MONTHS	Biscuits (cookies)
	Bread (unsliced)
	Filled pies
	Pizza
8–12 MONTHS	Beef
	Fruit
	Fruit cake
	Poultry
	Vegetables

FOOD STORAGE CHART

INGREDIENTS	IN THE FRIDGE	SPECIAL REQUIREMENTS
Butter	Wrap tightly to stop it becoming tainted or going rancid	Unsalted butter will not last as long as salted butter
Dairy, such as milk and cream	Keep cartons and bottles closed, as milk taints very easily	
Eggs	Keep eggs in the carton in which they are sold as they can easily be tainted by other smells in the fridge	Do not store loose in the egg holes in our fridge
Fish	Put on a plate, cover with plastic wrap and keep for as short a time as possible	Gut fish before storage, as ungutted fish go off quickly
Fruit	Store in the salad compartment. Strong-smelling cut fruit such as melon should be tightly wrapped or it will taint other items	Store bananas and avocados in cool places but not the fridge, if possible
Herbs	Store in their plastic bags or containers in the salad compartment, or put large bunches in a jug of water	Buy pot herbs if you can, as you often only need a few leaves out of each bunch. This way, you can pick them as you need them
Meat	Remove from packaging, put on a plate and cover with plastic wrap	Store on the bottom shelf of the fridge so no blood can drip onto cooked food
Poultry	If there are giblets included, remove them as soon as you get home. Unwrap the chicken, put it on a plate and cover with plastic wrap	Store on the bottom shelf of the fridge so no blood can drip onto cooked food
Shellfish	Store in a bowl in the salad compartment and cover with a damp cloth	If they're alive, don't put them in cold water or they will drown
Vegetables	Store in the salad compartment	Store root vegetables in the dark

The fruit bowl
To display fruit and vegetables, choose open-weave metal or wicker baskets, which allow the fruit to breathe. Glass bowls may look good but they restrict the airflow to the fruits on the bottom, which means they will ripen and rot more quickly.

Useful information

When you're following recipes in a cookbook, you will probably come across measurements you need to convert. On these two pages you'll find some useful measurement conversions. (Note that the conversion tables shown are an approximation of conversions — in reality, 1 oz = 28.35 g, but it is easier to call it 30 g, as scales do not measure small enough amounts to conveniently use any measurements of less than 1 g.)

WEIGHT CONVERSIONS

METRIC	IMPERIAL	METRIC	IMPERIAL
10 g	¼ oz	280 g	10 oz
15 g	½ oz	310 g	11 oz
20 g	¾ oz	350 g	12 oz (¾ lb)
25/30 g	1 oz	375 g	13 oz
55 g	2 oz	400 g	14 oz
85 g	3 oz	425 g	15 oz
115 g	4 oz (¼ lb)	450 g	16 oz (1 lb)
140 g	5 oz	550 g	1 lb 4 oz
175 g	6 oz	900 g	2 lb
200 g	7 oz	1 kg	2 lb 4 oz
225 g	8 oz (½ lb)	1.3 kg	3 lb
250 g	9 oz	1.8 kg	4 lb

LIQUID MEASURES

ML	FL OZ	OTHER
5 ml	1 teaspoon	
20 ml	½ fl oz	1 tablespoon*
40 ml	1¼ fl oz	2 tablespoons
60 ml	2 fl oz	3 tablespoons**
80 ml	2½ fl oz	⅓ cup ***
125 ml	4 fl oz	½ cup
150 ml	5 fl oz	
200 ml	7 fl oz	
250 ml	9 fl oz	1 cup
310 ml	10¾ fl oz	1¼ cups
330 ml	11¼ fl oz	1⅓ cups
375 ml	13 fl oz	1½ cups
400 ml	14 fl oz	
420 ml	14½ fl oz	1⅔ cups
435 ml	15¼ fl oz	1¾ cups
455 ml	16 fl oz	
500 ml	17 fl oz	2 cups
560 ml	19¼ fl oz	2¼ cups
1 litre	35 fl oz	4 cups

Notes

* The Australian tablespoon is 20 ml. The US and UK tablespoons are 15 ml; however, this discrepancy should not affect most recipes.

** ¼ cup.

*** 4 tablespoons.

OVEN TEMPERATURES

°C	°F	GAS MARK
70	150	¼
100	200	½
110	225	½
130	250	1
140	275	1
150	300	2
160	315	2–3
170	325	3
180	350	4
190	375	5
200	400	6
210	415	6–7
220	425	7
230	450	8
240	475	8
250	500	9

USEFUL MEASURES AND APPROXIMATE CONVERSIONS

INGREDIENTS	SPOONS	METRIC	IMPERIAL
Breadcrumbs, dry	2 tablespoons	30 g	1 oz
Cornflour (cornstarch)	1 tablespoon	30 g	1 oz
1 egg white	2 tablespoons	40 ml	1¼ fl oz
Powdered gelatine	4 teaspoons	15 g	½ oz
Juice of 1 lemon	4 tablespoons	80 ml	2½ fl oz
Juice of 1 lime	2 tablespoons	40 ml	1¼ fl oz
White flour	1 tablespoon	30 g	1 oz
White sugar	1 tablespoon	30 g	1 oz

CUP CONVERSIONS

INGREDIENTS (1 CUP)	METRIC	IMPERIAL
Brown sugar, soft	185 g	6½ oz
Butter/margarine	250 g	9 oz
Flour, white	125 g	4½ oz
Long-grain rice, cooked	185 g	6½ oz
Long-grain rice, uncooked	200 g	7 oz
Tomatoes, chopped	200 g	7 oz
White sugar	220 g	7¾ oz
Yoghurt	250 g	9 oz

Note
Cup measures are based on an Australian/UK cup (250 ml/9 fl oz).
A US cup (235 ml/8 fl oz) may also be used in the same way
without affecting most recipes.

Natural dyes
Use tea leaves, onion skins and turmeric as safe natural dyes for crafts.

Fresh ingredients

When shopping for fresh ingredients, knowing what to look for is essential, as is correct handling. Here are some tips on buying, storing and preparing meat and fish.

BUYING AND STORING MEAT

Look for meat that has a clear, fresh appearance — meat with a greyish tinge has been poorly handled and stored, and must be avoided. Other indicators that the product is unacceptable are an unpleasant odour and slimy surface. Reject offal (variety meats) such as kidneys and liver that have a strong smell of ammonia.

Meat should be kept refrigerated, so buy it last on your shopping trip and bring it straight home. Unwrap the meat and put it on a plate, then loosely wrap it with foil or greaseproof paper and place it in the fridge. Be sure to use it within a couple of days.

Meats wrapped in plastic do not last as well as unwrapped meat because they contain more water and the wrapping encourages bacterial growth at the surface, which can become slimy after about 3 days. If this happens, throw it out.

The surface of unwrapped meat dries out, which actually discourages bacterial growth, although it looks less attractive and may lose some flavour. To keep meat covered without letting anything come into contact with the surface, place it in a ceramic bowl covered with greaseproof paper, plastic wrap or a plate.

If you need to store meat for longer, remove the original wrapping and seal the meat in a freezer bag, first expelling as much air as possible. Double-bag the meat if there is any danger of the bag tearing, as meat exposed to air will suffer from freezer burn. Clearly label the bag, including the date. Most cuts of meat can be frozen for up to 6 months.

Make chicken one of the last items you buy so it's out of the fridge for the shortest possible time. Check that frozen chicken is solid and tightly wrapped. Take fresh chicken out of its packaging, cover it loosely with plastic wrap and place it on a plate to catch any drips. Keep it in the fridge, and cook it within 2 days.

Sealed in a freezer bag with the air expelled, chicken can be frozen for up to 3 months (make sure you write the date on a label). Thaw chicken carefully as bacteria, such as salmonella, can be activated if it gets too warm. Thaw in the fridge, not at room temperature.

Thaw chicken pieces in the microwave (arrange the thickest portions to the outside of the plate) but not whole birds — they thaw unevenly and some parts may start to cook. Use thawed chicken within 12 hours and never refreeze it. Cooked chicken can be kept in the fridge for up to 3 days.

FRESH SEAFOOD

Seafood is highly perishable, so take care when buying, storing and preparing it.

BUYING FRESH SEAFOOD

To ensure seafood is out of refrigeration for the shortest possible time, make it the last thing you buy on your shopping trip. Your fishmonger should wrap the seafood in a plastic bag to keep in the moisture and then several insulating layers of paper. All seafood should have a pleasant, fresh, fishy smell. Avoid anything that looks or smells at all unappealing. Instead check for these general signs of fresh produce.

▶ The eyes of fresh fish should be bulging and clear, not sunken and cloudy.

▶ The skin should be plump and moist. Fish fillets should be plump, moist and evenly coloured, with no dry edges.

▶ Shellfish such as lobsters and crabs are generally best bought live, although they are also available already cooked or frozen. If you are buying them live, they should be fairly active. If you're buying them cooked, make sure the shell is intact and there is no discolouration around the joints.

▶ Fresh, raw prawns (shrimp) should be plump and firm (not mushy), with no black spots.

▶ Cooked prawns should have a firm head and shell, with no black discolouration.

STORING FRESH SEAFOOD

Seafood has a very short storage life and is best used within a day of purchase. Place fish on a plate, to prevent dripping onto other foods, cover it with plastic wrap or foil and store it in the fridge. Seafood can actually taint other foods with an undesirable smell — another reason not to store it for too long. If necessary, you can freeze it — a great way to store fish you have caught yourself, as you can be sure it is fresh.

If you're freezing bought fish, ask the fishmonger whether it has already been frozen and thawed — if it has been, don't ever refreeze it (this applies to all food to be frozen, not just seafood).

▶ **Fish** You can freeze fish whole, but you must clean it first, then rinse it to remove any traces of blood (pat dry with paper towels). If you're going to fillet a white fish, do so before freezing. Put the fish into a freezer bag and extract as much air as possible. Seal firmly and clearly label with the date. To make separation easier when you need to use frozen fillets, place a sheet of freezer wrap between them. Freeze non-oily fish for up to 4 months, and oily fish for up to 3 months.

Cooked meat
One of the most common sources of food poisoning is cold cooked meat, often by cross-contamination from knives, hands and chopping boards. When preparing cooked and uncooked meats, either use different chopping boards and utensils, or thoroughly wash and dry them before switching foods. Never handle cooked and uncooked meats together.

Kitchen hands

To remove fruit stains from your hands, mix a little caster sugar into some olive oil to make a paste. Rub this into your skin, leave for a few minutes then wash your hands in warm soapy water. Stubborn stains may require three goes. To remove the smell of onions from your hands, rub them with celery or parsley.

Lay down your wine

Store table wines and ports lying down so that the cork remains moist. Only wines with metal caps are stored upright.

▶ **Shellfish** Lobsters, crabs, prawns (shrimp) and other crayfish can be frozen raw or cooked, and don't need to be cleaned first. Wrap larger shellfish in plastic wrap or foil, then place them in a freezer bag, extracting as much air as possible. Take care that any sharp parts of the shell don't pierce the bag. Freeze for up to 2 months.

▶ **Squid and octopus** Clean and cut into pieces for cooking. Freeze raw in a freezer bag, with as much air extracted as possible. Freeze for up to 4 months.

▶ **Molluscs** Mussels, oysters, scallops, pipis and clams should be cooked and the meat frozen, without the shell, in a freezer bag with as much air extracted as possible. Freeze for up to 3 months.

THAWING SEAFOOD

There is no need to thaw small or thin fillets of fish. Just cook them a little longer than the recipe recommends. If the fillet requires further preparation, such as coating with crumbs or batter, just thaw it enough to make it easy to handle. Alternatively, crumb fish before freezing — the coating will stick better and there is no need to thaw it. Other seafood should be thawed in the fridge, never at room temperature, and never in a sink full of water. Cook any seafood as soon as it has thawed.

Storing wine

Most households do not have, or need, a special wine cellar, but it is still worth storing your wine properly. If you always drink wine within a few weeks of buying it, place a small rack anywhere that isn't too hot or in bright light. But if you tend to keep even some of your bottles longer, and the conditions under which it is stored aren't right, the wine will age too quickly. Premature ageing doesn't mean the wine is ready to drink sooner — it simply ruins it. A valuable wine collection is always worth storing correctly.

▶ A cool, stable temperature of 10–12°C (50–54°F) is best, although most wines can be stored between 5°C and 18°C (41°F and 64°F) without adverse effect. Rapid fluctuations in temperature cause the wine to expand and contract, which eventually damages the cork.

▶ Even wines meant to be drunk chilled should not be kept in the fridge for more than a few days.

▶ Light can increase the ageing process, so keep wine in a dark place, away from windows, such as in the area under the stairs, a hall cupboard, an unused fireplace or a basement. Wine in light-coloured bottles is most affected, and sparkling wines are more susceptible than others.

▶ Moderate humidity is best for storing wine, as too little (below 50 per cent) will dry out the cork. High humidity is less damaging to the wine but it can cause the labels to rot and make it impossible to identify your wines.

▶ Some wine authorities believe wines should be stored where they will not be disturbed or subjected to vibrations such as those caused by passing road traffic, low-flying planes or even very loud noises.

▶ Wine can absorb odours through the cork, so don't store it in a place where there are strong odours or food that may ferment.

Kitchen pests

Using toxic pesticides exposes the whole household to a range of chemicals, and some people — the elderly, children, babies, pregnant women, asthmatics and people with allergies — are particularly vulnerable. When used outside the home, pesticides may also kill soil organisms, birds, fish and beneficial insects such as bees.

Alternative methods of pest control focus on using mechanical means such as screens, traps and other practices that do not involve harsh chemicals. Prevention is often a matter of commonsense, such as always putting food away in pest-proof containers and keeping your kitchen benches wiped clean.

As a last resort, some of the less toxic chemicals may be recommended.

Pantry pests

Some of the pantry foods most vulnerable to pest attack include grains and dried fruits, breakfast cereals, flour and spices. Store these products in pest-proof jars and containers, as even the tiniest hole may be a large enough entry for an insect. If you find an infested product, dispose of it immediately in an outside bin.

If an infestation is bad, empty the cupboard, clear it of all food debris and wash it down with a detergent solution. If the infestation returns and you want to try something harsher, first clear and clean the cupboard, then dust the cracks and corners with diatomaceous earth (food grade, suitable for use near food preparation areas). Alternatively, you could try pyrethrins or neem oil (from a tree that is native to western Asia). Try to avoid using persistent surface sprays in food areas.

ANTS

▶ Sprigs of fresh mint in the pantry will deter ants.

▶ Put 1 teaspoon of liquid dishwashing detergent in a spray bottle of water, and use the solution to spray ant trails as they trek into your kitchen.

▶ Follow the trail of ants and try to locate the nest. Pour a cup of water into the nest and spray the ants with a pyrethrin spray as they emerge from the hole. Alternatively, place a few borax and sugar baits around the trail and nest.

▶ Every few days, until they disappear, puff pyrethrin-containing powder down the holes where ants enter the house.

COCKROACHES

▶ Seal as many cracks and crevices as you can.

▶ Place sticky traps near breeding areas.

▶ Put low-toxicity baits such as 5 per cent borax and sugar in a small lid.

▶ Use a pyrethrum spray in crevices and underneath cupboards areas.

▶ As a last resort, use a pyrethroid spray such as permethrin, or a misting bomb containing permethrin and hydropene, which will cover every surface. You need to leave the house for at least 2 hours, but a weekend would be even better.

FLIES

▶ Make your own flypapers. Mix together equal quantities of sugar, corn syrup and water, and boil for 30 minutes. Spread the mixture on paper strips, and once they set to a sticky consistency, hang them near doors and windows.

▶ A potpourri mixture of cloves and dried orange and lemon peel, stored in open jars, is said to deter flies.

▶ Burn eucalyptus, lavender, citronella or peppermint essential oil in an oil burner.

RATS AND MICE

First try an old-fashioned spring trap baited with pumpkin or brazil nuts for rats, and dried fruit for mice. If you find a rodent in your trap, wear gloves while you handle the corpse. Place it in a plastic bag and dispose of it in the garbage bin, or bury it deep in the garden in an out of the way spot.

If you must use poisonous baits, multi-dose rodenticides are considered safest for both the environment and humans (in the case of accidental ingestion).

Natural pest repellent
To discourage flies inside your home, sprinkle dried tansy flowers on your pantry shelves.

The wash

Managing the household laundry can be a daunting task — not surprising when you consider that the average person generates over a tonne of dirty clothes every year. Even with the ever-increasing sophistication of washing machines, dryers and irons, we all need to know how to avoid those all-too-common disasters — a favourite item of clothing shrunk beyond recognition, or stuck to the iron!

Programming your wash

Many washing machine models have computerised controls, enabling you to program each load in specific ways. If you organise each washing load to make the most of this facility, you will save energy, and therefore money, each time you wash. For example, always wash heavily soiled garments together in one load.

Each time you sort out your washing, take the following factors into consideration.

TEMPERATURE
The hotter the water, the greater its cleansing power, but you need to balance the temperature setting of your machine against the needs of each fabric type — only cotton and linen can stand very hot temperatures, while silk may shrink and wool may felt. Hot water may result in a whiter wash, but it also uses more energy. To save energy, only use hot water for heavily soiled items. Alternatively, soak soiled items separately in a bowl of hot water before washing them in a cooler load.

WASH TIME
Wash lightly soiled items and delicate fabrics, such as wool, for a shorter time. Dirty gardening gear, for example, may need longer.

AGITATION STRENGTH
Regular agitation during the wash cycle may be too tough for lingerie or washable wool.

LOAD SIZE
It is more energy-efficient to wash with the fullest load suitable for the fabric type. However, be careful not to overload the washing machine or the items will not move freely, making soil removal inefficient. Repeated overloading will also shorten the life of the machine itself. Use the half-load setting when washing small bundles of similar items; if you wash a small amount on the full-load setting, you'll waste a lot of water.

SPIN CYCLE
For delicate fabrics, set the machine to a slower spin cycle and a shorter spinning time.

Fabric care

Nowadays there is an enormous range of fabrics and finishes — both natural and synthetic — from which to choose clothing and other household textiles. To prolong their life and keep them looking in optimum condition, it's worth taking the time to discover what they're made from, and how you should care for them.

Allergy alert in the laundry

Ingredients in detergents, fabric softeners and soaps can cause skin irritations and other allergic reactions. Some people are allergic to the solvent 1,1,1-trichloroethane, which is used in stain removers. It has a strong odour and can cause sneezing or a tightening of the chest in people with respiratory allergies.

If you or someone in your household is prone to allergies, take these precautions.

▶ *Consider using a non-biological detergent.*

▶ *Rinse clothes extra carefully, perhaps by using the rinse cycle twice.*

▶ *Before wearing new clothes, wash them to remove excess factory finishes.*

▶ *Wear gloves when hand-washing.*

SORTING THE WASHING

The obvious benefits of sorting are avoiding colour runs and saving on wear and tear, but it also makes your machine more energy efficient. How much time and trouble you take over it depends on your motivation and the time you have available.

Do these small jobs while sorting the clothes for washing.

▶ Empty pockets of paper tissues, coins, keys and any other items that could harm the washing machine or ruin the wash.

▶ Close buttons, zips and other fasteners to reduce the risk of your clothing tearing.

▶ Tie tapes and strings to prevent tangling in the wash.

▶ Brush clothes free of loose dirt and fluff.

▶ Mend any tears and holes to reduce the chance of holes enlarging during the washing process.

BY FABRIC TYPE

Fabric type determines the maximum temperature at which an article can be washed without causing damage. In some cases it also determines spin speed and washing machine cycle length. Consult the care label of the garment for information. If you wash all your clothes in cold water regardless of fabric type, you may simply need to separate woollens and other delicate items that you wish to wash by hand. It's best to wash towels separately to prevent lint spreading onto other garments.

Yellowing cotton
In most cases, ordinary bleach treatment will rid cotton of yellowing caused by age or excessive sunlight. If you have the facilities, you can try boiling the fabric for 45–60 minutes with detergent.

BY COLOUR

Even when washing in cold water, you should separate loads of washing into coloureds and whites. You can break these groups down further into darks, mixed white and coloured patterns. Treat mainly white prints that are colourfast as 'white'. Always check the care label on each garment. Instructions to 'wash separately' mean just that — excess dye may bleed out of the fabric for at least the first few washes.

BY DEGREE OF SOILING

Pull out the items that will benefit from pre-wash treatment, whether they are stained or heavily soiled. Never wash a single very dirty item with a load of lightly soiled clothes.

Testing for colourfastness

To test how fast a dye is — that is, how strongly it retains its colour — take these three steps.

1   Dampen a piece of the hem or seam allowance or any inconspicuous part of the article.

2   Iron a piece of dry white fabric onto it.

3   If any colour transfers to the white piece, the dye is not colourfast. Wash the article separately in cool suds and rinse at once in cold water. Dry immediately.

CARE LABELS

Care labels on textiles, which advise the consumer on the best way to wash a particular item, usually refer to four different care processes — washing, bleaching, drying and ironing. They may also give dry-cleaning advice and information. They tend to err on the side of caution — for example, many silk items that are labelled 'dry-clean only' may in fact be carefully hand-washed. But if you do hand-wash an item with such a label, and something goes wrong, you cannot complain to the manufacturer.

When there's no care label, follow these guidelines.

▶ Synthetic fabrics in particular benefit from frequent washing, as it prevents dirt from becoming absorbed into the fibres.

▶ To safeguard colour, finish and shape, and to minimise creasing, never wash hotter or longer, nor spin longer than recommended, unless you are absolutely confident of the results.

▶ Rinse thoroughly. Clothes and linen need at least two rinses to remove all traces of detergent and soil. Some finishes will not work effectively without proper rinsing — for example, towelling may become scratchy.

▶ Blends are made by spinning together different fibres to form a yarn, which is then spun and woven or knitted. Mixture fabrics are made by weaving or knitting together yarns made from different fibres. When washing blends and mixtures, determine which fibre needs the gentlest treatment before you decide on a washing method. For instance, wash a blend of polyester and wool as if it were all wool, in warm water.

GUIDE TO CARE SYMBOLS

SYMBOL	MEANING
⊻	Machine-washable (normal cycle)
⩌	Hand-wash only
△	Any bleach can be used
▣	Tumble dry after washing
▣	Tumble dry with high-heat setting
▣	Tumble dry with low-heat setting
⏚	Hot iron
⏚	Medium iron
⏚	Cool iron
○	Dry-cleaning
Ⓐ	Any solvent
Ⓟ	Any solvent except trichloroethylene
Ⓕ	Petroleum solvent only

Steam treatment
To smooth out a wrinkly wool garment, such as a suit, simply hang it up in a steamy bathroom.

Lint trap

To prevent lint from blocking your drains, fit the end of the water outlet with a section of pantihose (tights), and remember to clean it regularly.

Keep your machine clean

Many manufacturers recommend running an empty washing machine through a complete cycle with no powder in it every month or so. This will keep the machine clean and free of any greasy deposits.

Washing guidelines

Are your whites grey? Do some of your clothes have persistent grease spots you can't remove? Try some of these old-fashioned whitening methods. For special instructions for individual fabric types, check the table on pages 83–88.

▶ **Blue** Washing blue, made from the pigment indigo, counteracts the yellow tint that results from perspiration and the use of soap and soda.

▶ **Methylated spirits (denatured alcohol) and cloudy ammonia** Adding 1 cup of each to the washing water every so often helps to keep whites actually looking white.

▶ **Borax** Add ½ cup borax to a machine wash. This is particularly effective if you dry the items in the sun after washing.

▶ **Sunlight** If you leave cloth in strong sunlight for a day, the sun plus oxygen and moisture from the air create a slow bleaching effect.

▶ **Frost** Bleaching also occurs when damp clothes become iced over. However, frost also weakens fabric, so handle items with care. To prevent tears, wipe the clothesline with boiling water and salt before you peg the clothes out in the first place. Ideally, wait until the washing has thawed before bringing it in.

Fire risks

▶ *Synthetic fibres such as nylon and polyester may be slow to ignite, but eventually they will burn and melt at a very high temperature.*

▶ *Light materials such as voile and muslin burn faster than the heavy types of fabric used in curtains.*

▶ *Fabrics that are mixed from synthetic material and cellulose have a wicking effect — the synthetic polymer fibres melt onto the cellulose, which acts as a wick.*

▶ *Wool and silk readily char and do not spread the flame.*

▶ *Raised pile fabrics are more of a fire hazard, as they have a greater surface area in contact with oxygen.*

▶ *Cellulosic fabrics readily burn and also produce flammable gases.*

FABRICS AND THEIR WASHING REQUIREMENTS

FABRIC	DESCRIPTION	SPECIAL REQUIREMENTS	MAX. WASH TEMP.	AGITATION	RINSE	SPIN	IRONING NOTES
Acetate	Widely used fabric derived from cellulose	Wash gently in lukewarm water. Handle gently when wet. Take care with stain solvents	40°C (104°F)	Gentle	Cold	Short	Damp iron on wrong side with cool iron
Acrylic	Synthetic fibre that does not shrink	Treat heavy knitted articles with care to avoid stretching. Gentle machine or hand-wash, inside out to prevent pilling. Use fabric softener regularly to reduce static electricity. Use a low tumble dryer setting, dry knits flat	40°C (104°F)	Minimum	Cold	Short	Cool iron if required
Angora	Fluffy fibre from the Angora rabbit	Hand-wash with care. To dry, lay flat away from direct sun or heat. Brush with teasel brush or (a spiky brush) when dry to raise the surface	40°C (104°F)	Minimum	Warm	Short	If desired, warm iron over damp cloth, or use steam iron
Cashmere	Natural fibre from the downy undercoat of the Tibetan cashmere goat	Hand-wash with care. Will quickly felt if washed too vigorously. To dry, roll in a dry towel, press to remove excess water, then repeat with a second towel. Finally, lay flat to dry on a fresh towel 40°C (104°F)	Gentle; do not to wring or twist	Cold	Do not spin	Press on wrong side with warm iron under damp cloth, or use steam iron	
Clydella	Mix of natural fibres, wool and cotton	Do not rub	40°C (104°F)	Minimum	Normal	Normal; do not hand wring.	If required, warm iron on wrong side when damp
Corduroy	Cut weft pile fabric with corded effect, usually cotton	Wash deep and bright colours separately	50°C (122°F)	Medium	Cold	Drip-dry	Do not iron. Remove creases by steaming

FABRIC	DESCRIPTION	SPECIAL REQUIREMENTS	MAX. WASH TEMP.	AGITATION	RINSE	SPIN	IRONING NOTES
Cotton	Strong natural fibre which can withstand vigorous washing	Machine-wash if you wish but be more cautious with loose weaves, trims and linings. Bleach when desired but rinse well afterwards. Dry in the sunlight for a lightening effect. Don't leave out in the sun for more than a few hours or it will yellow	95°C (203°F) whites; 60°C (140°F) coloureds	Maximum	Normal	Normal	If required, warm to when hot iron dry
Cotton (drip-dry)	Cotton with special finish for crease resistance and minimum iron	Machine-wash	50°C (122°F)	Medium	Cold	Drip-dry	Warm to hot iron when dry if required
Denim	Twill weave, usually cotton or cotton blend	Allow for shrinkage. Not all denim is colourfast	95°C (203°F) whites; 40°C (104°F) coloureds	Maximum	Normal	Normal	Hot iron when damp
Dylan	Shrink-resistant wool	Sometimes machine-washable. Normal rinse. Normal spin, do not wring	40°C (104°F)	Minimum; do not rub	Normal	Normal; do not wring	Warm iron over damp cloth, or steam iron
Egyptian cotton	Fine-quality natural cotton fibre in closely woven cloth	Machine-wash	95°C (203°F) whites; 60°C (140°F) coloureds	Maximum	Normal	Normal	Hot iron on wrong side when damp
Elastane fibres	Synthetic stretch fibres	Wash according to other fibres in fabric and not above 50°C (122°F)	50°C (122°F)	Medium	Cold	Short spin or drip-dry	Do not iron
Fibreglass fabric	Woven from fine glass filaments. Flame-proof and resistant to bacteria	Handle gently; liable to fray if machine- washed. Abrasion can cause damage to the surface and loss of colour	40°C (104°F)	Gentle	Cold	Drip-dry	Do not iron
Flame-retardant fabrics	Various fabrics designed to decrease flammability	Do not soak, bleach or boil	40°C (104°F)	Minimum	Cold	Short spin	Press lightly with a cool iron on wrong side while slightly damp

FABRIC	DESCRIPTION	SPECIAL REQUIREMENTS	MAX. WASH TEMP.	AGITATION	RINSE	SPIN	IRONING NOTES
Flame-retardant finishes	Various fabric finishes designed to decrease flammability	Do not use soaps or soap products. Medium agitation. Rinse carefully with cold water. Do not soak or bleach	50°C (122°F)	Medium	Cold	Short spin or drip-dry	Cool iron
Foam backs	Fabrics to which a layer of polyurethane or polyester foam has been bonded to the back of the face fabric to give warmth without weight and to preserve shape	Not all foam backs are suitable for home washing. If in doubt dry-clean. Otherwise proceed as for face fabric	As for the face fabric	As for the face fabric	As for the face fabric	As for the face fabric	Iron as for face fabric
Glazed cotton	Cotton with special finish. Only perma-nently glazed cotton will retain sheen on washing	No special requirements	50°C (122°F)	Medium	Cold	Short spin or drip-dry	Hot iron on wrong side when damp. Finish by polishing on right side
Helenca	Process that gives high stretch to yarns such as nylon and polyester	No special requirements	60°C (140°F) white nylon; 50°C (122°F) other	Medium	Cold	Short spin or drip-dry	Warm iron when dry if necessary
Lamb's wool	Natural fibre, fine-graded, high-quality wool	Hand-wash with care	40°C (104°F)	Gentle	Cold	Roll in towel, then dry flat	Press lightly with warm iron under damp cloth or use steam iron. Brush up pile when dry
Laminates	Two or more layers of fabrics bonded together	Not all are suitable for home washing. If in doubt dry-clean. Washable laminates should be laundered according to face fabrics	As for the face fabric	As for the face fabric	As for the face fabric	As for the face fabric	Iron if necessary according to the face fabric

FABRIC	DESCRIPTION	SPECIAL REQUIREMENTS	MAX. WASH TEMP.	AGITATION	RINSE	SPIN	IRONING NOTES
Lastex	Natural stretch yarn made from extruded rubber (latex)	If no advice on label, proceed at your own risk	30°C (86°F)	Gentle	Cold	Short	Do not iron
Linen	Natural fibre made from flax	Wash at high temperatures. Can bleach and boil if white	95°C (203°F) whites; 60°C (140°F) coloureds	Maximum	Normal	Normal	Hot iron when damp
Linen (delicate)	Lace or fine linen blouses	Hand-wash or place item in old pillowcase before washing on gentle setting. Use mild detergent; avoid one with optical brighteners, which can cause white spotting	40°C (104°F)	Do not wring	Normal	Roll in a towel to remove excess moisture, then dry flat away from direct source of heat	Iron when still damp
Linen (sturdy)	Tablecloths, sheets, woven towels	Presoak overnight to remove stubborn stains. If tumble drying, remove while still damp to prevent overdrying, which can make linen brittle	50°C (122°F)	Minimum	Extra rinse	Fast; don't wring	Iron when still damp
Lurex	Specially processed metallic thread incorporated into other fabric	Wash according to fabric type	As for fabric type	As for fabric type	As for fabric type	As for fabric type	Warm iron
Minimum iron	Easy-care finish	Wash according to fabric type	40–50°C (104–122°F)	Minimum	Cold	Drip-dry	Warm iron if necessary when dry
Modal	Viscose in modified form with improved strength	No special requirements	40–60°C (104–140°F)	Maximum	Normal	Normal	Hot iron when damp. If necessary, warm iron for polyester blends
Mohair	Natural fibre from the Angora goat	Hand-wash only	40°C (104°F)	Gentle	Cold	Roll in towel, then dry flat.	Press on wrong side under damp cloth with warm iron. Brush up pile when it is dry

FABRIC	DESCRIPTION	SPECIAL REQUIREMENTS	MAX. WASH TEMP.	AGITATION	RINSE	SPIN	IRONING NOTES
Nylon	Strong versatile synthetic fibre	No special requirements	60°C (140°F) whites; 50°C (122°F) coloureds	Medium	Cold	Short spin or drip-dry	If necessary, cool iron when dry
Permanent press	Technique providing garments with permanent shape and creases	Wash according to fabric type	As for fabric type	As for fabric type	As for fabric type	Do not wring	Not necessary
Polyester	Very strong synthetic fibre	Wash regularly as attracts greasy soiling. Pre-treat greasy stains. Wash inside out to prevent pilling	50°C (122°F)	Medium	Cold	Short spin or drip-dry	If necessary, cool drip-dry iron when dry
Polyester cotton	Blend	Do not allow to become heavily soiled before washing	60°C (140°F) whites; 50°C (122°F) coloureds	Medium	Cold	Short spin or drip-dry	If necessary, warm iron when dry
Proban	Flame-retardant finish	Do not use soap	50°C (122°F)	Medium	Cold	Short spin or drip-dry	Cool iron
PVC	Synthetic thermo plastic fibre	Shrinks over 70°C (158°F). Coats and raincoats: sponge only	40°C (104°F)	Minimum	Cold	Short spin	Do not iron
Rayon	Read care label carefully as finishes and manufacturing processes are so varied. Specific care labels recommend more vigorous handling	Either hand-wash or use machine's gentle cycle if care label recommends machine washing. Use a mild, non-alkaline detergent. Dry knits flat; hang woven items	30–40°C (86–104°F)	Gentle	Cold	Squeeze rather than wring	If in doubt, cool iron
Rigmel	Shrink-resistant finish for cotton	No special requirements	95°C (203°F) whites; 60°C (140°F) coloureds	Maximum	Normal	Normal	Hot iron when damp
Sanforised	Shrink-resistant finish	Wash according to fabric type	As fabric type	As for fabric type	As for fabric type	As for fabric type	Iron according to fabric type
Sarille	Modified viscose with wool-like qualities	No special requirements	40°C (104°F)	Normal	Normal	Normal	Hot iron when damp

FABRIC	DESCRIPTION	SPECIAL REQUIREMENTS	MAX. WASH TEMP.	AGITATION	RINSE	SPIN	IRONING NOTES
Scotch-guard	Water- and oil-repellent finish	Wash according to fabric type. Rinse thoroughly	As for fabric type	As for fabric type	As for fabric type	Drip-dry	Warm iron if necessary
Silk and wild silk chlorine	Natural protein fibre made by silkworms	Use mild soap or detergent. Regular laundry detergent is alkaline and could damage silk fibres. Don't use bleach; use hydrogen peroxide or sodium perborate bleaches. Rinse thoroughly, dry gently. Don't soak for long periods	30–40°C (86–104°F)	Minimum	Cold	Short spin, do not hand-wring	Warm iron when slightly and evenly damp. Cool iron wild silk
Triacetate	Synthetic cellulose-derived fibre	More robust in wash and wear than acetate	40°C (104°F)	Minimum	Cold	Short spin	Cool iron when damp
Viloft	Tubular viscose fibre with high bulk and extra absorbency	Washes well often	50°C (122°F)	Medium	Cold	Short spin or dry	Not usually necessary
Viscose	Widely used cellulose fibre used on its own and in blends	No special requirements	60°C (140°F)	Maximum	Normal	Normal	Hot iron on wrong side when damp
Viyella	55% lamb's wool, 45% cotton	Treat gently	40°C (104°F)	Minimum; do not rub	Normal	Normal spin; do not hand-wring	Warm iron on wrong side while slightly damp
Wool	Natural sheep fibre available in many qualities	Hand-wash unless specifically advised to machine wash	40°C (104°F)	Minimum; do not rub	Normal	Normal spin; do not hand-wring	Warm iron under damp cloth, or steam iron
Wool (machine washable)	Process which makes wool shrink-resistant	Do not wring	40°C (104°F)	Minimum; do not rub	Normal	Normal spin; do not hand-wring	Warm iron over a damp cloth, or use a steam iron

Hand-washing

Hand-washing is still desirable for many items, such as woolly jumpers or delicate lingerie. For the best results, follow these steps.

1 Fully dissolve the granules of powder in the water.

2 Soak the article to loosen dirt, but never soak wool.

3 Agitate by kneading it gently.

4 Rinse thoroughly.

5 Drip-dry articles if you have the space, or roll them in a towel to remove moisture, then hang them up to dry.

SOAKING SUCCESS

Heavily soiled or stained articles may need soaking before washing. When soaking coloured items, follow this checklist.

▶ Check that the dye can withstand soaking (if in doubt, do not soak).

▶ Fully dissolve the washing powder (there may be spotting if concentrated powder is left in contact with the fabric).

▶ Select a water temperature that is not too hot for the fabric type.

▶ Make sure the article is not bunched up.

▶ Soak white and coloured articles separately.

REMOVING WASHABLE STAINS

Type of stain	Removal method
Excess liquid	Blot excess liquid with a dry cloth or paper towel before soaking
Food solids	Scrape off solids such as cooked egg before soaking
Fresh stains	Soak in cold suds for 30 minutes to prevent the stain from setting in the fabric, then wash normally
Dried stains	Apply a mixture of 1 part glycerine to 2 parts water to the stain. Leave for 10 minutes, then treat as a fresh stain
Residual marks on white fabric	Soak for 1 hour in a solution of hydrogen peroxide (1 part '20 white fabric volume' hydrogen peroxide to 9 parts water), then wash as usual

Out damned spot!

When dealing with stained fabric, act fast. A speedy response may prevent a stain from setting and allow you to use a milder remedy. Some delicate fabrics may withstand methods that are appropriate for removing a fresh stain, but the same fabrics may be damaged by the harsher methods necessary for removing set stains.

If you leave the wrong stain to set on the wrong fabric, you could end up with permanent stains; synthetic and drip-dry fabrics are more prone to this than natural fibres.

Here are some general guidelines for stain removal.

▶ **Remove the spill first** Use a cloth to mop liquid spills on washable fabrics, and the back of a knife to remove solids.

▶ **Never rub a stain** Rubbing only pushes the stain further into the fabric. Instead, use a pinching action with a clean cloth or paper tissue to remove as much of the staining substance as possible.

▶ **Outside in** When working with solvents on a stain, always work from the outer rim of the stain to minimise its spread.

▶ **Test first** If possible, first test a stain remover, especially a solvent, on a hidden or less conspicuous area of a garment, such as the hem or seam allowance. (See 'Testing for colourfastness', page 80.)

Using the absorbent pad method

To treat and wash stains, use the absorbent pad method, which requires two or more pads of cotton wool or something similar.

1 Soak one pad in the appropriate solvent.

2 With the solvent pad under the stain and the other pad on top, dab the stain.

3 When some of the stain has transferred to the top pad, turn it over so its clean side is in contact with the fabric, and repeat.

4 Change the top pad and continue working until no stain comes through.

5 Wash as usual.

The essential stain-removal kit

Keeping a household stain-removal kit in your laundry gives you a head start on stains. A basic kit should contain the following items, but take care with solvents and only use them if they are really necessary.

- Acetone or amyl acetate, solvents found in nail polish remover
- Bicarbonate of soda (baking soda)
- Blotting paper
- Borax
- Clothes brush
- Cotton wool, paper tissues, clean dry rags
- Cream of tartar
- Droppers
- Dry-cleaning fluid
- Eucalyptus oil
- Glycerine for lubrication

- Household ammonia
- Hydrogen peroxide
- Kerosene
- Lemon juice
- Methylated spirits
- Potassium permanganate
- Precipitated chalk
- Proprietary grease
- Salt
- Scraper
- Turpentine
- White vinegar

STAIN REMOVAL

TYPE OF STAIN	SOLVENT	METHOD
Ballpoint ink	Methylated spirits	Absorbent pad method (see page 90)
Bicycle oil	Proprietary grease solvent	Absorbent pad method
Black lead	Proprietary grease solvent	Absorbent pad method
Chalks and crayons	Detergent. Use methylated spirits for stubborn marks. Wash as normal	Brush off as much as possible while dry. Brush stained area with suds (1 dessertspoon to 2 cups water)
Chewing gum	Methylated spirits Ice cube	Absorbent pad method Rub the gum with an ice cube to harden it. You may be able to pick it off by hand, then wash as usual to remove any traces
Cod liver oil, cooking fat and heavy grease stains	Proprietary grease solvent	Absorbent pad method
Contact adhesives	Amyl acetate	Absorbent pad method
Dried fruit stain (for all but very delicate fabrics)	Boiling water	Stretch the fabric over a basin. Pour over almost boiling water
Dried fruit stain (very delicate fabric)	Lemon juice	Spread the fabric over blotting paper and sponge on the wrong side with hot water. If the mark remains, moisten with a little lemon juice and rinse with hot water
Felt pen ink	Soap Methylated spirits	Use hard soap to lubricate the stain. Wash as normal. For obstinate stains, use methylated spirits and the absorbent pad method.* Wash again to remove final traces
Fresh fruit stain	Salt	Before it has had time to dry, cover the stain in salt and wash without a soap (the alkali in the soap fixes rather than fades the stain)
Glue, tar, chewing gum on fabric and other surfaces; adhesive tape on vinyl	Eucalyptus oil	Place a few drops on the stain, leave for 2 minutes and wash. Repeat a few times if necessary. Finish with a wipe of methylated spirits and eucalyptus oil

TYPE OF STAIN	SOLVENT	METHOD
Grass stain	Methylated spirits, cream of tartar	If the fabric is too delicate to wash, daub with methylated spirits on a clean cloth. If it can be laundered, soak in cold water, then cover with a little cream of tartar and leave it in the sun
Hair lacquer	Amyl acetate	Absorbent pad method
Ink stain on coloured fabric	Milk, tomato	Soak the stained part immediately in slightly warm milk. Rinse. Or rub the stain with half a ripe tomato, then soak the fabric in cold water. The stain should disappear in the next laundering
Ink stain on white fabric	Salt, lemon	Sprinkle with salt immediately then rub with a cut lemon. Rinse and wash off
Iron mould on white cotton and linen only	Oxalic acid solution	Dissolve ½ teaspoon oxalic acid crystals in 1 cup hot water. Tie a piece of cotton tightly around the edges of the stained area to prevent the solution spreading and immerse the stained part. Leave for 2–3 minutes. Rinse thoroughly and wash in rich suds
Iron mould (rust marks) on wool, synthetic fabrics and all delicate fibres	Lemon juice	Flood the stain with lemon juice and leave for 10–15 minutes. Place a damp cloth over the stain and iron. Repeat several times as necessary. Rinse and wash as usual
Lipstick and blush	Proprietary grease solvent	Soak light stains, then wash in the usual way. For heavier stains, use the absorbent pad method
Lipstick alternative on washable fabrics	Kerosene	Sponge
Lipstick on non-washable fabric	Methylated spirits or eucalyptus oil	Absorbent pad method
Marking ink	Marking ink eradicator	Follow the manufacturer's instructions
Metal polish	Proprietary grease solvent	Absorbent pad method
Mildew on coloured articles	Detergent	Soak, then wash in rich suds. If the stain is not entirely removed, it may gradually fade with subsequent washes

TYPE OF STAIN	SOLVENT	METHOD
Mildew on linen or cotton	Precipitated chalk	Wet the mildewed parts, rub with ordinary laundry soap, cover with precipitated chalk and rub it in. Leave for at least 1 hour then rinse. Repeat if necessary
Mildew on white cottons and linens without special finishes	Household bleach and vinegar	Soak in 1 part bleach to 100 parts water with 1 tablespoon vinegar. Rinse thoroughly, then wash
Mildew on white drip-dry fabrics	Hydrogen peroxide solution	Soak in 1 part hydrogen peroxide ('20 volume') and 9 parts water until stain has gone. Rinse thoroughly and wash as normal
Mildew (old and persistent stain)	Potassium permanganate	Try soaking item in solution of 1 teaspoon potassium permanganate in 2 cups water.
Mildew (set in)	Salt	Rub the stain with damp salt and expose to warm sunshine if possible
Mildew (slight stain)	Lemon juice	Sponge with lemon juice and place in the sun until the spores have disappeared (about 1 day)
Nail polish	Amyl acetate	Absorbent pad method
Nicotine	Methylated spirits	Absorbent pad method
Paint (oil-based)	Turpentine or amyl acetate	Absorbent pad method
Paint (water-based)	Water	Sponge paint splashes immediately with cold water. Dried paint is permanent
Permanent ink	Oxalic acid solution (suitable for linens and white cottons only)	Dissolve ½ teaspoon oxalic acid crystals in 1 cup hot water. Tie a piece of cotton tightly round the stained area to prevent the solution spreading and immerse the stained part. Leave for 2–3 minutes. Rinse thoroughly and wash in rich suds
Perspiration (fresh)	Ammonia	Dampen with water then hold over an open bottle of household ammonia
Perspiration (old stains)	White vinegar	Sponge with white vinegar, rinse thoroughly then wash as usual
Perspiration (on wool)	Lemon juice	Sponge with a 1:1 solution of lemon juice and water then hang up to air

TYPE OF STAIN	SOLVENT	METHOD
Plasticine	Proprietary grease solvent or mineral spirits	Scrape or brush off as much as possible. Apply solvent using the absorbent pad method,* then wash to remove final traces
Scorch marks (light)	Glycerine	First try soaking in cold water and soap or detergent suds, then wash. If stain persists, moisten with water and rub glycerine into the stain. Wash. Try removing residual marks by soaking in a hydrogen peroxide solution. Heavy scorch marks that have damaged the fabric fibre usually cannot be removed. Alternative method: dampen the affected area and leave in the sunlight for a few hours. Soak a piece of linen in a solution of 3% hydrogen peroxide, place it over the scorch then press with a hot iron. (Test for colourfastness first)
Shoe polish	Glycerine and proprietary grease solvent	Lubricate stain with glycerine, then use solvent and absorbent pad method. Wash to remove final traces
Sour milk	Laundry detergent and cloudy ammonia	Rinse in cold water, then soak for 30 minutes in laundry detergent and lukewarm water with 1 teaspoon cloudy ammonia. Rinse and wash in lukewarm water
Stains on clothing (soluble grease, perspiration marks and oil)	Eucalyptus oil	Add 2 teaspoons eucalyptus oil to a wash load. Place an absorbent cloth under the stain. Moisten a clean rag with eucalyptus oil and gently but firmly brush the stain from its edge into the middle
Sunscreen	Proprietary grease solvent	Absorbent pad method
Tar	Eucalyptus oil, proprietary grease solvent, benzineor lighter fuel	Scrape off surplus. Apply solvent using the absorbent pad method.* Rinse and wash off as soon as possible
Verdigris (green stains from copper pipes) on wool, synthetic fabrics and all delicate fibres	Lemon juice	Flood the stain with lemon juice and leave for 10–15 minutes. Place a damp cloth over the stain and iron. Repeat several times if required. Rinse and wash as usual
Verdigris on white cotton and linen only	Oxalic acid solution	Dissolve ½ teaspoon oxalic acid crystals in 1 cup hot water. Immerse the stained part. Leave for 2–3 minutes. Rinse thoroughly and wash in rich suds

Special washing tasks

Here's a special guide for tackling some of those difficult washing tasks around the home.

DOONAS AND EIDERDOWNS

Dry-cleaning is usually the recommended option for doonas (duvets) and eiderdowns, but if you have the space to tackle them at home, use warm, soapy water and knead to aid cleaning. Rinse well in several changes of water. Do not wring or spin dry the doona, just squeeze out as much water as possible, then place it flat on grass, if you can, on an old sheet. Turn it over and shake it from time to time. When it is absolutely dry, shake it thoroughly and hang it on the line, then beat it gently to separate the filling.

BLANKETS

Don't wash a woollen blanket in hot water, as it will felt — that is, it will become matted in texture. Instead, use warm water with a mild detergent and a gentle washing action. Do not leave a woollen blanket to soak for more than 5 minutes. A cup of ammonia will help to soften the fabric. Spin dry, shake vigorously and reshape it before hanging it on the line to dry.

Non-woollen blankets are usually machine-washable. If yours is heavily soiled, it's a good idea to soak it for about 20 minutes first. Then wash it on a gentle cycle in the washing machine in warm water, followed by a cold rinse and a fast spin dry. Hang the blanket out to dry on a line and, if possible, spread the weight over two lines, or simply lay it flat on an old sheet on the grass.

CURTAINS

Many types of curtains are washable, especially if you wash them by hand. To get rid of as much dust as possible, take the curtains outside and shake them first. If you're washing curtains for the first time, soak them overnight in salty water to remove fabric dressings (finishing treatments).

PILLOWS

It is possible to wash feather-filled pillows, but take care not to strip the feathers of their natural oils. Follow these steps.

1   Use a mild detergent or soap and wash them either by hand or in a front-loading machine. (A top loader may be too rough.)

2   Rinse the pillows thoroughly and, if washing by hand, squeeze out any excess water.

3 Otherwise spin dry in any type of washing machine.

4 Do not hang up pillows to dry, as the filling will fall to one end. If you don't have a dryer, lay them flat. If you're drying them in a tumble dryer, use a low temperature. A couple of towels in the dryer will speed up the drying time, and two or three tennis balls will help break up any clumps of feathers. Make sure the pillows are completely dry before putting them away.

DELICATE ITEMS

Small lace handkerchiefs and other delicate items that could be damaged by rubbing can be placed in a screw-top jar filled with warm, soapy water. Soap flakes are fine. Shake vigorously. Rinse in clean, warm water in the same manner.

To wash delicate net or chiffon, place the item inside a clean muslin bag first. Wash it in warm, soapy water (again, use soap flakes) and knead it gently. Rinse in the same fashion.

Starching

Stiffening fabrics with starch gives them body and crispness, and also creates an extra barrier to dirt. Starches are available in dry, liquid and spray forms, but you can also make them yourself. Some starches are applied during ironing, while others can be put in the final rinse of the wash. Sprays are convenient when ironing or for a quick touch-up job on cuffs and collars.

If using liquid starch, dip clothes in the starching fluid after rinsing. Squeeze out excess water, hang the articles until nearly dry, or roll in a dry cloth ready for damp ironing. Iron the garment on alternate sides until it is dry.

To stiffen synthetic fabrics, use sizings. These usually contain a cotton derivative, sodium carboxymethylcellulose, which stiffens when it is exposed to heat.

Drying

If you can, dry your washing outside in the fresh air — a clothes dryer consumes energy and costs you money, while wet clothes hung over a clothes horse disperse a lot of extra moisture into the home, encouraging moulds and dust mites.

If you live in a flat or apartment, you don't have a clothes dryer and drying inside is the only option, use only one room, if possible, and keep a window open to provide ventilation. Shut the door of the room, sealing it off from the rest of the house. Of course, after several days of wet weather, especially if you live in a cold climate, you'll have no option but to hang damp clothes up to dry all over your home.

PEGGING OUT

Hanging clothes out is quite a simple task; however, if you follow these handy tips, your clothes will last longer and ironing will be easier.

▶ Hang clothes straightaway. If you leave wet clothes in the laundry basket, you risk colour runs and mould.

▶ Hang drip-dry clothes while they are dripping wet — they are designed to relax their wrinkles while drying.

▶ Lie knitted items flat in the shade.

▶ Place pleated garments in a stocking before hanging them up to dry. Roll them up if necessary.

▶ Dry white household linen and white clothing in the sun, but coloured items and woollens out of the sun. The sun's bleaching effect is welcome on whites, but it can fade coloureds as well as shrink wool and cause white silk to yellow.

▶ Use plenty of pegs to support garments so they won't be pulled out of shape.

▶ As a rule, peg the strongest part of the item — waistband, shoulders and toes, and the hems of T-shirts, dresses and shirts.

▶ Don't fold sheets before pegging them out, as they will dry faster if allowed to billow between two lines. If you must fold them because you don't have enough line space, fold each sheet in four, then refold and turn them from time to time to accelerate the drying process.

Caring for towels

As bacteria love a moist environment, towels and face washers or flannels should be allowed to dry thoroughly between uses; on a sunny or windy day, it's best to dry them outside. Making sure each household member has his or her own towel will cut down the transfer of bacteria from one person to another.

As some toiletries contain substances that can damage towels and face washers or flannels, rinse them in cold water if they come into contact with, for instance, skin creams. Skin creams containing benzoyl peroxide can cause colour loss. Hair perming and neutralising solutions are also particularly damaging.

Snip pulled threads on towels before they spread.

USING A TUMBLE DRYER

Here are some tips for using your tumble dryer efficiently.

- ▶ Make sure your tumble dryer is vented to the outside so the moist air is extracted.

- ▶ Use the washing machine's fastest spin option to squeeze as much water out of the load as possible. This will cut down the drying time.

- ▶ Sort the clothes first, grouping together items that need a similar drying time, otherwise you'll end up with some damp clothes and others that are over-dried and possibly damaged.

- ▶ Use the correct temperature for the fabric.

- ▶ Don't overload the dryer — the load should tumble freely. However, remember that drying full loads is more efficient.

- ▶ Reload the dryer while it's still warm from a previous load.

- ▶ Clean the dryer's lint screen after each load. Lint build-up limits air flow and so increases drying time.

- ▶ Do not tumble dry items that contain elastic or rubber.

Ironing

With so many easy-care, drip-dry clothes available these days, it's possible to avoid using an iron altogether, but there are still many people who regard a newly ironed, crisp cotton shirt as being worth the extra effort. And there are also some people who insist on ironing every item of washing, including towels and socks!

IRONING HINTS AND TIPS

What you choose to iron is up to you, but when you do, here are some tips on how to go about it.

- ▶ First, dampen the clothes. Steam irons automatically dampen fabric as they iron, but some items will still benefit from dampening before ironing. The most effective way of doing this is to sprinkle the item with warm water, then roll it up tightly and put it aside. If you're really organised, you could sprinkle them and leave them in a plastic bag overnight. Alternatively, sprinkle the clothes an hour before ironing. Failing that, spray or sprinkle while you iron.

Drying knits
If you have nowhere flat to dry a knitted top, run the legs of an old pair of pantihose (tights) through both sleeves and peg the waist and toes of the pantihose to the line. This technique helps support the weight of the garment and prevents peg marks.

Sweetly pressed
Add a couple of drops of an essential oil to a spray bottle of water, and use it to dampen clothing and linen when ironing.

▶ Ironing brings out the best in a fabric, but it's important to follow a few basic rules. The iron must be hot enough to smooth a fabric's wrinkles, but not so hot that it damages it. Some fabrics should be ironed on the wrong side to avoid making them shiny, and others (such as wool) should not be ironed directly, as this makes the fibres brittle.

▶ Unless the manufacturer specifically states that tap water is suitable for your iron, use either distilled water or demineralised tap water, both of which are available at supermarkets.

▶ Natural fabrics will simply burn if you iron them on too hot a temperature, but synthetic fibres may melt.

▶ Don't iron over plastic buttons and zips.

▶ Don't press over metal objects that may scratch the plate of the iron.

▶ Use a pressing cloth over metal objects, especially when using an iron with a non-stick plate.

WHICH IRON SETTING?

FABRIC	IRON SETTING	DAMP OR DRY	WHICH SIDE?
Acrylic	Cool	Dry	Wrong
Cotton (dark)	Warm–hot	Either	Wrong
Cotton (pale)	Warm–hot	Either	Either
Linen (dark)	Warm	Damp	Wrong
Linen (pale)	Hot	Either	Either
Nylon	Cool	Damp	Either
Polyester	Cool	Damp	Either
Polyester mixes	Warm	Either	Either
Rayon	Warm	Damp	Wrong
Silk	Warm	Either	Wrong
Wool	Warm	Dry	Wrong

Ironing clothes

1 First, iron thicker areas — such as collars, cuffs and waistbands — as these will wrinkle less while you complete the garment.

2 Next, iron structured areas that are not flat — for example, sleeves.

3 Finally, iron the flat areas such as shirt backs.

Ironing table linen

1 For a round tablecloth, start in the middle and work outwards.

2 Iron napkins flat. Do not iron in creases.

3 Iron damask, which is designed to be shiny, on the wrong side first, then on the right side.

PRESSING

Knitted woollens and tailored items, such as suits, need pressing rather than ironing. This is best done professionally, but when that's not possible, or you want to touch up a garment, you can do it at home.

To press, take a hot iron and a damp cloth made of calico or linen. Place the damp cloth on the garment and press heavily on the iron to remove creases. Continue pressing until the cloth is dry, but don't let it become singed. If the garment to be pressed is damp, do not dampen the cloth. Take care that the iron does not touch the garment itself or it may cause shiny patches.

CLEANING THE IRON

It's a good idea to keep the plate of your iron clean with this old-fashioned method — from time to time rub it with a cloth soaked in strong, cold tea, then wipe it with a soft, clean cloth. If you exercise some care when using your iron, you will avoid damaging the plate with melted fibres or rust. If something does go wrong, look at the table on page 102 for some cleaning and repair solutions.

Sterilise as you iron
A hot iron sterilises tea towels and handkerchiefs.

Ironing linen
If you have hung linen to dry or laid it flat, once it is the correct dampness for ironing, roll it up tightly and place it in a plastic bag. Put it in the fridge or freezer if you don't intend to iron it within a couple of hours.

HOW TO CLEAN A DIRTY IRON

PROBLEM	SOLUTION
Accumulated brown stains	Rub the cold plate with a cut lemon
Clogged steam vents	Use a cotton wool bud and warm soapy water. If this doesn't work, pour white vinegar into the water tank and turn on the iron for a few minutes. Iron a clean rag to remove deposits. Cool and rinse with cold water
Dirty non-stick plates	Clean with a cloth dampened in warm water and detergent
Dirty ordinary plate	Rub with bicarbonate of soda and a damp cloth
Melted synthetic fibre	Heat the iron and gently scrape away large pieces with a wooden spoon or ice cream stick. Wearing an oven glove, remove smaller traces with cotton wool dipped in acetone (nail polish remover) and/or rubbing alcohol. If necessary, rub a regular plate with very fine steel wool, and a non-stick plate with a nylon mesh scrubber dipped in mild sudsy water
Plastic	Sprinkle some aluminium foil with salt and then iron it
Rust	Scour with salt and beeswax
Scratched surface	Rub with dampened salt and crumpled newspaper
Sticky plate	1 Use a clean toothbrush. Heat the iron to warm and iron (e.g. with starch) over a piece of waxed paper. 2 Clean with metal polish. 3 While the iron is hot, run it back and forth over a sheet of clean paper that has been generously sprinkled with salt.

Maintenance

There are many simple maintenance jobs around the home that you can do, regardless of your skill or experience, from changing a fuse or a fluorescent light tube to unblocking the drain and cleaning the windows. Store your tools in a well-organised work area, and always keep dangerous chemicals in a locked cupboard.

2   If you have, remove the cover from the fluorescent light. If there are two screws at either end holding the caps on, which in turn hold the cover on, take one cap off and remove the cover.

3   Rotate the tube slightly, pulling on it as you go. The tube should pop out.

4   Line up the lugs of the new tube with the slot at each end. Slide the lugs in and rotate the tube. Turn on the power and test that it works.

Replacing the starter

If you've changed the tube but the light is still flickering, the problem could be one of the starters — the small, white cylinders poking out from the light body. Once again, turn off the power at the main switch.

1   Push up slightly and turn the starter. It will pop out.

2   Replace it. If you're still having problems, call an electrician.

Simple plumbing jobs

It's a good idea to familiarise yourself with these basic maintenance jobs, as they only take a few minutes but may save you a lot of money.

THE WATER METER

The first thing you should do when you move into a new home is find the water meter and make sure the washer works and actually shuts the water down. It's not unusual in an emergency to find the water meter needs repairs and you can't turn off the water. If this is the case, putting a new washer in the meter is a job for the plumber, but it will be money well spent. Otherwise, if the kitchen pipe bursts, and water goes everywhere, you won't be able to turn the water off at the main.

The water main is usually on the left-hand side of the front garden, or if you live in an apartment, it can actually be inside. Sometimes it's in the kitchen cabinet — just look in a cupboard for a tap that's on its own. Turn it off and test the water.

If there's a burst pipe in the house and you've turned off the water at the meter, but it's still not shutting the water down properly, turn on any other tap between the meter and the burst pipe. This will reduce the flow in the house, not stop it, but it might save some damage until you can call in a professional.

KEEPING THE DRAIN CLEAR

A little attention now and then can prevent serious blockages developing.

▶ **Selective disposal** The first step in trying to keep drains clear is to put as little as possible down the drain in the first place. Catch food debris and prevent it clogging the drain pipes by using a sink strainer, then dispose of the scraps in the compost. Use the compost bin for biodegradable matter, including tea leaves and coffee grounds, and scrape fat and oil into the garbage rather than wash up dishes and pans caked with fat.

▶ **Boiling water** Pour boiling water down the kitchen sink to melt grease and wash it away.

▶ **Drain cleaners** Keep the kitchen drain clear by regularly using a drain cleaner — it's much less time-consuming than clearing an already blocked drain. Commercial drain cleaners often use sodium hydroxide and aluminium, which rely on bubbling — from aluminium and the heat formed when the sodium hydroxide dissolves — to agitate and melt grease. It's cheaper and better for the environment to try one of the home remedies given on page 36.

Unblocking a sink

If you have a blocked sink, it's usually due to a build-up of grease or other matter in the trap. You could try using chemicals (proprietary drain cleaners), but if they don't work, try the following, or see the box on page 36.

1 Take the trap off.

2 Disconnect the top and bottom, and clean out the trap. If the trap is clean, this means the blockage is further down the line, so you'll need to call a plumber.

Fixing noisy water pipes

If you hear a loud bang when you turn off the tap, or a tapping sound while the water's running, this is probably due to water hammer, which is usually caused by poor installation of pipes.

The only way to fix this problem yourself is to isolate the rattling pipe and tighten it. If it's attached to the wall of your floor frame without enough fastenings, it can rattle around when you turn your taps on and off.

1   Find the noise first. Get under the house and ask a helper to turn the taps on and off.

2   If the pipe is loose, saddle it to whatever you can — brickwork, bearer or joist — and once you've done that, simply flick the pipe with your finger and listen for any movement.

3   Keep applying the saddles until the pipe is tightly in place. If there are loose pipes you can't get to, and it's still a problem, call the plumber.

Checking for burst water pipes

If you have some damp in the walls or a wet spot in the garden, you may have a burst water pipe. To test for a burst pipe, mark the meter and check it the next day.

1   Turn off all the taps tightly at night before you go to bed, and also turn off the toilets, as they may have a tiny leak you can't see. You'll still be able to flush each toilet once during the night.

2   At your water meter, use a felt tip pen to mark a line on the glass covering the numbers. Match what you've done on a piece of paper.

3   The next morning, compare the position of the line on the meter with the one you copied onto paper the night before. If the line on the meter has moved since the night before, then you have a water leak. This will avoid the plumber's lengthy inspection costs, and you may also be able to save even more time and money by digging up and exposing the burst pipe.

Unblocking a toilet

If the pan is clogged and overflowing with water, turn off the water supply to the toilet. The tap is usually just behind it.

1   First, wait a while to allow the water to subside — sometimes a blockage will clear of its own accord. If it doesn't, use a plunger. Some experts recommend a plunger with a metal disc above the rubber cup to prevent the cup turning inside out while you use it; plunging requires more vigour for a toilet than a sink, as there are no flat surfaces with which to make a good seal.

2   Wash the plunger by flushing the cistern while it is still in the pan, then adding a little detergent and bleach to the pan water.

3   Depending on your confidence, or your skills, plumber's eels (jointed flexible tubing that can be pushed into drains to remove blockages) are another possible solution, but it may be easier to call the plumber.

Fixing a constantly running toilet

This problem is often caused by a worn cistern washer. It's a little difficult to fix, but worth a try.

1 Remove the lid of the cistern. If an old blue toilet cleanser is stuck under the cistern washer, letting water out, then simply remove it. However, it's more likely that the washer has perished.

2 Turn off the water supply to toilet.

3 Flush the cistern so you have a dry unit. At the bottom of the cistern, sealing off the entrance to the flush pipe, is a washer. Reach in and prise this off.

4 Take this washer to the plumbing supply store so you can match and replace it.

Replacing a toilet seat

Purchase a new toilet seat at the plumbing supply store, as they'll have the best range. To replace the seat, follow these steps.

1 Reach down under the back of the seat. On each side you will find a wing nut, which you can undo with your fingers. Unless your toilet seat is very old, these nuts will be plastic.

2 The new toilet seat will come complete with new screws and wing nuts, so all you need to do is reverse the process.

Repairing the seals on the bath

The sealant around the edge of a bath will need to be repaired at some point during the lifetime of the bath. Removing the old seal and replacing it with a new one is a simple process.

1 Use a small paintbrush to apply a proprietary sealant-removal solution along the sealant bead. Allow this to soak into the sealant, according to the manufacturer's instructions.

2 Use a window scraper to ease the sealant away from the wall and bath surface, taking care not to scratch the surface of the bath.

3 Use a cloth to clean away any remaining sealant. Dampening the cloth with methylated spirits (denatured alcohol) will help prepare the surface for the application of new sealant to give a watertight finish.

Painting exterior surfaces

Exterior surfaces, which are subject to the vagaries of the weather, should be painted often. Modern paint finishes respond well to weathering, but still require occasional maintenance.

How much paint to buy

To work out how much paint to buy, calculate the total surface area to be painted. The surface area of a wall is obtained when you multiply its length by its height. For example, a 4 x 5 m (13 x 16½ ft) wall has a surface area of 20 sq m (215 square ft). Before buying your paint, check on the can to see how much coverage it will provide. Keep in mind, however, that this is only a rough indication, as the application method and the type of surface being painted are more likely to dictate the amount of paint you will use.

Ventilators

Vents in your house walls need checking and cleaning so the air can breeze through. Make sure you prune nearby trees and shrubs. Clean small holes with a bottle brush.

PREPARING SURFACES FOR PAINTING

Basic cleaning down every 12 months, or a freshening up of heavy-duty areas, should provide a longer-lasting paint finish on exterior surfaces. Remember that dirt, grime and the sun are continually working away at the painted surface, breaking it down. Regular maintenance will make exterior repainting a much easier task, largely decreasing the amount of surface deterioration.

Modern homes require little maintenance, if any, apart from a regular washing down, while older homes, which generally have more timber surfaces, require much more work.

TIPS FOR EXTERIOR PAINTING

▶ Work from the top downwards, both when cleaning and painting, to prevent dust, dirt or paint splashes.

▶ Avoid painting in direct sunlight. Glare off the surface can hurt your eyes and put you at risk of skin cancer, while sunlight can cause many problems with the drying process and the ultimate paint finish. Try working on the shady side of the house in the morning, finishing in the afternoon on the other side of the house.

Cleaning and maintaining brickwork

Bricks are best cleaned with a solution of hydrochloric acid and water, 1 part acid to 20 parts water. Always add the acid to the water so the acid will be less likely to splash you.

Complete all surface preparation before applying any paint or you'll end up with damaged work. Keep to a system — surface preparation first, then priming, undercoat and finish.

If the weather looks indifferent, consider painting areas that will not be damaged by wind and rain. Leave areas that are under cover until last, just in case it does rain.

Cleaning windows

There is something very satisfying about seeing sun stream through a gleaming pane of glass. You'll need the following equipment.

▶ Steady ladder to reach higher windows. (Call a window cleaner if you're unsteady on your feet or suffer from vertigo.)

▶ Bucket of cleaning solution — either a commercial one, or one of the home-made alternatives on page 112

▶ Sponge

▶ Squeegee (handle with a thin strip of sponge on one side and a rubber strip on the other)

▶ Clean cloth

▶ Newspaper

Cleaning windows

Wash windows on a cloudy day, as sun makes the glass dry too quickly and unevenly, resulting in streaks. If you plan to clean or wash the window frames too, do these before you wash the glass — wipe or dust the frames first and if that's not enough, follow with a wash and wipe dry.

1   First, starting at the top of the window, wash the glass with a cloth or sponge. Some people swear by rinsing with clean water then wiping with a chamois,

others not. It probably depends on how dirty the windows are and whether cleaning them is a grand annual ritual or a fortnightly routine.

2   Following the wash or the rinse, squeegee the surface or dry it with a clean, dry, lint-free cloth.

3   For really dry, sparkly windows, polish with a few sheets of newspaper.

WINDOW-CLEANING TIPS

▶   To prevent windows from fogging, rub over a little glycerine after cleaning them.

▶   For a quick clean, when the glass is not too dirty, try wiping the windows first with wet newspaper, then with dry. The ink on the newspaper polishes them.

▶   Never try to clean a window with a dry cloth, as the dirt could scratch the glass.

▶   Never use soap on windows, as it leaves smears that are very difficult to remove.

▶   To remove wet paint from glass, wipe with a cloth dipped in the appropriate solvent — turpentine for oil-based paints, water for water-based.

▶   To remove old paint marks from glass, gently scrape off the paint with a razor blade, taking care not to scratch the glass.

▶   To remove putty marks from glass, wipe with ammonia or cold tea.

Cleaning flyscreens
First, use a soft brush to remove dust and cobwebs from flyscreens, then wipe over with a sponge dipped in warm water. Rinse with clean water to which a few drops of citronella or tea-tree oil have been added. The oil will help repel pests.

Homemade window cleaners

Recipe 1
>   250 ml (8 fl oz/1 cup) white vinegar
>   4 litres (8½ pints) water

Recipe 2
>   125 ml (4 fl oz/½ cup) white vinegar
>   125 ml (4 fl oz/½ cup) household ammonia
>   4 litres (8½ pints) water

Recipe 3
>   250 ml (8 fl oz/1 cup) methylated spirits (denatured alcohol)
>   250 ml (8 fl oz/1 cup) water

Door problems

Here are a couple of common door problems that can be easily fixed by the home handyperson.

Fixing a rattling door

If even small gusts of wind cause the door to rattle, it could be that the doorstop has been positioned too far from the latch, which should be held firmly in place by the latch position and doorstop combined. Alternatively, the doorstop may be positioned too far forward or too close to the latch plate, and you can't physically shut the door.

To reposition the doorstop, follow these steps.

1 Use an old chisel to carefully lever the doorstop out of position.

2 Close the door, and mark a line on the door lining where the edge of the doorstop should be.

3 Reopen the door and nail the doorstop back in place, according to the new guidelines. You may also need to move the position of the doorstop on the head and hinged side of the frame, so check this once you have positioned the first piece of doorstop.

Fixing a stiff lock or keyhole

Sewing machine oil, WD 40 or grease may each ease a stiff lock for a short time but not for long. These substances attract dust and dirt, and will clog up the mechanism and make it stiff again. Instead, buy some graphite a fine powder form. It comes in a plastic container with a pointed nozzle.

1 Squirt the graphite on the key as well as into the keyhole.

2 For a deadlock or door handle, you may have to pull off the lock or handle and squirt the graphite into the lock.

3 The latch on the edge of the door is a separate unit to the handle. Squirt it with graphite as well so the whole action can move smoothly.

Keeping gutters clear

The only gutters worth having are clean ones — leaf- and dirt-filled ones don't work properly when it rains and are a fire hazard in dry, hot weather. To prevent a serious build-up of leaves and other debris, fit mesh along the gutter. This will protect the down pipes from blockage.

Clean gutters regularly. Use a trowel, plastic scraper or stiff brush to remove debris and built-up dirt, then give the gutters a good hose. Check the downpipe on a regular basis for blockages, and use hot water to loosen any encrusted dirt before flushing the pipe with the hose.

Personal belongings

Whether your fashion sense favours investment dressing or a quick raid on your favourite boutique each season, your clothes and other personal belongings deserve care and attention. Look for those little details — a missing button or a tarnished piece of jewellery — and fix them promptly

Get organised

Do you regularly have trouble finding things when you need them, or are reluctant to throw things out, even when they're broken? If your home feels a little chaotic, it's time to get organised and regain a sense of control.

THE BOX METHOD

Start going through the house in a systematic way, room by room, or if that seems like an insurmountable task, just clean out one drawer or shelf per session. Dump everything on the floor, then apply the clutter test to each item, sorting into six boxes as you go.

▶ **Box 1** Put away the things you want to keep.

▶ **Box 2** Throw away anything that's broken or can't be fixed, reused, recycled or given away.

▶ **Box 3** Get rid of clothes that don't fit, gifts you don't like and will never use, books you don't value and appliances you never use. Donate to a charity, give them away to friends, or sell them at a garage sale or on ebay.

▶ **Box 4** Store seasonal clothing and items you only use occasionally, such as camping equipment.

▶ **Box 5** This is the 'not sure' box, where you store anything you're not sure about for one year. If you don't use it in that time, throw it out.

▶ **Box 6** Set aside items that need repair, but be realistic — will you actually fix it? Otherwise, put it in Box 2.

Is it worth keeping?

Before you decide to keep something, ask yourself these six questions.

1   Is it in good shape?

2   Do I really need it?

3   Has anyone used it in the past year?

4   Would it be hard to replace if I ever need it again?

5   Would I pay to store it, and if so, for how long?

6   Does it have sentimental value?

THE GOLDEN RULES OF CLUTTER CONTROL

▶ Spend 10 minutes each morning or evening picking things up and putting them back where they belong.

▶ Institute family or household rules for clearing up after one activity and before starting another.

▶ Deal with things as they arise.

▶ Take things upstairs or downstairs when you're going there anyway.

▶ Dump junk mail the minute you receive it. If possible, keep a paper bin near your mail box.

▶ Limit yourself to a set number of bags, food containers and boxes that you keep because they 'might come in handy one day'.

▶ One in, one out — in other words, throw/give away one item each time you acquire something new. This may be worth trying if you are constantly acquiring new things.

Your wardrobe

Clothes need air to stay fresh. The cupboards, wardrobes and closets where you store your clothes should be dry and airy. Slatted shelves allow air to circulate — several shallow shelves are more effective than one or two deep ones and also make it easier to find items.

If you look after your clothes, they'll not only look their best but also last longer.

▶ Hang up your jacket as soon as you take it off rather than sling it on the nearest chair or bed.

▶ Don't launder more often than necessary — if you wear a shirt for just an hour or so, hang it up to air for a few hours before putting it back in the wardrobe. Fasten the top, middle and bottom buttons and, if necessary, spot-clean it rather than wash it.

▶ Dirt and sweat cause fabrics to deteriorate, so when clothes really need washing, do it sooner rather than later.

▶ When doing anything messy, protect clothes with an apron or overall.

▶ Use a scarf to protect the necks and collars of coats and jackets, especially leather ones, as hair and skin oils can stain.

▶ Don't be tempted to put slightly damp clothes away. Wait until they are bone dry, as even the slightest touch of dampness will give clothes a musty smell that will be difficult to remove.

▶ Air and brush tailored jackets and skirts or trousers that have been dry-cleaned before putting them away.

Hanging up

Wide, shaped clothes hangers prolong the life of tailored clothing by spreading the weight and reducing the stress on the fabric. They also help preserve the shape. Padded hangers are even better.

Before you hang up your clothes, fasten zips and do up the top, middle and bottom buttons — this will help them to hold their shape. Empty the pockets, especially in woollen garments, which easily become distorted when they are weighed down with loose change and other heavy but small items.

Hang trousers by the cuffs (the leg bottoms) or fold them over a hanger that has either a thick dowel bar or a paper guard to prevent a horizontal crease forming.

Heavenly scents
To add a fresh smell to your wardrobe or chest of drawers, use herb sachets. Place a couple of teaspoons of potpourri or dried lavender in a piece of lightweight fabric, such as muslin or cheesecloth, and tie it with a ribbon.

NEW LIFE FOR OLD CLOTHES
Back in the days when nothing was wasted, patching, mending, cutting down and reusing worn out clothes and old linen used to be a way of life — garments were cut into squares and sown into patchwork quilts, double sheets were revamped into single ones and and even rags were made into plaited and coiled floor rugs. A patchwork quilt could become a family heirloom and a highly valued collectors' item.

These days we tend to throw out or give away a piece of clothing as soon as we're bored with it. But you can give clothing a new lease of life. Here are some ideas to get you started.

> ## Basic sewing kit
>
> *Even if all you do is sew on loose buttons, every house needs a small repair kit.*
>
> ▶ **Scissors** A small pair with sharp points for cutting thread; dressmaking shears if you plan to tackle fabric.
>
> ▶ **Needles** A range is best, according to likely tasks — ordinary, embroidery, darners, upholstery.
>
> ▶ **Thimble** Protects the middle finger when pushing a needle through fabric.
>
> ▶ **Threads** White, black and beige are a good base.
>
> ▶ **Pins, tape measure and fastenings** Include a button collection.

DYEING

When the colours of a garment have faded but the fabric is not worn, dyeing — especially professional dyeing— revitalises and smartens. This is also a good option for faded towels and bed linen.

DARNING

Once darning holes in socks was the norm, but these days cheap factory products have made it an almost redundant skill. However, darning is still useful for repairing small holes that would otherwise make a woollen item unwearable.

1 Take care to match the colour of the thread. If darning a patterned garment, using two colours may disguise the repair better.

2 If possible, work on the wrong side.

3 Take stitches well beyond the hole into the strong part of the fabric.

PATCHING

This repair method is ideal for children's play clothes and also useful for adults' clothes that can take a bit of character — for example, elbow patches on a favourite woolly jumper. Circular or diamond patches wear better and show less than rectangles and squares. Choose soft, supple leather for elbow patches and for strips along the end of a sleeve or along the front of a pocket. Cut a generous size that amply covers worn areas with plenty of margin, and use a blanket stitch or buttonhole stitch with a little slack to allow for movement.

Trim it
If a favourite cardigan is looking a little dated, try dressing it up with new trims and buttons.

MENDING AN L-SHAPED TEAR

When clothes catch and tear on a sharp object, pull the edges together and tack them to a piece of finely woven cloth on the wrong side of the fabric. Using threads from the garment, if possible, make a series of diagonal stitches across the tear in one direction, then in the opposite way so they form a trellis pattern.

POCKETS

A worn pocket is a liability and an unnecessary one at that. For holes in trouser pockets, cut off the worn area and sew in a new piece in a tough fabric such as drill or calico. Alternatively, you could fit an entirely new pocket — these are available ready-made if you don't want to start from scratch.

To fix patch pockets that have ripped from the back, unpick the top corners, and place a strip of cotton behind the tear or weak area. Fix it with running stitches, then lightly darn on the right side. Finally, reattach the pocket firmly.

Recycling ideas

▶ *Eccentric hats, uncomfortable but glamorous shoes and other purchasing mistakes, especially ones made from unusual fabrics, make wonderful additions to a children's dress-up box.*

▶ *Old big shirts are ideal for dirty work, such as cleaning and gardening.*

▶ *Odd or old socks are useful for storing safety goggles, as ladder end pads and for various jobs around the house, including polishing.*

▶ *If a pyjama leg is not too worn, secure it in place over the ironing board.*

STORING CLOTHES

Before putting clothes away for long-term storage, or to store until next season, make sure you follow this checklist.

▶ Wash them in hot water, 50–60°C (122–140°F), or dry-clean them first. Dirt is more likely to attract pests such as insects, and encourage mildew.

▶ Air items, especially ones you've steam-ironed or damped down before ironing.

▶ Use muslin or canvas storage bags, or clean white or undyed sheets.

▶ Place items on wire racks rather than shelves to allow the air to circulate properly.

▶ Don't starch items to be stored, as starch attracts meal-seeking silverfish, which do not discriminate between the starch and the clothing fibre.

▶ Don't store clothes in dry-cleaning plastic or other garment bags that don't breathe, as moisture may be trapped inside. Over time, dry-cleaning plastic may cause yellow streaks due to the plasticisers it contains.

▶ Don't put clothes away while they are still damp.

Wrinkle less
When you're packing a suitcase or putting away valuable clothes, placing tissue paper (acid-free for storage) between the fabric layers helps reduce creasing and wrinkling.

Home dry-cleaning kits

Instead of sending your delicate clothes to the dry-cleaner, you can try freshening them in the tumble dryer by using a kit comprising stain removers, a dry-cleaning sheet and a dryer-safe plastic bag. These kits are good at removing odours such as stale cigarette smoke and cooking smells but they don't clean as well as the professionals. They do, however, help minimise the number of visits to the dry-cleaners. They also use chemicals that, while not considered 100 per cent environmentally friendly, are less harmful to the environment than 'perc'.

MOTHS

The webbing clothes moth *(Tineola bisselliella)*, the most common fabric moth, is particularly attracted to wool and furs, and its larvae eat the fibres, leaving a rash of holes. Stored, unused clothing is most vulnerable, as moths do not attack clothes that are in constant use. Regular airing and shaking does much to guard against moth attack. Turn out pockets and brush off fluff.

Toxic treatment

Commercial moth treatments kill moths, larvae and eggs in an airtight situation where they saturate the insects, but they are toxic not only to moths but also to humans. They include naphthalene and PDB (paradichlorobenzene), an organochlorine. If you must resort to these, use them only in spaces away from living areas, such as attics or garages.

To remove the smell of mothballs, scrub with equal parts of white vinegar and lemon juice. Repeat if necessary.

Seal it away

*If any of these treatments
cause irritation, you
may need to store
moth-vulnerable clothing
in sealed plastic bags.*

NATURAL MOTH TREATMENTS

▶ If you suspect moths have invaded an article of clothing, wrap it in a clean, damp towel and put it in a low oven to steam out the grubs, or place it underneath a damp towel and press it with a hot iron.

▶ If you can actually see moths, brush the article with a solution of 3 tablespoons turpentine and 2.8 litres (98 fl oz) water.

▶ To defend drawers and cupboards from moth invasion, keep them free from dust and fluff by regularly airing and vacuuming them. Wipe over with a natural repellent such as eucalyptus oil.

▶ Cotton wool buds dipped in essential oils are said to keep moths away from clothing. You could try lavender, lemongrass, camphor or rosemary, and place a couple of buds in each drawer between your items of clothing. Or dot a few drops of essential oil on sheets of blotting paper, fix the scent with orris root powder and use them as drawer liners.

▶ Herbal deterrents include sachets of cedar chips or dried lavender flowers, rosemary or southernwood. Place these among your clothes, where they not only help to deter moths and silverfish but also keep clothes smelling fresh.

▶ Line drawers with brown paper, butcher's paper or wallpaper off-cuts. Scatter herbal repellents underneath the paper.

▶ Make sachets from light fabrics such as muslin and fill them with a mixture of ground cloves, nutmeg, mace, caraway seeds, cinnamon (30 g/1 oz each) and orris root powder (90 g/3½ oz). This amount of mixture will fill several sachets.

Brushes and combs

To clean brushes the old-fashioned way, dissolve a walnut-sized piece of washing soda in hot water in a basin. Comb out the hair from the brushes then dip them, bristles downward, into the water, keeping the backs and handles out of the water as much as possible. Repeat until the bristles seem clean. Rinse in a little cold water, shake well and wipe the handles and backs, but not the bristles, with a towel. Place in the sun or near a heater to dry. Do not use soap on bristles or wipe, as this will soften them.

Tortoiseshell or bone combs are best not washed, as water may split and roughen them. Clean them with small brushes instead.

JEWELLERY

If you prefer to clean your jewellery at home, forearm yourself with a little knowledge, but always take valuable pieces to professionals for expert cleaning.

▶ Store precious jewels in padded boxes or bags to protect them against sunlight, dust and humidity.

▶ Avoid extremes of temperature.

▶ To protect precious pieces against scratches and tangles, keep them separate from each other.

▶ Take extra care when cleaning jewellery with loose stones, as the dirt may be all that's holding them in place.

▶ Use the gentler methods first — for example, use a paint- or make-up brush to clean very dusty pieces.

▶ Don't use any substance on jewellery without being absolutely sure it is recommended for all the materials the jewel is made from. This includes water, detergent, ammonia, bicarbonate of soda and jewellery cleaning cloths and dips.

▶ Don't accidentally spray jewellery with hairspray or perfume, as these can dull some surfaces.

PEARLS

▶ Do not wrap pearls in cotton or wool, as the extra heat this generates can dry them out and cause cracking.

▶ Dampen pearls from time to time in lightly salted water.

▶ After wearing pearls, wipe them with a soft cloth or chamois leather, dry or damp, to remove traces of perspiration, as the acid can damage the surface of the pearls.

▶ If your pearls are really dirty, you can wash them in water and a very mild soap, then clean them with a soft cloth. Lay them on a moist, clean tea towel to dry. The pearls will be dry at the same time as the towel.

WOODEN BEADS, BANGLES AND BROOCHES

Wipe with a damp chamois cloth and rub well with a little olive oil. Finally, buff with a soft cloth.

Washing jewellery
Once you are sure a jewel can be washed, proceed as follows.

1 *Put some water and some washing up liquid into a small bowl. Hot water (not boiling) is fine for diamonds, otherwise use lukewarm water.*

2 *Soak your jewellery for 15 minutes to loosen the dirt, then rinse well.*

3 *Use a small, soft brush, such as a paintbrush, work detergent into the crevices.*

4 *Rinse and dry on a lint-free cloth, such as a tea towel.*

Pearls of wisdom
Wearing pearls often is said to be the best way to care for them, as the oils in your skin give them a gentle lustre.

GLASS BEADS

Shake glass beads in a plastic bag with 2 tablespoons bicarbonate of soda. Dust with a soft brush and buff with a damp chamois cloth.

Not for washing

The following substances are relatively soft and may absorb not only water but also chemicals, including soap or other cleaners.

- *Amber*
- *Bone*
- *Coral*
- *Ivory*
- *Lapis lazuli*

- *Malachite*
- *Mother-of-pearl*
- *Shells*
- *Turquoise*
- *Opal*

SHOES

- Give your shoes a day's rest after each wear — this allows moisture to evaporate, so have at least two pairs for each season.

- Keep your shoes on shoe-trees when they're not in use — this keeps them in shape and avoids cracking. If you store shoes for a long period, place them in individual shoe bags or wrap them in tissue paper.

- Caring for the leather helps prevent cracks (see the box below).

- Use a hard brush to remove mud; never scrape with a knife.

- Repair damaged shoes as soon as they need it. Delaying repair is a false economy.

To soften leather

- *Rub with lemon juice or castor oil. Olive oil helps prevent the leather from cracking and drying.*

- *To wear in new shoes, carefully pour a small amount of methylated spirits into the shoes at the heels and let it soak in. Wear the shoes while they're still wet.*

- *Where a shoe pinches over a toe or joint, press a very hot damp cloth over the spot, and leave it for a few minutes so that it expands and softens the leather.*

REMOVING STAINS

Always proceed with caution, especially for pale-coloured footwear.

▶ **Grease stains on leather** Daub with petrol, then egg white.

▶ **Grease stains on suede** Rub with a rag dipped in glycerine.

▶ **Tar** Remove with petrol.

▶ **Other stains** Sponge with a solution of warm water and vinegar. When dry, polish with a soft cloth soaked in linseed oil. Remove all traces of the oil with a soft, clean cloth.

DRYING SHOES

Leather that remains wet can become irreversibly damaged, while drying wet shoes too quickly can cause cracking.

▶ Never dry shoes in front of a fire or heater.

▶ Stuff shoes with balls of newspaper or sand — the latter dries them quickly without altering their shape.

▶ Revive fine leather shoes by coating them in oil or petroleum jelly. Rub down boots and tougher shoes with saddle soap.

▶ To polish leather that is a little damp, add a few drops of kerosene to a cloth, then use it to rub the leather.

To deodorise shoes
Sprinkle bicarbonate of soda inside the shoes. Leave for a day or two, then shake out and air.

GLOVES

How you clean gloves depends on the material.

LEATHER GLOVES

As a rule, you should not wash suede and lined leather gloves, but some leather gloves are washable. If you want to try washing leather gloves, follow these steps.

1 Empty the fingers of dust and lint.

2 Wash the gloves in warm water and mild soap suds.

3 Squeeze gently.

4 Rub extra soap on any stained patches.

5 Turn the gloves inside out and repeat the gentle squeezing.

6 Rinse the inside, then the outside.

7 Dry the gloves flat, working them several times with your hands as they dry to prevent them from stiffening. When they are half dry, put the gloves on to shape them.

8 When they are completely dry, rub them with a little leather conditioner. If they do dry stiff, wet them a little and work them with your hands to soften them.

WOOLLEN GLOVES

Wash woolly gloves by hand, as they may pull apart in a machine wash.

1 Remove lint and dirt from the inside.

2 Wash them by hand with a mild detergent.

3 Rinse.

4 Roll them in a towel to dry.

LACE

If your lace gloves are machine washable, place them in a mesh bag. Use a gentle cycle, mild detergent and warm water only. If they are too delicate for the washing machine, use the method described in 'Delicate items' on page 97. Dry them by first rolling them in a towel, then laying them flat.

Leather bags and luggage

Before cleaning a bag or suitcase, check the manufacturer's care label, as both leather and suede are available in two different types — one can be washed but the other should be dry-cleaned. Use different methods of cleaning for different types of leather.

▶ Brush suede with a suede brush or an off-cut of suede.

▶ Finish leather with wax polish to keep it supple.

▶ Smear petroleum jelly on patent leather, then buff it dry.

▶ Rub leather bags with neat's-foot oil from time to time, or polish them with boot polish.

▶ To renovate an old leather bag, use a warm, not hot, solution of washing soda to remove grease and dirt. Apply it with a soft rag or a brush if it is very dirty. Oxalic acid, used after the soda, may remove stains. After cleaning the bag, wash with lukewarm water, place in a warm spot to dry and once dry, treat with a wax polish.

Safety in the home

You may be surprised to learn that accidents in the home are a major public health issue, particularly for young children, whose curiosity can lead them to all sorts of dangers. But it takes only a handful of simple measures to protect your family — for example, install smoke alarms, rehearse a fire drill, keep a well-stocked first aid kit and check the house for anything that may cause problems.

- Petroleum jelly
- Cold/allergy remedy
- Antihistamine and decongestant
- Expectorant cough medicine
- Methylated spirits (denatured alcohol)
- Teaspoon or other dose measure, such as syringe, for children
- Hydrogen peroxide
- Syrup of ipecac
- Sunscreen
- Thermometer
- Family medical guide
- Hot water bottle
- Heat pack
- Ice pack (stored in your freezer)

Homemade antiseptic

Here's a simple homemade recipe that can be used for minor cuts and grazes. Dissolve salt in boiled water. Dip a cotton wool ball in the warm, salty water and apply it to the injury.

First aid kit

Keep a first aid kit in your car as well as in the house. Pharmacists sell ready-assembled kits; check against the following list and supplement where necessary.

- 1 small roller bandage
- 1 large roller bandage
- 1 small conforming bandage
- 1 large conforming bandage
- 2 eye pads with bandages
- Scissors
- Safety pins
- Calamine cream
- Pack of gauze swabs
- 2 triangular bandages
- Hypoallergenic tape
- 2 sterile pads
- Waterproof plasters or bandaids
- 1 finger bandage
- Tweezers
- 1 sterile dressing with bandage

Emergency phone numbers

A little forethought saves time and hassle later. Photocopy this list of emergency phone numbers and stick it next to the phone so that all members of the household can find them easily if they need them, and make sure the medicine cabinet and first aid kit are kept well stocked at all times.

Police, fire, ambulance (emergency only) _____

Family doctor _____

Nearest hospital with accident and emergency unit _____

Local police station _____

Local fire station _____

Plumber _____

Locksmith _____

Glazier _____

Electrician _____

Electricity company's emergency phone number _____

Gas company's emergency number _____

Local builder _____

Vet _____

Work numbers of the adults in the household _____

_____

_____

Mobile numbers for key family members and friends _____

_____

_____

School/day care numbers (as appropriate) _____

Relatives or friends whom children can ring in an emergency _____

_____

_____

_____

_____

Entranceway lighting
*Lamps that light up
driveways, paths and
front and back doors
help young and old alike
to avoid falls, and deter
intruders from lurking
in the shadows.*

How hot?
*Children are more
sensitive to hot water
and usually prefer it
at a maximum of 35°C
(95°F), while babies are
better off with bath
water at 30°C (86°F).*

Child safety around the home

When babies and toddlers are on the move, they want to inspect everything in the house, where some of the biggest threats to child safety can be found. Here are some useful child-proofing tips for the whole house.

▶ Place safety latches on all the drawers and cupboards that contain potentially harmful products, such as dishwashing powder and plastic bags, or implements such as knives, skewers, toothpicks and any object that could cause choking. Reserve a special cupboard or drawer for your child, and fill it with safe items that can be used as musical instruments, for shop games or measuring and pouring fun.

▶ Avoid sharp edges and corners on furniture that can injure.

▶ Cover electrical outlets with safety caps.

▶ Place electrical cords out of reach: run them along the wall or behind furniture.

▶ Many children are injured by furniture falling on top of them as they hold onto it to pull themselves up, or try to climb on it. Bookshelves and wardrobes can be particularly dangerous. If furniture is in danger of tipping over, it's a good idea to bolt it to the wall.

▶ Push appliances to the back of shelves or tables, away from the edge.

▶ Don't leave tiny objects — such as coins, marbles or beads, which a small child could pick up and choke on — lying around on the floor.

▶ Never leave a nappy bucket on the floor or in a place where your child could fall into it.

▶ Place safety gates at the top and bottom of stairs, and check that a toddler is not able to climb over them. Closely examine balcony areas for safety.

Toy safety checklist

Avoid toy boxes with heavy lids, and use baskets in the rooms where your child plays. Before you give your child a toy to play with, run through this safety checklist.

▶ *Is it safe?*

▶ *Is it age appropriate? Check the label.*

▶ *Is it unbreakable?*

▶ *Is it washable?*

▶ *Is it too big to swallow?*

▶ *Is it smaller than a film canister? If so, it is a potential choking hazard.*

▶ *Does it have any sharp edges or other pointy bits?*

▶ *Does it have any strings, cords or ribbons that are longer than 15 cm (6 in) attached?*

▶ *Is it made from non-toxic materials?*

▶ *Does it run on batteries or electricity? (Batteries are dangerous if children suck them.)*

▶ *Does it have any small gaps that can pinch fingers?*

▶ *Does it make any loud explosive sounds that could damage a baby's hearing?*

IN THE KITCHEN

The best rule is to keep young children out of the kitchen. Consider installing a child gate, which will block the entrance while allowing your children to see you.

▶ Keep glassware in above-bench cupboards or shelves.

▶ Young children are insatiably curious — if they can't see what's on top of the stove, their natural instinct is to reach and grab! To prevent this disastrous scenario, fit a stove guard that blocks access to the front and both sides of the stove. If the stove top is part of a freestanding stove/oven unit, ensure that it's anchored to the wall. Add an oven lock to prevent your child pulling open the oven door.

▶ Turn saucepan handles away from the stove front and cook on the rear plates whenever possible.

▶ Cordless kettles mean one less cord to be able to pull; empty kettles are one less source of hot water.

▶ Carry plates to the pans rather than carry pans to the plates.

Microwave
Don't turn on your microwave when it's empty, or you will damage the magnetron. If you have small children who may turn it on by accident, always leave a jug of water in the oven.

Outdoors

Efforts to reduce your home's impact on the environment can be particularly rewarding in the garden, where you can reduce the amount of water you use, compost your kitchen waste to create a thriving, healthy soil, and grow fresh fruit and vegetables for your table, all while minimising your use of chemicals.

Soil

Whether you're embarking on creating a new garden or the custodian of an established one, remember that healthy, flourishing plants are the by-product of a healthy soil that's enriched with organic matter.

Earthworms
Worms and other soil organisms transform organic matter into humus — nature's plant food and soil conditioner. Their tunnelling activities carry organic matter through the soil and allow for the easy penetration of air and water.

Soil types

The ideal soil is deep, crumbly, or friable, fertile, well-drained and rich in organic matter — the foundation of a healthy garden in which plants will thrive. However, in reality, few garden soils fit that description.

There are three main types of soil.

▶ **Clay soil** This type compacts when dry and becomes waterlogged with too much moisture, but it does hold nutrients well. Both drainage and aeration are poor, making it very difficult for the roots of young plants to grow.

▶ **Sandy soil** Sand never compacts, and it provides excellent aeration and drainage, but it has no ability to hold either nutrients or water.

▶ **Loam** This beautiful soil, a combination of clay and sandy soil, has excellent properties for plant growth. Unfortunately, few gardeners are blessed with this ideal soil type.

IDENTIFYING YOUR SOIL TYPE

The first step in improving your soil is to finding out what type you have in your garden. Just feeling the soil can teach you a great deal about it. Take a handful of moist topsoil and squeeze it gently to form a lump. Soil with a high clay content will form a tight, sticky ball, while the sandy type will lose its shape and fall readily from your hand. Soil of good, friable texture will hold its shape but break away easily when further squeezed or prodded.

Adding gypsum to clay soil

You can improve clay soil by adding gypsum, a mineral that can help the fine particles to clump together into bigger ones, thereby opening up the soil and improving its drainage. However, it doesn't work on all clays, so you should carry out the following test first.

1 Drop a 6 mm (¼ inch) fragment of dry soil into a glass of distilled or rain water and let it stand for 24 hours. Don't shake or stir it.

2 If the water turns cloudy around the fragment, your soil will be improved by the addition of gypsum. The more obvious the discolouration, the greater the improvement will be.

3 If there is no discolouration, repeat the test with moist soil that has a plasticine-like consistency.

4   If the water then turns cloudy, adding gypsum will help prevent wet weather damage to your soil.

5   Add gypsum at the rate of 500 g per square metre (1 pound per square yard) but don't dig it in.

Soil pH

The soil pH is a measure of acidity determined on a scale of 1 to 14 — a pH of 1 is extremely acid while a pH of 14 indicates extreme alkalinity; 7 is neutral, as it is neither acid nor alkaline. Most plants prefer slightly acid soil and do well where the pH reading is between 6 and 7. Some plants — such as azaleas, camellias, magnolias and rhododendrons — like quite acid soil with a pH of between 4.5 and 5.5, but only a few plants could tolerate a strongly acid soil of pH 4 or less. Plants that prefer alkaline soils generally do best with a pH of between 7.5 and 8.

The pH of soil affects the level of nutrients available to plants. Thus, if you grow a plant native to alkaline soils in a more acid soil, it will overdose on some nutrients but be deficient in others. The result will be poor growth, yellowing leaves and/or eventual death.

You can adjust overly acid soil (less than a pH of 5) by adding lime, or adjust excessively alkaline soil with flowers of sulphur. Apply at the rate of about one handful per square metre (square yard) and lightly dig into the soil, then water the treated area deeply.

Don't suddenly make large changes in the pH or you may shock your garden to death. Instead, apply the appropriate remedy, as described above. Let the soil lie for 2 months, test it again and make another application if necessary. Repeat at 2-monthly intervals until you achieve the correct pH.

Coffee reduces pH
Coffee grounds (from real coffee, not instant) added to alkaline soil will bring down the pH.

Testing soil pH

You can test your soil pH with a soil-testing kit, available from garden centres.

1   Remove a small handful of soil from the area to be tested and add it to the test tube provided. Then add the soil-test powder included in the kit.

2   Next, add distilled water to the soil and the test powder, filling up to the level marked on the side of the test tube.

3   Secure the lid and shake the test tube. Wait a few seconds for the liquid to change colour, then compare it with the pH colour chart supplied.

4   A yellow or orange liquid indicates an acid soil, bright green indicates a neutral one, and dark green indicates an alkaline soil.

Hydrangeas and pH
In acid soils hydrangea flowers are blue, but in alkaline soils they are pink. If you want blue flowers, your soil should have a pH of between 5 and 5.5. For pink flowers, maintain a soil pH of 6 or more by adding lime to your soil if it is acid.

Adding lime to acid soil

Do this on a windless day and make sure you wear long sleeves and gloves, as lime is caustic. Apply at the manufacturer's recommended rates.

1   Shake the lime over the area to be covered, spreading it well to ensure even coverage.

2   Lightly fork the lime into the soil and cover. Do not add manure to the soil for at least 6 months.

Soil drainage

Only aquatic plants or those native to swamps or bogs survive sodden roots. Dry land plants must have air in the soil around their roots or they will drown.

If all or part of your garden is poorly drained, you can grow plants that will tolerate it, build a raised bed or install subsurface drainage.

TESTING YOUR SOIL FOR DRAINAGE
Dig a few holes about 50 cm (1¾ feet) deep and fill them with water. Allow them to drain, then refill them. If water remains after 24 hours, your soil is badly drained; the more water in each hole, the worse the drainage problem.

Another way to test your drainage is to observe what happens after rain — does water lie in pools, or does the soil just remain sodden? If so, subsurface drainage will allow you to grow a much wider range of plants. If the poor drainage is restricted to a small area, an alternative is to raise the area about 30 cm (1 foot) above the natural level by building retaining walls. Fill the area within the walls with good quality, weed-free topsoil from a landscape supplier.

Construct beds from railway sleepers (railroad ties), rocks or a variety of other strong materials. Monitor the moisture levels, as raised beds tend to dry out faster than ground-level beds.

DOUBLE DIGGING TECHNIQUE
With this technique, the soil is cultivated to a depth of two spade blades. It's best used on land that is being cultivated for the first time or where a hard subsurface layer (called a pan) of soil has formed, impeding drainage and the penetration of plant roots.

This method improves the friability of the subsoil without bringing it closer to the surface, so the most biologically active layer of topsoil is always closest to the roots.

It's important to avoid mixing subsoil with topsoil, otherwise you will be diluting the fertility of the topsoil instead of improving the fertility of the subsoil. It's hard work, but the benefits of double digging can last up to 15 years, provided you manage the soil correctly.

To double dig an area so you can grow deeper-rooted plants such as roses, shrubs, trees or fruit bushes and trees, add a layer of well-rotted manure or compost into the bottom of the trench before you reincorporate the topsoil.

Double digging

1   Starting at one end of the plot, use a string line and canes to mark out an area 60 cm (2 feet) wide. Dig a trench the width and depth of one spade. If it is very large, you can divide the plot in two.

2   Remove the soil from this first trench and take it to the far end of the plot, laying it quite close to the area where the final trench is to be dug. When the soil is removed from the first trench, fork over the base of the trench to the full depth of the fork's tines. If required, fork compost or manure into the lower layer of soil or scatter it on top after cultivation.

3   When you've cultivated the base of the trench and broken through the compacted layer, use a garden line to mark out the next area 60 cm (2 feet) wide. Using a spade, start to dig the soil from this second area, throwing it into the first trench, while making sure you turn over the soil as you move it. This process will create the second trench at the same time as you fork over the base.

4   Repeat the process until you've dug the entire plot to a depth of about 50 cm (1¾ feet).

Nettles mean fertile soil
Stinging nettles thrive in fertile soil. For an organic liquid fertiliser, fill a bucket with water and add a bunch of nettles. Allow the nettles to rot down for 2–3 weeks. Use the resulting liquid as a nutrient-rich foliar spray, which is also useful against aphids, blackfly and mildew.

The no-dig garden

The Australian gardener Esther Dean first became known in the late 1970s for a specialised form of sheet composting called the 'no-dig' garden. You can use this technique anywhere, even on the most compacted soils, or directly onto lawn, to provide a fertile garden bed. You'll see a great improvement in the soil's texture and also an increase in the earthworm population.

1   Provide an edging for the future garden, then give the soil a good soak.

2   Next, lay overlapping thick layers of newspaper, cardboard or even old carpet on the ground, and follow this with a layer of lucerne hay, a layer of organic fertiliser, a layer of loose straw, and another thin layer of organic fertiliser. Water well.

3   Make depressions in the surface and fill them with compost. Plant well-established seedlings, large seeds, tubers and bulbs immediately. If you have enough compost, place a layer of compost right over the top of the garden, rather than just in pockets.

Improving the soil

All soil types can be improved by adding organic matter, which can take several forms, such as old farmyard manure, compost, leaf mould or composted sawdust. These natural substances are further broken down by soil organisms, such as bacteria, fungi and earthworms. In the process, humus is formed. With repeated applications, a booming population of soil organisms distributes the organic matter through the top layers of soil, opening up clays and making sands rich and more water-retentive.

COMPOSTING

By far the largest proportion of household garbage consists of kitchen scraps, which are highly biodegradable and can be composted or processed by a worm farm. Composting takes a little more room, but as well as diverting garbage away from landfill, it provides you with valuable fertiliser for your garden. Alternatively, check with your local government authority — they may be able to tell you about community gardens that would welcome composting materials.

What to compost

Almost any biodegradable household waste can be composted.

▶ **Garden waste** *Grass clippings, fallen leaves, faded cut flowers.*

▶ **Kitchen scraps** *Fruit and vegetable scraps (banana peel is high in potassium).*

▶ **Coffee grounds and tea leaves** *Coffee contains protein as well as oils while tea is rich in nitrogen.*

▶ **Household dust** *Empty the contents of the vacuum cleaner into the pile.*

▶ **Waste paper** *Cardboard and paper are useful because of their carbon content. Place cardboard at the bottom of the heap or pack it around the sides. Paper works best if it's shredded.*

▶ **Prunings** *Shred woody prunings from trees and shrubs before adding them to the pile. If you produce enough of this waste each year, consider hiring or buying a mulcher. Cut thin, sappy stems with a rotary mower before adding them.*

HOW TO BUILD A COMPOST HEAP

The secret to good composting is layering. Whether you create your own heap in a corner of your garden or use a compost bin, available from garden centres, start with some basic layers.

1   Start with a layer of woody prunings to raise the heap off the ground and allow air to circulate.

2   Add garden trimmings such as prunings and old plants, plus vegetable and fruit peel.

3   Add a third layer of grass cuttings and leaves.

4   Repeat these three layers to speed up the rotting process.

5   Finally, cover the heap with a piece of old carpet or a layer of straw to prevent moisture escaping and to retain heat within the compost heap.

6   Use either stable (or poultry) manure or blood and bone (bonemeal) to add nutrients to your compost heap.

7   Straw, sawdust, manure, seaweed or waste from food-processing plants — such as pea trash, rice hulls and nut shells — can also be added.

Heat it up
Meat and fish tend to attract flies and vermin, as the home compost heap is rarely hot enough to kill the pathogens. If your compost is attracting cockroaches, maggots, rats or mice, add grass clippings to raise the internal temperature of the heap and keep pests at bay.

As you add to the compost, intersperse alternate layers of moist and dry materials. Encourage the breakdown of material by keeping the heap damp but not wet. Turn the heap regularly to improve aeration, which will in turn speed up the rotting process.

Green manures

To improve the quality of the soil, plant green manure crops. These are usually nitrogen-fixing plants, often with strong, deep root systems that help to break up compacted soil and draw nutrients up to the surface. After a certain period, dig them back into the soil. Choose from, for example, deep-rooted lucerne (Medicago sativa); lupin (Lupinus angustifolia); daikon or white radish (Raphanus sativus) — its flowers attract beneficial insects while its huge roots break up soil; and rye (Elymus sp.) — its fibrous root system improves soil structure.

Making straw compost

Old straw makes bulky organic matter to improve soil drainage, moisture retention and fertility. It can also be used as an organic mulch, spread over the soil surface to preserve moisture and suppress weeds. This layer will be gradually incorporated into the soil by the activity of worms, bacteria and other soil-borne organisms.

1   Cover the base of the area chosen for the compost heap with 30 cm (1 foot) of loose straw. Soak the straw thoroughly with water.

2   Sprinkle a light covering of nitrogenous fertiliser over the straw. This will help speed up decomposition.

3   Add another 30 cm (1 ft) layer of loose straw to the stack; again, water it thoroughly, and add more fertiliser.

4   As the straw decomposes, it will become covered in white mould and begin to resemble well-rotted manure.

WORM FARMS

Gardeners know the value of the earthworm, toiling away, aerating and refining the soil. In worm farms, they are also fastidious recyclers of kitchen waste, turning your scraps into rich soil you can use in the garden, or indoors for houseplants. Local government authorities often have information on worm farms, and may even sell subsidised ones.

A typical worm factory consists of a series of stacked plastic trays inhabited by a starter population of, for instance, 1000 compost worms on a compost-like bedding. These worms naturally exist in the top 30 cm (1 foot) or so of soil, as opposed to earthworker worms, which burrow much deeper. Compost worms eat almost anything of plant or animal origin, converting it to castings (worm excrement) and liquid fertiliser, which is drained off through a tap at the bottom of the trays. Once they have adapted to a new food source, worms eat up to their own body weight every day. As they eat the food in one tray, they move up to the next, leaving their castings behind.

A worm farm takes 2–5 years to mature, at which point it may support up to 20,000 worms. You can leave the worms to their own devices for 3–4 weeks as long as they already have a good food supply, and you place the farm in a cool spot under cover with the tap open.

WORM-FARMING TIPS

▶ While mashing scraps for the worm farm may not be practical, it's worth bearing in mind that worms prefer soft foods. You can feed them vegetable and fruit scraps and peelings, tea leaves, tea bags and coffee grounds, vacuum cleaner dust and hair or fur clippings, soaked and torn newspapers and cartons, and crushed egg shells.

▶ While worms will eat acidic foods such as citrus peel and onion skins, they will always eat other, preferred food first.

▶ Garden lime helps to counteract the effect of acidic food. A handful or so every few weeks is sufficient.

FERTILISING

Fertilisers can make the difference between success and failure in the garden, but how much and how often you need to apply depends on whether you use nature's own, free, miracle food — compost (see page 146).

WHY PLANTS NEED FERTILISING

Plants exist by converting water and minerals from the soil into stems, leaves and flowers. In the wild, those minerals would be constantly replaced — leaves, twigs, fruit and bark fall to the ground, and every animal deposits plant food in its droppings. Nature is in perfect equilibrium — what goes up (into plants) must come down (and go back into the soil).

In gardens, however, things are different. The plants are not an eco-system but an unrelated mixture of species from a wide variety of habitats and soils. Each may have different nutrient needs. More importantly, there is no build-up of fallen vegetation, and few animals to enrich the soil. Gardeners sweep up fallen leaves, and remove dead plants before they can rot. The result of all this tidiness is a gradual but steady impoverishment of the soil.

The answer is not to stop sweeping and clearing up, but it is helpful if the sweepings are composted and returned to the soil. Compost has virtually all the nutrients plants need and it also does the soil good by creating humus — a vital natural ingredient, present in all fertile soils.

Unfortunately, the average suburban garden does not produce nearly enough compostable matter to supply all the garden's compost needs, but if you compost what you can and distribute the product, you will not need to buy anything like the amount of fertiliser that an uncomposted garden requires.

Handy feeding hints

▶ *Always fertilise when the soil is moist, and water thoroughly after you have completed the application.*

▶ *If in doubt, apply fertiliser at half-strength, twice as often.*

▶ *Plants don't use much food in winter, so don't bother feeding then. Spring, summer and autumn feeds are generally better value.*

▶ *Nitrogen is responsible for leaf growth, but too much nitrogen can cause floppy growth and poor flowers.*

▶ *Phosphorus is vital for strong roots and stems.*

▶ *Potassium maintains the rigidity of plants and helps promote flowering.*

MAJOR PLANT FOODS

The elements nitrogen, phosphorus and potassium (usually abbreviated to their chemical symbols, NPK) are the main and essential ingredients of all complete plant foods.

▶ **Nitrogen (N)** This is the most important, as it is responsible for the growth of healthy leaves and is also present in chlorophyll and many other plant parts. If plants lack nitrogen, leaves gradually turn yellow, and new growth is stunted.

▶ **Phosphorus (P)** Without any phosphorus, photosynthesis is not possible and there would be no new roots, shoots and flower buds. A phosphorus deficiency in your soil causes stunting, spindly growth and blue-green leaves. However, an excess of phosphorus can also be harmful, even toxic, to many plants, especially Australian and South African natives.

▶ **Potassium (K)** Potassium regulates and aids the chemical reactions within plants and also promotes stem growth. A deficiency causes leaves to turn a lustreless grey-green, perhaps also developing yellow spots. Affected leaves often brown at the edges, die and fall.

Packaged complete plant foods usually include percentages of calcium and sulphur as well as the three main elements. Magnesium, the sixth important element for plant growth, is normally present in sufficient quantities in the soil. A garden fed with complete plant food should not lack any major nutrients.

MINOR PLANT FOODS

The minor plant foods, on the other hand, are a completely different story. Vital to all plants, trace elements are usually present in well-composted soils. In other soils, deficiencies can occur because plants use up the supply or because other plant foods are applied too generously. For example, iron is abundant in most soils, yet plants can suffer deficiencies in iron if too much lime has been applied to the garden. But there are other causes of discolouration and poor growth, such as too much or too little water, attacks by pests and diseases, salty soils, misuse of poisons, too much or too little shade or an inappropriate pH reading of the soil.

If none of these applies to an affected plant, then suspect a trace element deficiency. However, they are not called 'trace elements' for nothing. Only a tiny amount is needed and it is vital that they be applied strictly as directed, as overdoses are fatal. Balanced mixtures of all the trace elements can be bought at nurseries and may be needed in gardens that are not regularly mulched with rotted organic matter. Apply trace elements annually or as directed on the pack.

Blackjack

Blackjack is an excellent, nutritious plant 'pick-me-up', which is very useful during the plant's flowering or fruiting periods. The first thing you will need is a quantity of animal manure that has been well rotted down. Add some soot (which provides nitrogen) and wood ash (good for potassium) to the manure. Put the mixture into a plastic-net bag. Seal the bag carefully, suspend it in a barrel of rainwater and leave it in position for several weeks. Once the solution is ready, decant it as required into a watering can, diluting it until it's the colour of weak tea, and apply it to your plants.

Making leaf mould

Leaf mould makes an excellent soil conditioner, but it also has low levels of nutrients (0.4 per cent nitrogen, 0.2 per cent phosphate and 0.3 per cent potassium) and is usually slightly acidic. In nature, leaf mould is a material that slowly forms beneath trees over many years, so making your own at home is a long-term project. The leaves can take up to 2 years to decay into a dark, compost-like material.

1   Rake up the fallen leaves into heaps. Alternatively, run a lawnmower with a grass-catcher over the leaves. This will not only gather up most of the leaves, but it will also chop them up, accelerating their decay. The best time to gather the leaves is just after it has rained when the leaves are moist, but you can also collect them when they are dry and dampen them later. Make sure you remove any foreign material, such as plastic wrappers.

2   Collect the leaves and place them in either plastic bags or heavy-duty black garbage bags. The latter are better as they block out most of the light and encourage fungal activity. To every 30 cm (1 ft) layer of leaves add a small amount of organic fertiliser, such as dried, pelleted chicken manure or a measure of organic nitrogenous fertiliser, such as sulphate of ammonia (which contains 16–21 per cent nitrogen).

3   When the bag is almost full, place it in the position where you are going to leave it while its contents decompose, and water it thoroughly so that the contents are soaking wet.

4   Over a period of about 2 years, the leaves will decompose and settle in the bag. These leaves will be pressed tightly together, with some remaining almost whole and others disintegrating completely. When the leaves are ready for use, the bag can be split open and the leaves used as garden mulch or soil conditioner.

MULCHING

Mulch is a layer of material spread evenly over the soil, about 5–10 cm (2–4 in) thick. Organic mulches — such as compost, rotted manure and dry grass clippings— slowly rot down, releasing valuable plant foods. Inorganic mulches — such as stones, gravel, crushed rock, coarse sand and black plastic — conserve moisture but do not condition or feed the soil. They make it difficult to incorporate soil additives and tend to raise the soil temperature.

The best way to save water — as much as 25 per cent — is to regularly apply mulch to all garden beds. There are other benefits too. A layer of mulch:

▶   shades soil from the sun and shelters it from drying winds, which keeps moisture in the soil by reducing the rate of evaporation;

▶   improves the structure of garden soil, resulting in better aeration and drainage, and an ability to hold more moisture for longer;

▶   encourages beneficial soil organisms such as earthworms, which, in turn, improve the fertility and aeration of the soil;

▶   suppresses weeds by smothering seedlings as they germinate;

▶   evens out the temperature of the soil, which can lead to a longer growing season; and

▶   reduces erosion during heavy rain, which means water soaks in to where it is needed rather than running off.

Seaweed fertiliser
Visit your nearest beach and fill a sack with seaweed that has been washed up onto the shore. Tie the sack, immerse it in a large container of water and leave it there for 7–14 days. This makes an invaluable, although very strong-smelling, liquid garden feed which can be sprayed or poured onto your plants.

Best time to mulch
Depending on the time of the year at which you mulch, you can influence your garden's soil temperatures. For example, if you mulch at the end of autumn, you will keep the soil warmer for longer, while mulching during the early spring months will keep the soil cooler and prevent heat being trapped in summer.

Five great organic mulches

1. Compost adds humus to the soil and also helps improve the soil's overall structure in your garden. In addition, compost allows good moisture penetration in the soil.

2. Grass clippings are high in nitrogen and other nutrients. Dry them before use and mix with leaf mould or manure for easy air and water penetration. Used alone they may make a water-repellent mat.

3. Leaf litter is attractive and quick to break down into a rich humus. Shred it before use and reapply annually.

4. Cocopeat is made from waste coconut fibre. Apply it moist in a layer about 3–5 cm (1¼–2 in) thick. It is a good substitute for peatmoss, which is a non-renewable product.

5. Rotted cow manure is an excellent soil conditioner as well as being high in nutrients. Don't use it fresh as the ammonia may burn plants.

High-nitrogen mulch
Some mulches, such as lucerne (alfalfa), compost and sugar cane, have a high nitrogen content. These types of mulches do improve the soil fertility, but they also rot down quickly, so replace them at least once every few months.

LIVING MULCH

Many low-growing plants make ideal living mulches. To exclude weeds in ornamental gardens, plant groundcovers such as bugle flower (*Ajuga reptans*) into mulched soil. Periwinkle (*Vinca minor*), ideal for dry shade areas, is easily controlled at a suitable height with a string trimmer used twice a year. Any of the prostrate-growing plants are effective in reducing weeds.

However, weeds may not always be a nuisance. They can, in fact, be helpful. A carpet of weeds can act as a protective blanket, another 'living mulch' of sorts. Many gardeners make their lives a misery worrying about weeds, but organic gardeners tend to be a bit more relaxed about invasion by 'unwanted' plants. They know that weeds are essential to the health of the soil. Bare earth is easily eroded by wind, and compacted by heavy rain or foot traffic. It is more easily leached of soluble nutrients and can also lose important gases.

You can slash the weeds just before they begin to flower and leave them on top of the soil as a green mulch, or dig them through the soil to add valuable organic matter.

Propagation

Individually, plants aren't very expensive, but when you're starting a new garden, or even revamping an established one, the number of plants you'll need adds up and can cost big money. Propagating your own plants is fun, saves you cash and is sometimes the only way to obtain a rare or unusual plant.

What is propagation?

There are two basic methods of propagation — raising plants from seeds and reproducing plants using vegetative propagation.

Raising seeds

This is the most basic form of propagation. A seed is a miniaturised plant, packed and stored within a protective coat, waiting for the perfect conditions that will give it a start in life. Some plants will easily self-seed, while others may need collecting, treating, sowing and transplanting. Seeds from dry seed heads can be shaken or rubbed from the plant, and any debris removed. In many cases, collecting seed heads in paper bags will help contain the seeds as they fall.

Most plants grown from seeds are annuals (plants that grow from seed to flower in one growing season) or biennials (plants that grow from seed to flower over two growing seasons). Another group comprises plants that are frost-tender, but are actually perennials in warm climates.

In principle, growing seeds is very simple. Sow them in fine-textured soil, cover them to a depth equal to the size of the seed, and keep the soil moist until they come up. When the seedlings are big enough to handle, transplant or 'prick out' into another pot or bed that will give them more room until they are large enough to plant out in the garden.

Propagation unit
For convenience, you can buy a ready-made propagating unit, which will help ensure successful seed germination. The unit consists of a tray with a hinged clear plastic lid. Or simply place your trays of seedlings on top of the refrigerator — it's just the right temperature to give bottom heat.

The pros and cons of seeds

The advantages of raising plants from seeds are saving money, access to interesting new genetic material, variation and variety, ready availability, and minimal storage and space requirements. However, you should weigh this against the possible loss of particular characteristics (such as flower colour), which may change in the second generation of plants, particularly in the case of annuals and biennials.

SEED-RAISING MIX

The ideal growing medium for germinating seeds under cover is made up of two layers. The first, or base layer, comprises seed-raising mix while the upper layer comprises free-draining horticultural grit or vermiculite. The advantage of this two-layer system is that the seeds are sown in the layer of grit, but the seed-raising mix in the layer below provides the nutrients that are required once the rooting process begins. The alternative is to simply fill the container with proprietary seed-raising mix. Soil-free mix is popular for this purpose.

SOWING SEEDS IN CONTAINERS

The great advantage of sowing seeds in containers is that it gives you complete control of their growing conditions, which is especially important with seeds sown in spring, when cold snaps may be a problem.

You can buy wide, shallow seed trays from nurseries, or use egg cartons, flat plastic take-away food boxes or even waxed paper trays or polystyrene boxes from grocers. Just remember to make some holes in the bottom for drainage.

Sowing fine seeds
When sowing very fine seeds — such as those produced by African violet, azalea, campanula, ferns, gloxinia, impatiens, lobelia, polyanthus and primula — mix some fine, dry sand with the seeds to make spreading them a little easier.

Stimulating seeds for best germination

Certain types of seeds need to be stimulated and shocked out of dormancy before they will germinate. Some cold-climate plants need an artificial cool time (called stratification) for germination to occur. This is an adaptation to prevent seeds from germinating until the last of the cold weather is over, so that late frosts or snow don't harm the young seedlings.

Other seeds respond to drought or heat and smoke (which is in effect the simulation of a bushfire). Hard seed coats can prevent plants from germinating by keeping out air and water — two vital ingredients in the process of germination — and the seeds will therefore need to be chipped or rubbed with abrasive paper (a process called scarification) before sowing.

Sowing seeds in trays

Germination depends on heat, and many plants will not easily germinate without some additional warmth. A large number of the plants used for summer bedding are half-hardy annuals, and their seeds will not germinate in garden soil until early summer, so sow them in spring under glass.

1   Fill a seed tray to the rim with a suitable seed-raising mix. Firm gently until the mix is 1 cm (½ inch) below the rim. If you are planting very fine seeds, it is a good idea to sieve another, thin layer of fine mix over the surface and firm it down lightly.

2   Sow the seeds as evenly as possible over the surface. Sow half in one direction, then turn the tray and sow the remainder in the opposite direction to ensure even distribution.

3   Sieve a thin layer of fine seed-raising mix over the seeds and firm gently. If you have very fine seeds, press them lightly into the surface of the mix, rather than cover them.

4   Lightly water the seed tray before covering it with a sheet of clear glass, and a sheet of newspaper for shade if required.

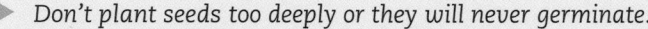

Seed-sowing tips

▶ *Don't plant seeds too deeply or they will never germinate.*

▶ *Barely cover fine seeds with very fine soil.*

▶ *Sow bigger seeds slightly deeper.*

▶ *Never allow the soil to dry out before seedlings have emerged.*

The time required for seed germination varies. Most annual and vegetable seedlings appear in 10–14 days after sowing, but shrubs and trees may take much longer, so don't be in a hurry to throw out a container of seeds that haven't come up yet.

After germination, the seedlings will become overcrowded if you leave them too long. Once they have grown 3–4 cm (1¼–1½ in) tall, they are ready to be pricked out. Be very gentle — lift them with a small, pointed stick, and relocate them to either a new container or a fresh part of the nursery bed, setting them about 5 cm (2 in) apart.

Water them in, and give them some shade for a few days. When they have settled in, give them some slow-release fertiliser. Once they have made 3–4 sets of leaves they are ready to go in their final positions. You may want to pot up trees, shrubs or perennials for a few months or a year until they are big enough for the garden.

SOWING SEEDS OUTDOORS

Many seeds can be sown directly where they are to grow. Big, easy-to-handle seeds are usually sown this way. With direct sowing, it is important to have the bed cultivated to a fine tilth so that the soil won't cake over the emerging seedlings. You should also water very gently, with a fine mist. Put out snail baits (see page 251).

It's easiest to sow in rows, making a shallow furrow with a pointed stick. Sow big seeds at their final spacings, but sprinkle smaller seeds along the furrow, then thin seedlings to their correct spacings when they come up. For an even distribution of fine seeds, mix them with dry sand and sprinkle the mixture.

Broadcasting seed

This is a useful sowing technique for hardy annuals, salad vegetables such as radishes and spring onions (green onions), and green manure crops — for example, comfrey or mustard.

1   Rake the soil, remove any stones and break down clods of earth to form a seed bed with a fine tilth. This will leave the soil with a fine layer on the top surface.

2   It's a good idea to pour a few of the seeds at a time from the packet into the palm of your hand, so you will be able to sow carefully.

3   Sow the seeds by scattering them evenly over the soil surface. Sow from a height of about 30 cm (1 ft) above soil level.

4   Lightly rake over the bed in at least two different directions. This will ensure that the seeds are incorporated into the soil and also that you avoid clustering. Label the seed bed.

Optimum temperature for germination

All seeds have an optimum temperature range at which they germinate best. This range is generally between 15°C and 25°C (60°F and 75°F), so (depending on your climate) spring and the early part of autumn generally make the most appropriate times to sow seeds.

Drill sowing

An excellent technique for growing various annuals and perennials, as well as popular vegetables, this technique allows you to see immediately when seeds have germinated and to easily remove weed seedlings from between the drills.

or winter when the shoots are about a year old, and are rooted outdoors or in a cold frame. They will not root readily unless hormone rooting powder is applied to the wound, and root formation can be very slow, but most will have rooted by the following spring.

Most cuttings, of whatever type, make roots best from a node in the stem, the point from which a leaf arises, and that is where to cut. Remove all leaves that will be buried and cut the remaining leaves in half to reduce moisture loss. Always take a few extra cuttings to allow for some failures. If you have a choice, take cuttings from young, more vigorous plants rather than from old, sedate ones, or at least from vigorous shoots, and always take the cuttings from the choicest, healthiest plants. Finish by watering well.

The time it takes for roots to form varies with the species, but as long as the cutting hasn't died, the process is under way. You can speed it along by dipping the cut ends in fresh rooting hormone (the preparation loses its potency quickly, so an old or opened packet is useless).

Hardwood cuttings can be struck in the ground in the same sort of bed in which you would grow seeds, but soft and semi-ripe cuttings need some protection. The simplest method is to put them up in pots of very sandy soil (3 parts sharp sand to 1 part regular potting mix/potting compost), and enclose each pot in a plastic bag to keep the cuttings moist and humid.

Taking root cuttings

Some plants produce very short stems and shoots, which can make taking cuttings very awkward, so another part of the plant has to be used. The roots of many herbaceous plants and alpines, and a number of trees, shrubs and climbers, can be used for propagation.

1 Carefully dig up the roots of the plant to be propagated, then wash them carefully to remove as much soil as possible.

2 Cut thick roots into sections of 5–8 cm (2–3¼ in) long, and make a flat cut at the top, and a slanting cut at the bottom.

3 Insert the root cuttings by gently pushing the slanted ends into a pot of growing mix so the top of each cutting is level with the surface.

4 Cover with grit, which ensures good drainage and also allows air to reach the top of each cutting without letting it dry out.

Collecting cuttings in warm areas

If you live in a warm area, remember that the best time to collect your cuttings is in the early morning before the sun heats up and the plants become fatigued.

Fleshy stems

It's easy to encourage plants with extremely fleshy stems to root in water. Place the cut stem of the plant in a jar of water and wait for the roots to appear. When they start to emerge, pot up the stem in the normal way.

Taking leaf cuttings

You can propagate some plants, such as African violets (*Santpaulia* sp.), *Begonia* sp. and Cape primroses (*Streptocarpus* sp.) by cutting and planting their leaves in a pot of potting mix (potting compost). New plantlets grow from the base of the leaf or the veins that run across it.

1   Lay the leaf upper-side down. Use a sharp knife to cut along the leaf close to the thick fleshy midrib, to leave two sections of leaf blade. Discard the midrib.

2   If you are dealing with particularly long leaf strips, cut them into halves or thirds so they will fit comfortably into a tray or pot of growing mix.

3   Insert the strips so the cut surface is just below the top of the mix. Lightly firm the mix, water and leave on a warm windowsill or in a propagator.

GRAFTING

Grafting, the union of one plant (the scion) with the roots of another (the stock or understock), requires more skill than other forms of propagation. If, for example, you have a camellia that is too good to discard but produces unappealing flowers, you can convert it to a plant you like by grafting, or you could try grafting several different varieties on it to create a multicoloured tree.

Grafting is also used to change varieties on grapevines. Most often, however, this technique is used to control the growth of the scion, either by giving it the benefit of more vigorous roots than it would make for itself (as when roses are budded on wild rose roots) or, conversely, by using a less vigorous, 'dwarfing' stock, a technique used with fruit trees to create smaller, more manageable trees.

The process requires making a wound on the stock plant and inserting into it a piece of scion (a cutting), in the hope that both stock and scion will callus together and grow as one. To do this, you must match the cambium layers (the green section of stem immediately below the bark) together perfectly. Use clean razor-sharp blades to make the cuts, and a steady hand to make the match precisely. To minimise the chance of transmitting infection, disinfect the blades after each cut.

Rooting powder
A rooting hormone preparation applied to the cut end increases the rooting capacity of the cutting. Dip the base of the cutting in the powder, then blow away any surplus.

Types of grafting

▶ *Budding (shield grafting) This is the simplest form of grafting. Around midsummer is usually the best time. Lift a flap of bark on the understock, which has been grown from seeds or a cutting, and slip in a growth bud from the scion, trimmed so it has just a sliver of bark to support it. Cambium matching is automatic, and you bind everything together with raffia or plastic tape. Then let the stock grow, cutting it off just above the bud the following winter. Come spring, the bud will grow away to start the branches of a new plant on the more desirable roots of another species.*

▶ *Cleft grafting The best time for this process is towards the end of dormancy (early spring). With cleft grafting, cut off the stock first, cleave it with a sharp knife and insert a scion into the cleft (or make two clefts and insert two scions, one on either side), matching the cambiums exactly. Cover all the wounded surfaces with grafting wax and enclose the graft within a plastic bag to keep the scion moist. The understock can be a young plant or a mature branch, which will need several grafts.*

Rose grafting

1 Start hardwood cuttings, taken from the 1-year-old shoots of a rose rootstock, in a warm place or greenhouse in midwinter. Remove the lower buds, then heel them into a soil bed. Graft in spring, when semi-ripe shoots of the rose you want to propagate are available.

2 Prepare the rootstock by cutting it down to 15 cm (6 in). Make a single, shallow, upward-slanting cut 4 cm (1½ in) long at the top of the rootstock, thus exposing the cambium, the plant tissue that allows the stock and scion to heal together.

3 Select a semi-ripe shoot about 8 cm (3¼ in) long from the rose cultivar you want. To form the scion, remove all of the leaves apart from the uppermost one.

4 Make a single downward-slanting cut about 4 cm (1½ in) long on the bottom section of the scion, just behind a bud. This cut will expose the cambium.

5 Gently place the two sections of plant together, so that the cut surfaces match. When they are correctly positioned, carefully bind the graft with an elastic band. This will hold the graft firmly until the two sections join.

6 Place the graft into a pot of growing mix. Water it well, cover with a plastic bag, and place it on a warm windowsill until the graft has taken.

Good plants for grafting
The following plants all take well to grafting — apple, camellia, cherry, grevillea, hibiscus, plum, pear and rose.

Maintenance

Unless you have an amazingly low-maintenance garden, you'll have to get out there on a daily or weekly basis. A little, done often, is the best prescription. And if you get into a routine of regular outdoor cleaning, you will come across jobs that you can attend to before they become major problems.

Garden tools

No gardener can function without appropriate tools in good working condition. There's an immense range of gardening aids available, so make sure you spend your money wisely.

Every gardener needs a spade, fork, trowel, hose and pair of secateurs. Other useful tools, although not essential, will make gardening easier — rake, hoe, hand fork, shears, dibber, hedge trimmers, wheelbarrow, watering can, portable sprayer, saw and sprinkler. Never buy hand tools that are too large or heavy — some firms make 'lady's weight' items, which are lighter and smaller, and also tools for left-handers.

CARING FOR TOOLS

▶ Keeping your tools clean and sharp will make them easier and safer to use, and they will also last longer.

▶ Clean tools by wiping them with a damp cloth or, if necessary, washing them in a detergent solution. Dry them with a clean, dry rag and hang them up if possible.

▶ Disinfect pruning saws and secateurs after each use to prevent the spread of fungal diseases.

▶ Keep a can of rough grease or oil with a rag in it and rub it over the metal parts of tools to prevent rusting.

▶ Wipe over the wooden handles of your tools with linseed oil at least once every few months.

▶ Sharpen the backs of cutting edges by rubbing them on a sandstone or an oilstone every year.

Maintaining secateurs

1 First, loosen the bolt with a spanner.

2 Remove the spring and take the secateurs apart.

3 Spray the parts with lubricant.

4 Holding the blade away from you, sharpen the cutting or bevelled side of the blade on an oilstone.

5 Clean the cutting blade with an old rag.

6 Soak the spring, nut and bolt in a bowl of turpentine. Rub the spring with an abrasive pad.

7 Reassemble the secateurs.

Storing hand tools
In a small bucket, add oil to dry sand. Mix the sand and oil together well. Use the bucket for storing your hand tools.

Restoring a wooden spade handle

For this job you'll need steel wool, a rag, a mixture of linseed oil and turpentine in an old jar, a sanding block and a fine- and a medium-grade abrasive paper.

1 Use medium-grade abrasive paper to sand back the spade handle, then clean the handle thoroughly.

2 Rub the handle with a rag that has been dipped into the linseed oil and turpentine mix, then leave it to dry overnight.

3 Lightly sand the handle again, this time with fine-grade abrasive paper. Repeat the whole process again if necessary.

4 Finish by rubbing the handle with some steel wool.

Watering

There's a golden rule that all gardeners should follow — only water when your plants actually need it, and then water thoroughly. You might need to experiment a bit to work out how much water you need for a thorough soaking. When the soil is dry, turn on the sprinkler, or hold the hose for a timed period of 10 minutes. Then, when any puddles have disappeared, dig down to see how far the water has gone (wet soil looks different to dry). If it's wet to, say, 10 cm (4 in), then you'll know that you probably need to water for half an hour to get the water down to 30 or 35 cm (12 or 14 in), which is where you want it.

HOW OFTEN?

If you watch your plants carefully, you'll learn to recognise the advance warnings of parched plants — leaves and flowers will look limp and lack lustre, and grass will lose its springiness and will retain footprints. Don't be deceived by the surface soil looking dry — if you're in doubt, dig down a little to check.

Of course, you'll need to water more often when the weather is hot and or dry. But unless it's an emergency, try not to water your garden in the heat of the day, when much of your precious water will evaporate at once. As a general rule, it's better to get the water directly to the soil, but don't apply it faster than it can be absorbed or you'll not only lose water from run-off but also run the risk of compacting the surface, which will further reduce water penetration. On clay and silty soils this may mean that you can't turn the hose on full, so just be patient and keep it on for longer.

Pruning in frost-prone areas
Pruning stimulates regrowth but frost will destroy the soft, new shoots. In frost-prone areas don't prune until frosts are past, which will be just before the new spring growth appears. If you live in a frost-free area, prune in the second or third month of winter.

Pruning

Gardeners remove part of a plant in order to encourage it to grow the way they want it to. Although pruning can call for some artistry, it is really not very hard to master.

HOW PLANTS RESPOND TO PRUNING

Whether the stem in question is a trunk, branch or twig, it is essentially a tube conveying sap, and if you cut it off, you divert the sap to some other stem, which will then grow more strongly.

A stem can be cut back to another, preferred stem or it can be cut back to a bud, from which a new stem will arise. On most plants buds can be seen as small nubs, either at the end of a stem (the terminal bud) or along the sides (the lateral buds). Lateral buds almost always grow in the axil ('armpit') of a leaf. Once a stem on a plant matures, the buds may lie dormant beneath the bark until pruning or some type of injury removes the growth above them and provokes them into growth.

When you cut back a stem, you remove the terminal bud, forcing the lateral buds to make side shoots. This usually makes the plant bushier. Conversely, you might choose to pinch back some side shoots, diverting the plant's energy into the terminal bud to make the branch grow longer. And by cutting back hard into old wood, you may also force dormant buds into growth. Beware, not all plants will tolerate being cut back to old wood, and some may die as a result.

The way you prune a plant depends on the sort of growth that will come from each bud. If you're training a climbing rose, for instance, you might remove the ends of the long shoots to force the side shoots that will bear the flowers; if you are training a young tree to grow tall, you might well shorten the side shoots back to encourage the main shoot (the leader) to grow up faster.

THE THREE BASIC PRUNING GROUPS

Plants are pruned according to their pruning group.

GROUP 1

Plants in this group are deciduous shrubs that require very little pruning by the time they reach maturity. They don't require any regular pruning, other than to remove dead, diseased or dying wood as and when it appears, and to lightly tip the old flowering shoots.

GROUP 2

Plants in group 2, deciduous shrubs that flower on the previous season's growth, are pruned to remove old flower-bearing wood straight after flowering has finished, giving as much time as possible for next year's flowers to grow.

GROUP 3

Plants in this group bear flowers on the current season's growth and are pruned hard during early spring. Prune back to a framework of older wood from which new shoots will eventually emerge.

WHEN TO PRUNE

A lot of minor pruning — pinching, removing dead wood, shortening that wayward branch — can be done any time you notice the need. But all major pruning of trees and shrubs is best done when the plant is dormant or least actively growing. For most plants, including many evergreens, this means in winter, but there is a large class of plants that flower in early spring on stems that were produced during the previous summer. This is often referred to as 'old wood'. If you prune these in winter you will be cutting away the flower buds and nothing but leaf growth will be produced in that year. Instead, prune them immediately after the flowers have finished but before the new season's growth is properly under way.

If you like, you can combine pruning with cutting long branches of flowers for the house, taking the branches that you plan to prune out, and finishing off the job as soon as the rest of the flowers have finished for the year.

Summer and late spring-flowering shrubs mostly bloom on the current season's growth — stems produced after winter, called 'new wood' — and can be pruned at any time from the end of autumn until the signs of growth in spring. Whatever you do, you won't kill a plant by pruning it at the wrong time of year. The worst that can happen is the loss of that year's flowers or fruits.

THE FOUR BASIC PRUNING TECHNIQUES

If you decide to prune, there are four basic techniques you can use, depending on what you want to achieve and the way the particular plant grows. These techniques — pinching, shearing, heading (or cutting back) and thinning — all start the same way, with the removal of any dead and obviously weak and sickly branches or shoots. Sometimes that is all that is needed. Take a critical look at your plant before going any further with pruning.

PINCHING

Pinching is the removal of the tip of a shoot, which causes the lateral buds of the plant to begin growing. Repeated pinching will result in many new shoots and a compact, bushy plant. This technique can be used on annual flowers such as petunias and marigolds and also on bushy shrubs such as lavender. Usually you only need to pinch a plant twice, and you shouldn't pinch once the plant begins to show signs of wanting to flower and is large enough to do so (otherwise you will be pinching off the flowers).

SHEARING

Shearing is like pinching but on an even more drastic scale. To shear, clip the outer parts of the plant to an even surface, using a pair of hedge shears. Repeated shearing will destroy the plant's natural form, but that could be exactly what you want to achieve. Shearing a hedge is the most obvious example of this, but you might also want to shear back a groundcover to make it grow lower, stronger and more evenly, or to remove a multitude of dead flowers.

This technique is not suitable for plants that have large leaves, such as camellias — you will end up cutting a lot of the leaves in half, which can create an unpleasant effect. It is much better to trim these large-leaved plants by cutting back each shoot individually with secateurs.

HEADING BACK

Heading back shortens a branch without removing it entirely, forcing growth from one or more lateral buds. You might use this technique to reduce the size of the plant, to encourage growth from lower down, where it will be stronger or more productive of flowers or fruit, or to remove part of a branch that has been damaged.

Always head back to a point from which growth will come — to another branch or to a bud — and consider whether that growth is likely to go in the direction you want (it will grow the way the bud is pointing). Don't leave the stubs to rot, and remember to go easy when heading back. You can always cut off more, but you can't stick branches back on.

THINNING

Thinning is the removal of whole stems, cutting them right back to their point of origin, with the aim of reducing the plant's bulk and bushiness but not making it any smaller. You might do this to let in more light and air, to reveal the lines of the branches or to channel the plant's energies into younger and more productive branches by removing old and unproductive stems. Often you will combine thinning and heading back, as in the pruning of bush roses where you cut out old branches and head back the rest.

Pruning tools

To make a good pruning cut that is clean and smooth, not ragged, keep your pruning tools clean and sharp. Most gardeners can get by with a pair of secateurs and a pruning saw. You might also add hedge shears and long-handled loppers, which are secateurs with long handles. Use them for higher stems and those branches that are too big for secateurs but not quite big enough for a saw.

The most useful type of saw has a tapering, curved blade, which can get into those hard-to-get tight corners. Bigger hand saws are useful for large limbs, and you can buy pruning saws with coarse teeth on one side and fine teeth on the other. To extend your reach, consider buying the ordinary curved saw with a long handle. If you are faced with limbs large enough to call for a chainsaw, pay a professional, as chainsaws are dangerous in inexperienced hands.

CHOOSING THE CORRECT PRUNING TECHNIQUE

Every plant is different, and how you apply the basic techniques will vary from plant to plant, but here are a few generalisations to guide you.

TREES

Some young trees may need pruning to encourage them to develop into shapely adults. But training a young tree is never a hasty business and it is best to take several years over the initial pruning. You might need to remove only old wood from an established tree, but it is sometimes desirable to thin out the branches to allow more light to reach the garden beneath. Thinning is almost always better than trying to reduce the size of a tree by cutting it back all over.

Always go easy when pruning trees. Ideally, the results should not be immediately obvious. First, cut out weaker branches and then any that are growing immediately above or below others. Now stand back and take a look before cutting any more. If a tree is branching too low, you can cut out the lowest branches to raise the crown, but it is much better to do this over a few years than all at once.

SHRUBS

Shrubs fall into two main groups — those that have several permanent branches growing from a single, short trunk and those that form clumps or thickets of more or less evenly sized stems growing straight from the ground. Shrubs with a trunk, such as daphne and most grevilleas, are usually headed back, although you might want to thin out the occasional weak or badly placed branch to keep them from becoming too bushy. On the other hand, thicket shrubs such as philadelphus, abelia and may bush are generally thinned by cutting a few of the oldest branches right to the ground.

Large shrubs such as camellia and the bigger bottlebrushes can be trained as small, multi-stemmed trees by removing the lowest branches. Not all will take being severely headed back into bare wood, and in most cases, it is usually better to begin pruning when the shrubs are still quite young and flexible.

Pruning an evergreen shrub

Generally speaking, evergreen shrubs need very little pruning when compared to deciduous shrubs. However, as with all types of shrubs, young plants benefit from some encouragement to form a good branching structure and evenly spaced lateral stems. In the first year after planting, prune the leading shoot to encourage a stronger system of side shoots to form. Thereafter, you need only remove weak or damaged shoots, or clip the bush lightly all over.

CONIFERS

Conifers range from creeping groundcovers to the world's tallest timber trees. With few exceptions, they are evergreen and their leaves are needles — either long as in pines and cedars or short as in cypresses and junipers. They fall into two broad classes — those such as pines, cedars and firs that bear their branches in whorls, radiating out from the trunk or limbs like the spokes of a wheel, and those such as sequoias, cypresses and junipers that branch at random along the stem.

This is important when pruning because, while the random branches have dormant buds all along their shoots, so that you can cut anywhere and expect growth, the whorl branches have buds only at the points where the whorls arise — at the tips or the bases of new shoots. The danger is that, if you cut between them, there will be no growth and the cut branch will eventually die right back: cut only to a lateral or, if you can see it clearly, to the cluster of buds that mark the base of a year's growth.

Most conifers are naturally shapely trees, and if you choose a conifer that suits your situation, you should not need to prune it. In any case, if you do have to prune, never cut into bare wood — the dormant buds lose their viability when the leaves finally fall and so it won't regrow. The plum pines (*Podocarpus* sp.) and the English yew (*Taxus* sp., so valued for hedging and topiary), are notable exceptions.

GROUNDCOVERS

Groundcovers are a very mixed group. Some groundcovers, such as ivy, are climbers that trail along the ground for want of something to climb up; some, such as *Hypericum* and *Vinca* species, are spreading herbaceous perennials, while others are prostrate, spreading shrubs. An occasional shearing or general heading back will keep these types of groundcovers dense and low.

Your first topiary
Try to select a plant that is already vaguely the same shape that you want to eventually achieve. For example, if you would like a triangular or pyramidal shape, look for a plant that is wide at the base and has a natural taper towards its top. For rounded or ball shapes, choose a multi-stemmed shrub that already has a good overall cover of foliage, such as a bay tree.

Special pruning techniques

Some plants are trained into shapes and screens using special pruning techniques.

▶ **Bonsai** *This is the art of dwarfing plants by regular pruning and cramping root growth. Theoretically, any type of plant can be treated this way.*

▶ **Coppicing** *This technique was developed to give a constant and renewable supply of wood for cane work and firewood. Basically, plants are cut back regularly to near ground level, which encourages a mass of new growth. This new growth is often more striking than older wood, and so it has ornamental value. Typical candidates for this sort of pruning are cornus and willow.*

▶ **Espalier** *Sometimes called fan-training, espalier is simply pruning plants flat against a frame or wall. Camellia, cotoneaster, fruit trees, pyracantha and roses are commonly used for espalier.*

▶ **Pleaching** *A popular device used in garden design during the sixteenth and seventeenth centuries, pleaching is the art of creating a hedge on stilts. European limes (Tilia sp.) are often used for this type of pruning, although any tree with a bushy habit is suitable.*

▶ **Pollarding** *This technique is similar to coppicing, except that growth is cut back to a permanent framework. Suitable plants include crepe myrtle, cornus, plane tree and willow.*

▶ **Topiary** *Pruning plants into shapes such as balls, cones, spirals and animals is an ancient pruning technique. Suitable species include box, conifers and shrub honeysuckle. Standardising is a particularly popular form of topiary, where climbers as well as shrubs can be grown up on a single stem, then shaped on top into a ball, or series of balls, or a weeping plant.*

Too many fish

Overstocking your pond with fish can lead to polluted water, algae and the spread of disease. For every square metre (square yard) of pond surface, allow a maximum of ten fish about 5–8 cm (2–3¼ in) long. Unless you are willing to install filtration systems, avoid koi carp. They make a lot of mess that will need to be cleaned up regularly.

Planting tip

A good idea when planting aquatic plants in a pot into a water feature is to place a layer of gravel or shingle on the surface of the potting mix (potting compost). This prevents soil particles from floating to the water's surface.

Water features

Water features are a delightful addition to the garden, and don't require much maintenance to keep them looking good. However, don't leave them unattended for long periods of time or they will deteriorate.

PONDS

A healthy pond looks after itself: its ecosystem of plants and animals acts like a living filter. But if this system gets out of balance and the pond becomes choked with vegetation, or fish become diseased, you need to take action. Seek the advice of an aquarium expert before emptying the pond and possibly fitting a filter.

Cleaning a pond

Clean your pond annually to remove debris that has accumulated throughout the year.

1   Empty the pond by bailing it out with a bucket, or pump the water out by attaching a hose to the pump outlet.

2   Remove any soil, mud and plant debris from the bottom of the pond. Place any pond creatures, such as water snails, in a tray of water.

3   Use a stiff brush to give the sides of the pond a thorough clean. Apply a weak solution of sterilising agent.

4   Clean the sides and bottom of the pond with a powerful jet of water. Allow the pond surface to dry, then refill. Return the creatures to their home.

Lengthen the life of the filter

Provide extra protection for the water pump and reduce the risk of any damage by simply covering the filter intake with a section cut from a pair of old pantyhose. Its fine mesh will block many of the particles that might otherwise block the filter. If your pond water gets particularly dirty, it may still need cleaning regularly.

SWIMMING POOLS

You'll need plenty of equipment to keep your pool hygienic and clear of leaves and other debris. Chlorine or other chemicals keep bacteria and algae counts down. You can test for the right chlorine and pH levels with special kits. Scrub algae off the steps and pool sides with a nylon brush. Specialised vacuum cleaners and filter systems clean the water but you'll also need to regularly skim a leaf net over the surface.

Keeping the area around the pool tidy and free of leaves will help keep the pool clean too. Sweep regularly and keep plants trimmed, and make sure pavers are free of mould by cleaning them regularly with a mild solution of bleach. Leave for 48 hours, then rinse and brush with a stiff outdoor brush.

SPAS

Regularly empty and clean your outdoor spa by following the manufacturer's instructions. If you plan to keep the spa constantly full, you'll need a filter system.

Garden furniture

Any softwood in the garden needs to be protected against the ravages of the weather with occasional coats of preservative. For most pre-treated woods, linseed oil offers an efficient form of protection, as it conditions the wood as it preserves it. A good time to treat the wood is in early winter, on a fine, reasonably warm day. The wood will then be protected against the winter rains and frosts.

Wooden decks, particularly in wet climates, will need occasional scrubbing with a stiff-bristled brush and an algicide to remove any accumulated (and slippery) green slime. Hardwood decks need not be treated, but softwood will need treating with preservative once a year.

Cleaning outdoor furniture

▶ *Wipe down furniture made from sealed wood with a damp sponge that has been dipped in a detergent solution. Keep an eye on cracks in the sealer and renew it regularly to maintain effective protection.*

▶ *Give unsealed wood a protective coat once a year by rubbing in a mixture of 4 parts raw linseed oil and 1 part turpentine.*

▶ *Wash cane furniture with warm salty water and leave it to dry in the sun. Protect cane pieces by painting them with an outdoor lacquer.*

▶ *Wash canvas furniture just as you would wash canvas awnings (see page 178).*

▶ *Use a chamois cloth to wipe over metal frames, and apply liquid wax polish to help prevent the metal from rusting.*

The benefits of aquatics
To keep the water clear and clean in your ponds, keep the sunlight off with a layer of floating aquatics that cover about 70 per cent of the surface area. This will stop the algae from growing and keep your fish fed with their greens when you're away. Fairy moss (azolla) is one of the plants that will do the job.

The barbecue
Brush off as much of the burnt remains as you can with a wire brush, then wipe with scrunched up old newspaper. Give metal cooking plates an extra rub with a little salt or sand while they're still warm and oil them before storing.

Spruce up concrete
Sprinkle cement powder over wet concrete and leave it for 10 minutes before sweeping up the excess.

CANVAS AWNINGS AND GARDEN UMBRELLAS

▶ Brush off any dirt and debris, then scrub with a stiff-bristled brush dipped in warm water and detergent. Rinse. For stubborn stains, sprinkle with bicarbonate of soda, leave for 5 minutes, then rinse.

▶ Remove mildew stains with a weak solution of bleach, but test for colour-fastness first. Leave the bleach solution for 48 hours, then rinse.

▶ If you prefer to avoid bleach, try rubbing the mildew with half a cut lemon dipped in salt. Always allow canvas to dry completely before putting it away.

Paths and paving

Sweeping with an outdoor broom is usually enough to keep well-laid bricks and stone pavers looking good, especially as a little weathering improves their appearance. However, too much dirt can cause surfaces to become slippery, which is especially dangerous on natural stone lying in shaded areas that might also attract algae. If mould and mildew become a problem, scrub the bricks and pavers with a mild solution of household bleach, leave for 48 hours, then rinse with a hose.

Removing weeds between pavers by digging, snipping or pulling out is kindest on the environment. You can also try killing them with hot water. Borax is a low-risk weed killer, but don't use it where it could leach onto beds or lawn, as it is poisonous to all plants.

A jet wash can work wonders, bringing a surface almost back to brand new condition, but it is not ideal for all paved areas. The jet is so powerful that any loose laid aggregates set between paving slabs will be sent flying. If there are any poor-quality mortar joints that need to be replaced, jet washing can present you with a quick method of removing any old and crumbling mortar.

KEEPING THE DRIVEWAY CLEAN

▶ If you always park your car in the same spot and you're concerned about grease and oil drips, place a shallow metal tray filled with sawdust or fine sand under the engine area.

▶ To remove oil stains, first blot any excess with something absorbent such as old newspaper or cat litter (work it in with a stiff broom), then blot again with a rag soaked in a grease solvent such as turpentine. Or try a strong household bleach cleaner. Make up a high-strength solution according to the manufacturer's instructions, apply liberally on the stain, leave for 10 minutes, then wash away.

Saving seeds

If you want to save seeds for the follo...
and the seed-bearing organ (the cap...
have dried and fallen, to ripen and dr...

Remember that the flowers grown f...
the crop from which they are grown...
as F1 hybrids. To produce their seed...
strains of the plant. To achieve ider...
crosses must take place naturally, ...
flowers from saved seeds is always...
and unexpected variations appeari...

SELF-SEEDING ANNUALS

Many annuals and even some peren...
and then fade away as quickly as the...
that remain in old gardens.

If you want to create a relaxed cotta...
to self-seed. This may mean tempora...
for the seed heads to form fully. It al...
as possible, as the tiny new plants a...
keep the garden moist, and wait unt...
are large enough to be noticed and...

Annual favourites include forget-me-...
vellous plants if kept in check; Johnr...
heartsease; and columbines, also knc...
include sweet Alice, primulas and cc...
skianus) can also be a lovely ground...
given the chance.

Perennials

Unlike annuals, which are relatively...
Choose those that are suited to you...
a bigger and better display, year aft...

Ornamentals

In a successful garden the seasons, shape, colour and form all play a part in creating drama and ambience. Shrubs and trees form the backbone of the garden while annuals, perennials and bulbs can provide quick and easy colour accents, sometimes producing chance associations that are far more effective than anything you could design.

Annu

Annuals g
other plan
They're ea

GROWIN

▶ Annua

▶ Grow
not o

▶ Befor
water

▶ Buy a
in qu
cell, t
remo

▶ Pinch
for a
will u

▶ All ar
are,

▶ Rem

▶ Wate

▶ Mos
an e

▶ Afte

DESIGN

When se
rows. If y
can then
for a rea
groups c

TYPES OF PERENNIAL

There are two types of perennial flowers — herbaceous and evergreen.

HERBACEOUS PERENNIALS

Most herbaceous perennials are native to areas with very cold winters, and in order to survive, they close down their above-ground parts in autumn but the roots remain alive. In spring, they reshoot. If you grow these winter-dormant perennials where winters are mild, they won't go completely dormant but will soon die, exhausted by their continuous growth.

EVERGREEN PERENNIALS

If you live in a warmer area (frost-free or nearly so), you'll have more success with evergreen perennials, which may slow their growth in winter but keep all their leaves. Of course, you can still grow herbaceous perennials in frost-free climates, but those from the coldest places will probably behave more like annuals, and the warmer your climate, the more this will be so.

GROWING TIPS

▶ Perennials need full sun and plenty of shelter from strong winds.

▶ The garden bed can be any size, but the smaller it is, the fewer types of perennials you should try to grow. Remember, many perennials will become big, and will not be suitable for narrow spaces.

▶ Because perennials are relatively long-lived, good soil preparation is essential. Start by clearing the area of weeds and nuisance grasses.

▶ Always water deeply but infrequently. In hot weather on sandy soils you may need to water twice weekly, but generally once a week is ample.

▶ Perennials should not need a lot of fertilising. Apply a complete plant food just as their growth begins. If the soil has been prepared well, this should be enough for the whole growing season. A mulch of decayed manure or compost placed around the plants will also improve growing conditions.

▶ Keep the area weeded until the plants cover the ground, or grow annuals as filler plants around them.

▶ Once your perennials are in bloom, deadhead them regularly.

▶ In autumn, when herbaceous perennials begin to die back, they can be cut to ground level. Evergreens are not cut back.

▶ Divide and replant perennials whenever the clump becomes overcrowded and congested, usually after 3–4 years' growth. Divide evergreens after flowering, and herbaceous perennials when they are dormant. Division rejuvenates them.

The value of the vertical

Although a sea of colour can be spectacular, you could create a different look by punctuating the horizontal level with spear-like plants that spire into the sky, adding definition and accent. Flowers that provide this effect in the garden include acanthus, delphinium, foxglove, larkspur and verbascum. Some, such as hollyhocks, can flower up to 2 m (6 ft) skywards.

PERENNIAL BORDERS

Perennials can be planted among shrubs, as a complement to a display of bulbs or annuals, or in separate beds — the perennial border. A border is a planted area designed to be seen mostly from one side. You can also grow shrubs or annuals there, in what's known as a mixed border. Most perennials need full sun, although there are some that will take shade.

The great attraction of a perennial border or bed is the wonderful massed display of colour they produce. Of course, choosing the colours and their placement within the border is where your artistry comes in. Your job is to know when each species flowers and in what colour, and to place those that bloom at the same time in pleasing colour combinations.

It's a good idea to do this on paper first. Draw the bed to scale on graph paper and allot a space to each type of perennial you want to grow. They don't all have to flower at the same time, but those that do should look good together. By choosing species that bloom at different times you can have a succession of flowers in a succession of colour schemes.

Dividing perennials

1 To divide plants, lift (dig up) the whole clump, shake off the excess soil and pull the clump apart or cut it into sections. With very large, heavy clumps, you may have to use an axe, a cleaver or a sharp spade.

2 Replant the divided sections straightaway, trimming off any very long roots. Remember the outermost growths are the youngest and the most vigorous. In some cases, the centre of the plant may have died out and so it can be discarded.

Spare pieces

If you are unable to replant at once or if you have pieces to give away, wrap them in damp newspaper or hessian (burlap) and keep them in a shaded, sheltered spot.

Bulbs

Few plants offer as much pleasure for so little effort. Even people without gardens can enjoy bulbs in pots and, while most people think of them as spring flowers, there are also bulbs that bloom in the other seasons.

GROWING TIPS

▶ Available in pink, white and cream as well as yellow, daffodils are probably the most popular bulbs. As with all bulbs, they look their best when they're planted in informal clumps or drifts.

▶ Some bulbs have a wonderful perfume. Freesias, hyacinths and jonquils in particular are noted for their heady scents.

▶ Ranunculus grow from tiny tubers. One tiny ranunculus tuber can produce up to thirty blooms, ideal for cutting. Make sure you don't overwater them, as they are susceptible to rotting in wet soils.

▶ Are your daffodils no longer flowering? Remember to divide them every 3 years or so by removing the offsets and replanting them separately into freshly dug-over, improved soil.

▶ If lifting your bulbs and replanting them sounds like a drag, try selecting old-fashioned favourites that pretty much look after themselves. If you have the space, plant them in bold drifts with cool-season grasses that don't need mowing as regularly. This technique is called naturalising. Try autumn crocus, baby gladiolus, babiana, bluebell, freesia, ixia, sparaxis, triteleia and watsonia.

▶ While most bulbs like a full-sun position, some are able to tolerate more shade. If you have a shadier garden, plant bluebell, freesia, grape hyacinth, snowdrop and triteleia.

▶ Because bulbs have evolved to withstand cold winter temperatures, it is important to wait until the heat of the summer is completely over before planting them. Early autumn is probably the best time to plant most bulbs, although tulips should be planted in late autumn once the soil temperature has dropped.

▶ If you're growing bulbs as cut flowers, place potted bulbs in the shade for a while to lengthen the flower stems, which is ideal for cutting. Gradually bring them out into full sun, then plant some seedling annuals between the new shoots.

▶ Use a premium potting mix (potting compost) when you are growing bulbs in containers. Free-draining, enriched composts with added peatmoss are vital.

Planting bulbs

1 Dig a hole for each bulb, allowing the appropriate depth for each. For example, daffodils need a depth of about 10 cm (4 in). For small groupings, use a trowel, but for larger plantings, use a special bulb planter, which will make the job much easier.

2 Position each bulb with the pointed end facing up.

3 Plant the bulb firmly in the soil, avoiding any air pockets. Backfill the hole with garden soil, then apply a layer of mulch to help conserve moisture, protect the soil from temperature fluctuations and reduce weed growth. Finish by watering the plant thoroughly.

Shade-loving bulbs

- ▶ *Achimenes* hybrids
- ▶ Calla lily (*Zantedeschia aethiopica*)
- ▶ Clivia (*Clivia miniata*)
- ▶ Cobra lily or Jack-in-the-pulpit (*Arisaema sikokianum*)
- ▶ Cyclamen (*Cyclamen persicum*)
- ▶ Dog-tooth violet, trout lily (*Erythronium dens-canis*)
- ▶ Fritillary, crown imperial (*Fritillaria imperialis*)
- ▶ Liliums (*some only*)
- ▶ Spanish bluebell (*Hyacinthoides hispanica*)
- ▶ Squills (*Scilla sp.*)
- ▶ Tuberous begonia
- ▶ Wood anemone (*Anemone blanda*)

CHILLING BULBS

Spring-flowering bulbs usually require a period of cold temperatures below 9°C (48°F) in order to kick off the flowering process. When the optimum temperature is reached, a biochemical reaction occurs within the bulb. This is followed by a response in the plant to increasing day length and warmer temperatures. Indoor forcing is a way of inducing that reaction artificially. In cool zones, you only need to plant bulbs out in autumn and wait for the shoots to appear in spring because the cold winter ground provides sufficient chilling for them to flower.

In warm areas, where the soil does not become cold enough in winter for the bulbs to successfully flower, they will respond to an artificially induced chilling period. To do this, buy bulbs as soon as they first go on sale and place them in your refrigerator crisper until mid- to late autumn, or until the garden soil is cool enough for planting.

Planting bulbs in lawn

A low-maintenance way to grow bulbs is to leave them in the ground to multiply. Bulbs suitable for planting in grass include *Colchicum*, *Crocus*, *Ixia*, *Leucojum*, *Muscari*, *Narcissus*, *Ornithogalum*, *Scilla*, *Sparaxis* and *Triteleia* species. The easiest method is to use a bulb planter.

1. Scatter a handful of the bulbs to achieve a natural look. Plant them where they land.

2. Twist the bulb planter into the ground to the desired depth and, still twisting, pull it out again.

3. Gently place the bulb in the hole in an upright position but do not press it down too firmly.

4. Place some of the plug around the bulb until it's level with the top. Add the remainder and press into place.

Supporting perennials, bulbs and annuals

Soft-stemmed herbaceous plants need support, otherwise delicate stems may snap in the wind, particularly when they are in flower. There are various staking options, and much depends on the setting for the plants. In a border where the plants are quite closely packed, the supports will not show and you can use types that have little aesthetic appeal. Link stakes, which slot into each other to form a ring around the plant, are useful for this kind of job.

For plants grown in containers, which are normally on show, more attractive forms of staking are useful. You can use branching twigs, inserted around the edge of the pot, as these look much more attractive than either link stakes or bamboo canes held together with string. Alternatively, you can make your own supporting cage from supple stems such as bamboo or willow. Insert about eight stems around the edge of the pot and tie them at the top with raffia to make a feature of the support. This also works well with heavy flowers that tend to flop, such as hyacinths.

The garden palette

Historically, the most successful garden designers have used colour in much the same way as artists do, selecting from their palettes and blending colours to create a harmony that results in a certain mood or effect. The result may be restful or flamboyant.

The three primary colours — red, blue and yellow — are the building blocks of all other colours, while the three secondary colours — green, violet and orange — are mixtures of these. Together, the primary and secondary colours make up the colours of a rainbow. Shades or hues vary, depending on the strength and intensity of each primary colour, while tone is a measure of the black and white component in each colour. Black, white and grey are inert colours, which means they don't change the colour, only the brightness.

The colour wheel can usefully be divided into two halves — in one half you'll find the 'cool' colours of green, grey, blue and mauve, and in the other the 'warm' colours, such as yellow, red, orange and hot pink. Colours next to each other on the colour wheel, or nearby, are called harmonious colours, while colours opposite each other are called contrasting colours.

You can use this knowledge as a tool in garden design. For example, if you want to plant a vibrant garden, use contrasting colours from opposite sides of the wheel — red and green, purple and yellow, blue and orange. Start with a cool colour as a base and add the hot colour as a highlight to intensify the effect of both colours.

If you're trying to create a tranquil haven, select complementary colours — such as pink and mauve — on the same side of the wheel. Gardens planted in one colour can also be very restful.

TIPS FOR USING COLOUR

▶ Colour outside should be used to back up the function and mood of the garden, the flower colour adding to the effect of the foliage, form and texture of shrubs, trees and groundcovers.

▶ Colour has a big effect on mood. Use bright colours in lively environments, and softer, subtle tones in restful areas.

▶ Locate the strongest colours in the foreground, and allow the colours to become paler with distance. Too much strong colour at a distance foreshortens the space.

▶ Work with any surrounding colour schemes, including the house as well as the boundary and distant views.

▶ Grey or silver foliage 'cools down' bright colours, and white flowers help contrasting colours to blend effectively.

▶ Colour changes, depending on the intensity of sunlight. Pale colours look soft and gentle in the morning and evening, yet can appear bleached and washed out during the day, while colours that work in the heat of the day can look garish in softer light.

▶ When you want something to stand out and be noticed, a loud splash of colour nearby will capture and hold the eye.

▶ Select a range of colours that suits your home and personality, but try deviating from this range to allow contrast into your garden.

▶ Try working with foliage colour as the backbone of your garden's year-round interest. Darker foliage makes colours more pronounced.

▶ Large flowers are harder to blend successfully than smaller ones.

Shrubs

You can create a lovely garden almost entirely from shrubs, which give the garden form and definition and much of its colour and texture. With careful planning you can have shrubs in flower every month of the year.

When you're planning your garden, select shrubs to suit the position. Will the shrub thrive in full sun, or does it prefer shade? Consider how high and wide it will grow. Don't buy a large-growing shrub for a small space, thinking you will keep it pruned. You will probably get tired of pruning and end up removing it.

Planting a shrub

Container-grown shrubs can be planted out almost any time of the year, except in areas that have heavy frost in winter. Before planting, check that the position you have chosen suits the shrub's requirements in terms of sun or shade, shelter, drainage and the area available for healthy growth.

1 Dig a hole that is at least twice as wide as the potted plant and about the same depth. Loosen the soil in the bottom of the hole but do not dig down into a clay layer or you may create a well in which the plant roots may drown.

2 Do not put compost or manure in the planting hole. You can sprinkle blood and bone (bonemeal) or slow-release fertiliser in the bottom of the hole but you must cover it with 3–5 cm (1¼–2 in) of soil so the roots don't come into contact with it.

3 Thoroughly water the plant in its pot, then loosen it by tapping the base and sides of the pot. Finally, slide the plant out gently.

4 Place the plant in the hole so the soil level is the same as it was in the container. Backfill the hole with the soil you have dug out and firm the soil in well, but don't compact the soil and crush the roots by stamping around too much.

5 Water the planted shrub thoroughly again to eliminate air pockets and settle the soil around the plant's roots.

6 Mulch the area around the shrub, but keep the mulch well clear of the stem.

Pruning shrubs
Many shrubs will never need pruning except to rejuvenate a very old plant or to remove the odd wayward stem and generally tidy up its appearance. If you do want or need to prune, do so immediately after the plant has flowered (see pages 170–75). The exception is shrubs grown for their berries, which form after the flowers, but these types of shrubs rarely need pruning.

Choosing a shrub at the garden centre

▶ *When buying shrubs, biggest is not always best. Look for well-shaped plants that have a good cover of healthy leaves.*

▶ *Check for insect damage, weeds or fungus rots.*

▶ *Avoid pot-bound shrubs — those with woody roots protruding from the drainage holes, those that are too tall for the pot size and those with knobbly, thickened bases to their stems. Their roots will be so tightly packed they may never spread out after planting.*

HEDGES AND SCREENS

A hedge or living screen looks beautiful, provides privacy, shade and shelter, and is relatively cheap and easy to grow, adding value to your home.

For clipped, formal hedges, evergreens with small leaves are the best. For informal hedges, which do not have neat outlines — and can be maintained with only one or two clippings a year — plants with dense foliage all the way to the ground are ideal. Screens, on the other hand, can be created with any plants that will achieve the desired result. Evergreen shrubs are generally the best for screening. However, remember that even the mass of bare branches on deciduous shrubs can have a dramatic effect and provide some screening, and they also let in the wonderful winter sun.

Good hedging plants

Evergreen plants
Box *(Buxus sp.)* to 1.2 m (4 ft)
Elaeagnus × ebbingei to 3 m (10 ft)
Escallonia sp. to 2.4 m (8 ft)
Holly *(Ilex sp.)* to 4 m (13 ft)
Prunus laurocerasus to 3 m (10 ft)
Viburnus tinus to 2.4 m (8 ft)
Yew *(Taxus baccata)* to 6 m (20 ft)

Deciduous plants
Berberis thunbergii to 1.2 m (4 ft)
Carpinus betulus to 6 m (20 ft)
Copper beech *(Fagus sylvatica,*
    Atropurpurea Group) to 6 m (20 ft)
Fuchsia magellanica to 1.5 m (5 ft)
Hawthorn *(Crataegus monogyna)*
    to 3 m (10 ft)
Rosa rugosa to 1.5 m (5 ft)

PRUNING TIPS

▶ Always prune any sort of hedge so that the top is slightly narrower than the bottom. This gives the lower growth enough light to live. This is especially important with conifers, such as cypresses, because once that lower growth dies, it usually doesn't regenerate.

▶ Start pruning a formal hedge early in the plant's life. To encourage low branching, cut the vertical growth severely as soon as the plant is established, and continue to trim the plants to shape as they grow. It will take several years for them to reach the desired height, but if you let them grow to the height you want before you start shaping, you may never achieve the dense foliage necessary for privacy, and you will almost certainly have bare branches at the base of the hedge.

▶ Prune conifers little and often, and never prune into older wood, as many of them will not reshoot from bare wood (see also page 170).

▶ Lightly shear informal hedges and screens at least once a year. If you start doing this at an early stage, the plant will develop an attractive thick, bushy habit.

▶ In mild climates, you can maintenance prune at almost any time of year, but remember, quick regrowth is desirable. In frosty areas, don't prune after midsummer, as the existing growth should have time to harden off so it won't be damaged by frost.

▶ Most hedges can be managed with secateurs and sharp hand-hedging shears. If, however, you have big hedges to maintain, a powered hedge clipper will make the job quicker and easier.

ROSES

These glorious plants are generally quite adaptable, but they do grow and flower best in cool to mild climates — those that don't suffer from extremes of cold or excessive heat and humidity.

GROWING TIPS

▶ Roses must receive at least 5 hours of direct sun every day, more if possible. Where summers are very hot, position them so they receive plenty of sun in the morning and early afternoon, as late shade helps preserve the flowers.

▶ The more humid your climate, the more open, sunny and breezy the rose-growing site should be. Humidity and a sheltered, still position are an open invitation to fungal diseases. The perfect place for growing roses is a breezy position, but without constant wind.

▶ Roses are at their best in very fertile soil that retains moisture but is never sodden for long periods of time. They will grow well in clay-based, fairly heavy loams as well as in lighter, more sandy soils. If you grow them in clay soils, make sure the soil drains freely, and make sure sandy soils contain plenty of rotted organic matter.

▶ Roses have big appetites but you can satisfy them by mulching at least once a year with rotted manure and a ration of rose food.

▶ Keep roses moist at all times but never allow the roots to sit in water.

▶ Prune back heavily once a year in winter.

Once-flowering or repeat-blooming

▶ *Some roses, usually the older varieties or natural species, flower only once, in spring. From beginning to end, the show lasts up to 6 weeks and can be truly spectacular.*

▶ *Today's popular hybrid tea roses and many others have a repeat-blooming or 'remontant' habit — that is, flowers come in flushes throughout spring, summer and autumn. Often there is an abundant display in spring and a second show in autumn, with a succession of individual blooms in between.*

▶ *Repeat-blooming may seem the better deal, but don't automatically choose a remontant variety over a once-bloomer. In hot climates, the summer flowers are often burned, and in rainy or humid climates they can be destroyed by the weather and diseases.*

Planting potted roses

Roses bought in pots can be planted out like any other potted plant.

1   Dig a hole that is 2–3 times wider than the pot but about the same depth. Loosen the soil in the bottom of the hole.

2   Crumble some of the excavated soil back into the hole so it forms a high mound in the middle. Don't enrich the soil in the rose-planting hole with compost or rotted manure, or you'll create a well of fertility that will discourage the roots from spreading into the surrounding soil.

3   Take the rose from its pot and carefully untangle and tease out the roots. Place the plant in the hole, making sure the roots are over the mound. Spread them downwards and outwards.

4   Refill the hole with the crumbled excavated soil, ensuring the rose is planted no deeper in the ground than it was in the pot. Tamp down the plant gently to firm the soil around the roots, and water in thoroughly. Top up with more soil if there is subsidence.

5   Mulch around the plant with compost or some other rotted organic matter and again water thoroughly.

6   After a few weeks, new growth will appear, and you can sprinkle a ration of complete plant food or slow-release fertiliser around the rose.

Roses for containers

Any rose can be grown in a pot, as long as it has adequate fertiliser and water and is grown in a rich soil, but some roses have been bred with dwarf root systems, making them ideal for containers. Look for these patio roses at your local nursery. Mini roses are easily grown in tubs and look beautiful in posies. White 'Popcorn', a soft lime called 'Green Ice', a ginger called 'Teddy Bear' and lolly pink 'China Doll' are tiny and delightful roses.

Planting bare-rooted roses

In winter, dormant or 'bare-rooted' roses are sold with their roots wrapped but with very little soil around them. When you bring your rose plants home, unwrap them and immediately soak the roots in a bucket of water while you prepare the planting hole.

1 Make the holes wide and about 30 cm (1 ft) deep, and make a mound as described for potted roses opposite.

2 Spread the roots downwards and outwards over the mound and refill the hole with the excavated soil. If any of the roots are damaged or too long, trim them back with very sharp, disinfected secateurs — you can shorten the roots to about 20 cm (8 in) without harming the plant. Make sure you don't bury the rose too deeply, as the graft union (the bend or lump on the stem between the roots and branches) must be above soil level when planting is complete.

3 Mulch around the plant after you have watered it in. Use well-rotted cow or poultry manure, compost, straw or any combination of these materials.

4 Water once a week if necessary — feel the soil under the mulch first and if it is moist, don't water.

5 When you see new growth, sprinkle a ration of complete plant food, rose food or slow-release fertiliser around the plant and water it in.

PRUNING ROSES

Just about all kinds of roses will send up vigorous new shoots from the base of the plant each year. After about 3 years, each of these shoots will have grown old — fewer flowers will be produced, and the decrepit stems will become easy targets for various pests and diseases. To make room for, and encourage, the fresh new stems, prune out the oldest branches each year, right at the base, and cut the younger ones back to a healthy bud.

CLIMBING ROSES

These produce many long canes from their bases, and these should always be tied to their support horizontally. The flower stems will then arise along the tied-down cane. In autumn, prune off 25–30 cm (10–12 in) from each cane and, in winter, remove any old woody canes. Shorten all new canes that have not yet grown long enough to be tied down. Also during winter, shorten all the lateral branches from the tied-down canes that have flowered back to the third set of leaves from their bases. Those lateral branches that have not flowered should be tied down horizontally but not shortened.

Hints for cutting roses

▶ *Use a sharp blade and always cut to an outward-facing bud.*

▶ *Avoid picking flowers in the first year of growth.*

▶ *When pruning, never take more than one-third of the flower stem; this helps to keep the rose bush productive and in shape.*

▶ *Cut roses early in the morning when the plant's moisture and sugar levels are at their highest.*

▶ *Remove thorns and leaves that will be below water level in the vase.*

▶ *After cutting, immerse the stems in warm water and cut them once more, this time under water. Add a teaspoon of sugar to help prolong the life of the blooms.*

Trees

Trees planted around your home not only improve its appearance but also make it a more comfortable and pleasant place in which to live, and add considerably to its value. Remember, however, that eventually the trees you plant will grow to dominate your block, so it's vital to choose them carefully.

GROWING TIPS

▶ Find out how big your tree will grow and make sure it will fit your garden without the need for constant pruning.

Caring for bare-rooted roses

If you are not able to plant your bare-rooted roses immediately, open the packaging to allow ventilation of the stems and to keep the plants cold but not frozen or exposed to frost. Don't allow the roots to dry out but don't sit them in water either. Plant them as soon as possible.

Disbudding roses

For fewer, but larger, prize-winning blooms, 'disbud' the rose bush by removing all the side buds while they are still quite small. This will allow the plant to concentrate its energy on the top bud.

▶ Avoid planting trees during the extreme temperatures of summer and winter. In the first year, water deeply to help the tree to grow strong, deep roots.

▶ Feed your tree appropriately to encourage vigorous new growth, and make sure you stake it for the first year only.

▶ Don't plant your tree closer than 5 m (16 ft) to your house. Its roots could damage your foundations and block drains.

▶ Allow space for the trunk to develop and for air and water to penetrate down to the roots, so don't pave too close to your tree.

▶ Prune your tree in autumn, as the sap flow slows down at this time of year.

Danger spots for planting trees

▶ *Never plant a tree under electric wires. If the trees grow to touch the wires, it can be very dangerous and you will be charged with the cost of clearing them.*

▶ *Avoid planting trees near sewer lines — if they ever leak, fine roots will enter and cause plumbing problems. This is due to the fact that as tree roots grow, they thicken considerably, widening the crack in the pipe and admitting more roots. Eventually they block the pipe. Modern, plastic pipes laid in long lengths are less likely to be penetrated than old terracotta pipes with their many leaky joins.*

▶ *A tree's surface roots can crack and lift paths and paving if planted closer than about 5 m (16 ft).*

▶ *Roots have also been blamed for cracking houses, and the problem is worse if the house is built on clay soils. In dry spells, as the tree takes up water, the clay shrinks and the house cracks as it settles. When it rains, the clay expands, causing further movement cracks. Generally, the bigger the tree will become, the further from the house it should be planted, especially in clay soil.*

Avoid overplanting
Saplings look small, but they will soon be a hundred times bigger. Trees that are planted too closely together may force each other to adopt unnatural, unappealing shapes. Also think about your neighbours — consider the shade your tree will cast on their property, the amount of their precious garden space its branches will invade and the litter it will drop.

Climbers in pots

A large container, filled with good-quality potting mix (potting compost), can be ideal for growing a climber that's needed to cover a pergola over a paved area. However, do consider the area you want the climber to cover in relation to the size of the pot, for the pot holds all the water and nutrients available. Will it be big enough to keep all those stems and leaves full of water? To provide cover for a pergola, you will need a very large container, and possibly several, with a climber in each. All will need frequent watering and fertilising.

The less vigorous climbers, such as waxflower (Stephanotis floribunda) and Hoya sp., are best for pots. Such climbers are too small to cover big areas but look lovely on wall-mounted trellises or twining up a pole. In tubs, very vigorous growers, such as wisteria, are best trained as standards or free-standing shrubs rather than as climbers. They need a very sturdy support until they become self-supporting.

FRAGRANT CLIMBERS

One of the most glorious features of many climbers is their scent. Consider the following tips for using fragrant plants effectively in the garden.

▶ *In the area immediately outside the house, grow perfumed climbers around the windows and doors, especially the ones you open regularly during the summer.*

▶ *Fragrant climbers are ideal for training on the walls of the house, including wisteria, Chinese jasmine (Trachelospermum sp.), roses and honeysuckle. The exact choice of plant, however, will be largely governed by the orientation of the house, as different plants tolerate different conditions.*

▶ *Try to select the right plant for the location. For instance, if you'd like a fragrant bedroom, choose honeysuckle. This produces most of its scent during the evening because it's pollinated mainly by moths, so it's ideal for growing near a room that's occupied mainly at night.*

▶ *If you often dine under a pergola during the day, when you need shade from the sun, plant a leafy perfumed climber overhead. If you use the area in the evening, choose climbers that have scent at that time of day, such as climbing moonflower (Ipomoea alba).*

Edibles

Growing your own herbs, fruit and vegetables is one of the most rewarding of gardening activities, and not as difficult as you might think. As long as you choose the right crops for your climate, keep the edible garden a manageable size for you and your lifestyle, and give your plants some ongoing care, you can enjoy fresh, delicious home-grown produce.

The herb garden

No garden is complete without herbs. They're invaluable in the kitchen and can also be used in cosmetics, craft arrangements and natural remedies. Even if you never use them, most make delightful garden plants, and some even repel insects.

You'll probably need several plants of your favourite herbs to avoid harvesting them to death. Try out a plant or two of a herb with appealing looks or fragrance that you're not familiar with.

GROWING TIPS

▶ Herbs grow naturally in many different soils and climates. Some thrive in extremely dry areas, others in tropical rainforests and temperate forests, so if you choose the appropriate herbs for the prevailing conditions, you can't go wrong. However, most herbs prefer full sun and free-draining soil.

▶ Don't pick more than one-third of a young plant or more than half of a mature specimen at the one time. The more often you pick, the bushier and healthier herbs become.

▶ Don't overfertilise, as this will cause too much soft, leafy growth at the expense of essential oils.

▶ Many herbs grow better when planted next to other herbs, but some will struggle in the wrong combinations. For example, mint hates growing near parsley. If your herbs aren't doing well, and you think they're growing in the right conditions, they might be in with the wrong crowd.

▶ To develop their full flavour, most herbs require at least 5 hours of sunlight a day.

▶ Always gather herbs just as they come into flower, when their flavour is strongest.

Ornamental herbs

▶ **Silver foliage** Artichoke, cotton lavender, curry plant, Euphorbia marginata, lavender, rue, sage, southernwood, Thymus 'Silver Posy', wormwood

▶ **Golden foliage** Golden box, golden lemon balm, golden marjoram, golden sage

▶ **Variegated leaves** Variegated apple mint, oregano and scented geraniums

▶ **Purple leaves** Bronze fennel, Japanese perilla, opal basil, purple sage

Planting a mint garden

Mints have long been grown for their oil-rich leaves. However, they are vigorous plants that can easily take over if you don't take steps to control it.

1 Place the mint in a pot and add potting mix (potting compost).

2 Dig a hole in the garden bed and insert the pot — the lip of the pot should protrude so that the runners won't easily spread into the surrounding soil.

3 Mulch the pot and water well.

Freezing herbs

Herbs suitable for freezing include basil, borage, chives and parsley.

1 Collect tender young shoots and keep them out of direct sunlight so they stay cool and fresh before freezing.

2 Wash the herbs thoroughly in cold water before using a sharp knife or scissors to cut them into small sections.

3 Place the chopped herbs into the compartments of an ice cube tray and fill each compartment with water, or bundle them into plastic bags. Place the herbs in the freezer.

Vegetables

Nothing beats garden-fresh vegetables, and you don't need much space to grow them. Any sunny spot, even a pot, can produce a few favourites, but with an area of just 4 x 4 m (13 x 13 ft) you can grow an amazing range.

If you have space for a large plot, keep the garden beds accessible for planting, weeding and harvesting. Many fruits, vegetables and herbs are highly decorative, so even if you don't have room to devote a whole patch to them, you can grow them in borders with your ornamental garden plants.

THE IMPORTANCE OF GOOD SOIL

Fertile, free-draining soil is essential for good crops. Start by clearing the site, then dig the soil over, breaking up clods as you go. Work in plenty of well-rotted manure and compost and a small handful of complete plant food per square metre (yard). The dug-over soil should be dark, fine and crumbly.

Potted herbs
Most varieties grow very well in pots, so even if you live in an apartment you can still have the pleasure of growing fresh herbs. If the window receives the sun, you can keep them on the kitchen windowsill — just reach out and harvest them as you need them.

Herb or spice?
Have you ever wondered what the difference is between a herb and a spice? Herbs are the leaves of plants, while spices are produced from the other parts, such as flowers, seeds and roots.

Edible thinnings
The thinnings of many vegetables are delicious in salads, or used lightly wilted. Try beetroot, chicory (endive), radish, silverbeet (Swiss chard) and turnip.

If your soil is sticky, heavy clay, don't dig. Instead, build a 25 cm (10 in) high retaining wall around the site and fill it with imported good-quality soil.

If your soil is very sandy, it will drain well and be very easy to dig, but you'll need to add lots of organic matter to make it fertile and give it some body. In any type of soil, adding organic matter will increase its bulk, but don't worry about that. The raised soil level helps ensure good drainage. Rake over to make it level, then water the whole area deeply.

CHOOSING THE RIGHT CROPS

Select only varieties that you enjoy eating. As vegetables planted at the same time will mature at the same time, it's a good idea to plant small batches 2–3 weeks apart — this should each yield no more than you can eat in 2 or 3 weeks. That way you will have a continuous supply without any wasteful and discouraging gluts. Few vegetables can be grown all year round, so choose varieties that are right for the season.

GROWING VEGETABLES

Vegetables can be started from either seeds or seedlings. Seeds are far cheaper, and there's a much wider range of varieties available. You can also plant a few seeds now and save the rest for later sowings. Follow the directions on the pack, especially the sowing depth, and never allow the soil to dry out while the seeds are germinating (which may take 2 weeks). When the seedlings do appear, thin the excess seedlings so the spacing between each one is correct.

Bought seedlings, being already several weeks old, are ready to eat much sooner and can be spaced correctly from the outset. On the downside, you'll have to plant all of them at once, regardless of whether you want a dozen of that variety maturing at the same time.

Vegetables are usually grown in rows. Single rows are the traditional choice but some garden experts are now recommending wide rows — that is, 3–5 rows closely spaced to form one wide row. This increases the yield per square metre or yard.

Crop rotation

This age-old technique is the natural way to keep your garden soil and plants healthy. Long before fungicides and pesticides came onto the scene, farmers discouraged pests and diseases by not planting the same crop or crops of the same plant family in the same patch of soil 2 years in succession. Instead, they rotated their crops into different beds over a 3 or 4 year cycle — pests that fed on particular plants died when their food source was not replanted. Here's a 3 year crop rotation plan based on a vegetable garden that's been divided into three beds.

▶ **Bed 1** *Grow all or some of these — any bean, lettuce, peanut, any peas, silverbeet (Swiss chard), spinach, sweet corn.*

▶ **Bed 2** *Grow all or some of these — broccoli, Brussels sprouts, cabbage, cauliflower, kohlrabi, radish, turnip.*

▶ **Bed 3** *Grow all or some of these — beetroot, carrot, celery, cucumber, garlic, leek, onion, potato, tomato, zucchini (courgette).*

The next year, grow the contents of bed 1 in bed 2, of bed 2 in bed 3 and of bed 3 in bed 1. Keep rotating the beds after every harvest.

Planting seed potatoes

Keep some seed potatoes until they sprout. This is called 'chitting' potato tubers, and will give your plants a head start.

1 Using a spade or hoe, double-dig a trench.

2 Create a flat-bottomed or V-shaped trench 15 cm (6 in) wide.

3 Cut the seed potatoes into pieces so that each piece contains an eye.

4 Plant the pieces of potato in the trench with the eye facing upwards.

5 Backfill the trench and water in thoroughly.

ROUTINE MAINTENANCE

Make sure you water your vegetable garden often — daily, or even twice daily when it's hot and dry. However, frequent watering will wash the nutrients out of the soil, so you should also feed the vegetables at fortnightly intervals (monthly in winter). You can use liquid or soluble fertiliser, or sprinkle complete plant food alongside each row. If you have a good supply of rotted manure, using it to mulch the vegetables will eliminate the need for fertiliser and help conserve soil moisture.

various permutations of these two. If your cloche is tunnel-shaped, or if you have a row of tent cloches, remember that end pieces are necessary to prevent the wind from blowing through the tunnel and killing off your precious plants.

You can buy cloches from garden supply stores or, if you prefer, make your own. Small individual cloches can be made from empty plastic bottles with the base cut out. These provide useful protection for small, tender plants and create an effective barrier against slugs and snails. In many instances cloches can allow you to get two crops a year out of the same plot, but you must fertilise the soil adequately to ensure the soil can support such a high yield.

GREENHOUSES

Greenhouses are available in various different styles and materials, each with its own advantages and drawbacks.

- ▶ Softwood frames need regular painting, and western red cedar needs occasional treatment with preservative, whereas aluminium is maintenance-free.

- ▶ A traditional span roof is ideal for vegetables at ground level.

- ▶ Half-boarded or those on a low wall are more economical to heat.

- ▶ A lean-to retains heat well.

- ▶ A conservatory is similar to a lean-to but generally sturdier.

- ▶ A plastic walk-in tunnel is inexpensive but not a good insulator, although it is ideal for vegetables in summer.

Citrus care tips

- ▶ *Citrus trees need regular feeding and watering. Feed them in winter with citrus fertiliser. Water first — never apply powdered fertiliser to dry soil, as it can burn the roots.*

- ▶ *Limes and cumquats grow well in pots. The best way to feed pots is with controlled-release fertiliser.*

- ▶ *Watch for citrus leaf miner, a tiny insect that causes deformity and hinders growth. Spray affected trees with white oil.*

Lawns and groundcovers

A healthy, lush green lawn can be a beautiful feature in its own right, but in order to create and maintain a good-looking lawn, you'll have to put in the necessary time and effort, as well as do a bit of forward planning. If you prefer a more low-maintenance solution, the answer is to grow groundcovers instead.

Concrete strips

Concrete mower strips make edging easier but don't install them until after you have established the turf. If the strips are installed before the turf and the soil subsides even slightly, they will be more of a hindrance than a help.

Time and money

All lawns are a long-term investment in terms of both time and money. Even if you are content to have your lawn grow reasonably well and not be too overrun with weeds, you will need to spend some time on maintenance. Achieving the perfection of a velvety smooth, immaculate lawn requires a great deal of time and effort.

Planning a lawn

The amount of time and care you give a lawn depends on the type of grass you choose and how obsessed you are with maintaining a healthy sward. There is no plant that grows as relentlessly as grass, and the time spent behind a lawnmower can be torture for some but relaxing therapy for others.

Don't rush into establishing your lawn — if you take the time to plan it carefully it will pay off in the long run.

▶ If you live in an area with low rainfall and/or water restrictions, your garden might use much less water if a part, or all, of the lawn is replaced with groundcovers or shrubs, or even with paving or gravel. Lawns are not an essential element in good garden design.

▶ Before you plant, prepare the soil well (see opposite) and consider both the climate and the amount of direct sun the area receives.

▶ Think about the primary use the lawn will have — a lush foil for a bed of ornamentals, or a children's play area? Some grasses withstand heavy wear and others cope with shade, but none do both.

▶ Plan your lawn area so that it will be easy to mow and maintain. Avoid sharp corners and wiggly edges, and don't have lots of small garden beds — they not only make mowing hard but also spoil the effect of a sweeping lawn.

Choosing your grass

Lawn grasses fall into two main categories.

▶ **Warm-season grasses** These perennial, running grasses — such as buffalo, couch, Durban and kikuyu — are best suited to frost-free areas. Many lose colour in winter but they do not die off unless winters are severe.

▶ **Cool-season grasses** Bent grass, fescue, Kentucky bluegrass and ryegrass, for example, are mostly tufty and tussock-forming, although there are a few that will run. They grow well in cool climates and during the cooler months in a warm climate but are very difficult to maintain during hot, humid summers when they are highly prone to attack by fungal diseases.

Preparing the ground for a new lawn

To establish turf successfully, you need friable, sandy loam that's workable to a depth of 15–25 cm (6–10 in). To improve aeration and drainage, incorporate large quantities of organic matter into the soil well ahead of turf laying or seed sowing; in sandy soils this will also aid moisture retention.

If you have a clay subsoil, you may need to import soil and cover the area to be turfed to a depth of at least 10 cm (4 in). Ask the soil supplier if the soil is weed-free, and check that it is not full of silty clay, which will set like concrete after watering. Mix the added soil with the existing soil so that water, air and roots can penetrate easily.

Treat heavy clay soils with an application of gypsum at a rate of roughly 300 g per square metre (10½ oz per square yard), or if the soil is known to be very acidic, garden or agricultural lime can be applied at a rate of 100 g per square metre (3½ oz per square yard). Only cultivate clay soils when they are just moist, not wet or dry.

CHECKING DRAINAGE
To check the drainage, dig a hole, fill it with water and see how long it takes to drain away. If water remains in the hole for more than 24 hours, you may have to lay subsoil drains or creating a slight slope on the area. A slope of 1 in 70 will prevent wet spots.

LEVELLING THE GROUND
There are various ways to level the ground, and the method you use will depend on the size of the area. For large areas, the simplest solution is to knock wooden pegs (on which height markers have been indicated with black pen) into the ground, each to the same depth. You can then run string between the pegs at the desired height, and adjust the soil surface so it is level with the string. If you decide to lay turf rather than sow seeds, allow 5 cm (2 in) on top of the desired height to account for the thickness of the turf.

REMOVING WEEDS
The area to be turfed should be free of stones, roots and any other debris. Be sure to remove all weeds, paying particular attention to those with bulbs, as they are very hard to control once grass is established.

ADDING FERTILISER
The surface should be raked level and be fine and crumbly. Apply lawn starter fertiliser or blood and bone (bonemeal), then lightly rake or water it in. Water the area lightly for a few days before sowing seeds or laying turf in order to firm the soil and provide a moist layer on which grass can establish.

Establishing a lawn

You can establish a lawn by laying turf, which will give you an instant lawn, or sowing seeds. The latter option is much cheaper but you will need to keep the sown area free of any traffic for several weeks.

TURF

Turf — living grass that is available in machine-cut rolls — provides an almost instant effect. It has been severed from most of its root system so it needs to be laid as soon as possible after delivery. If there is any delay in laying, keep the rolls damp, in a shaded place. Covering them with wet hessian (burlap) also helps, although it may be several weeks before it is fully stable.

Ideally, turf should be laid in autumn. However, if the soil is too wet to work on in autumn, the turf can be laid in spring.

To lay the rolls, place them on the prepared ground with their edges pushed firmly together, and check they make good contact with the soil. Set each piece like bricks in a wall, so the joins are staggered. If the ground slopes, lay the rolls across the slope, not down it, and stagger the joins to prevent erosion. Work from a flat board to avoid damaging the turf by walking on it, and to firm it into place.

Spread over a top-dressing of sandy loam and brush or rake it into any gaps to stop the edges from drying out and shrinking. Then thoroughly water the turf and keep it moist for the first 10–14 days. This may mean watering more than once a day in hot or windy weather. Then cut back watering to every second day. In 3 weeks the grass should be established and you can reduce watering to a heavy soaking once a week. Mow lightly after about 3 weeks.

SEEDS

Seeds take a lot longer than turf to establish as a lawn, but if they are sown during the spring or autumn months, they will produce a good-quality result. Also, you can select a grass seed mixture to suit your own purpose, while specialist turf has to be ordered well in advance.

The germination time varies according to the grass type, and may be anywhere from 5 days to 3 weeks. Warm-season grasses are usually sown in spring or early autumn, while cool-season grasses may be sown in mid-spring or late summer. Don't mow until the grass has reached 4–5 cm (1½–2 in) high.

Drought-tolerant grasses

As summers are becoming hotter in many areas, you should look for drought-tolerant lawns that are less dependent on watering. Hybrid couches and fescues are the hardiest, while bluegrass and buffalo grasses are reasonably tolerant. The grasses to avoid include ryegrass and bent.

Sowing lawn seeds

1. Rake the prepared soil to form a seed bed with a fine tilth, removing any stones and using the rake to gently break up any clods of soil in the bed.

2. Mark out the area into equal squares. Weigh out the seeds for each square and, for even coverage, mix lawn seeds with some dry sand or dry sawdust.

3. With your hand at about knee level, sow the seeds evenly, half in each direction.

4. Lightly rake the seeds into the surface soil and water gently, being careful not to allow pools to form, as these may wash the seeds into patches. You may need to water several times a day if the weather is windy or hot. Keep the surface just moist at all times after seeding or the results will be poor.

The best time to sow lawn seeds
Always sow lawn seeds in mild weather on a day that isn't rainy or windy.

Mowing

As a general rule, all lawns should be high cut rather than shaved. Cutting a lawn too short weakens the grass, which gradually becomes thinner. Weeds soon take over, worn patches develop, and the ground becomes compacted before hardening in the heat of summer. When grass is left longer, it will grow vigorously to form a thick, healthy turf. This in turn will allow the grass to grow much stronger as the roots will penetrate deeper into the soil.

A handy hint is never to remove more than one-third of the leaf blade at any one cutting. If grass has been allowed to grow very long it is better to reduce the height gradually rather than cut it low with one mowing and risk scorching what is left. As winter approaches, raise the mower height to help maintain the grass through the colder months. Grass growing under trees should be cut very high, to 8–10 cm (3¼–4 in), otherwise it may die out.

Mowing in hot-summer areas
Make sure you keep your mower blades sharp, as torn grass edges brown quickly in the summer heat.

Lawn equipment

▶ *If you have a large lawn, choose a motor mower with the correct horsepower and an appropriate catcher. Hand-held trimmers, motorised or manual, make quick, light work of neatening rough areas along paths, around trees or next to fences.*

▶ *The lawnmower most commonly used is the rotary mower, which has an adjustable cutting height and horizontal cutting blades that revolve at a high speed. This type is fairly easy to maintain, and if you keep the blades well set and sharpened you'll be rewarded with a most satisfactory cut.*

▶ *On a mechanical cylinder mower, the blades are on a turning cylinder that moves against a fixed base plate. There is also a roller behind the cutting cylinder. The cutting height is adjustable but this type requires more regular sharpening and maintenance. It does, however, give a finer and much better finish to the lawn.*

▶ *The hand cylinder mowers of today are so lightweight, they can be pushed with only a little effort. These mowers are ideal for small, flattish lawn areas, and are very simple to maintain. If you keep the blades sharpened, they give a good finish.*

▶ *Ride-on mowers are expensive but the only practical way to mow extensive lawn areas, such as a large private lawn or a huge park.*

Edging the lawn

If you have a mower strip or neat and well-spaded edges on your garden beds, edging will not prove to be too much of a chore. Well-trimmed edges can be counted upon to create a general appearance of neatness and if you have them you can sometimes get away with mowing less often. Grass tends to grow faster on the edges as there is generally no foot traffic there, and edges often receive more water than the rest of the lawn from overspray when watering garden beds. After trimming your lawn edges, rake or sweep up the lawn clippings and add them to your compost heap.

Edging tools

There are several different kinds of edging tools available. Keep them clean and well sharpened and they will last twice as long, be easier to use and do the job well.

▶ *String trimmers, or 'whipper snippers', are efficient, but they should never be used to trim the grass around your trees — there are many sad tales of dead or dying trees that have been accidentally ring-barked with one of these. If you use this kind of tool, make sure you wear strong boots and safety goggles to protect yourself, and don't allow children to play in the area until the job is complete.*

▶ *On a firm surface, beside a path, a mechanical, long-handled edging tool does a very neat job and is easy to use. There are two types that can be operated by hand, giving you a choice of cutting head — one has a sharpened disc that rotates as it's pushed along, while the other has sharp-angled blades. A more expensive type has a petrol-driven motor. If the cutting edges of these tools are kept sharp, they are not difficult to use.*

▶ *There are also some very satisfactory hand tools. Long-handled clippers are made with blades set at the vertical or horizontal. Vertically set blades are easiest to use along spaded edges of garden beds, while horizontally set blades may be better against a mower strip or other firm edge. Both can be used from a standing position, an advantage for anyone who finds bending or kneeling difficult.*

▶ *For smaller lawns or for gardeners who are happy to work on their hands and knees, there are cordless electric hand shears and the simple but very effective sheep shears.*

Maintaining the lawn

Once you have established a beautiful swathe of lush, green lawn, you will no doubt want to keep it that way.

TOP-DRESSING

This has no intrinsic benefits for the lawn and is only necessary for filling in hollows and maintaining levels. If there is a large hollow, in spring or early autumn apply only 1–2 cm (½–¾ in) of top-dressing at a time and wait until the grass grows through it before applying more. Washed river sand or good-quality sandy loam is best.

**Lawn tip
for hot areas**

*In hot areas it is wise to
sprinkle your lawn with
a soil-wetting agent
once at the beginning
of summer. It will help
moisture penetrate and
works wonders on any
type of soil. If a lawn is
watered too frequently
there is no need for the
grass to make good long
roots — this means
that shallow roots will
be cooked in very hot
weather and the turf
will deteriorate further.*

FERTILISING

Hungry, impoverished lawns will very quickly become infested with unwanted weeds. Feed your lawn at least four times a year, at the beginning of each season; however, fertilise very high-quality lawns every 4–6 weeks during the growing season.

The trick to successful fertilising is to use a specially formulated, slow-acting lawn food that will sink down past the shallow roots of the grass, encouraging the roots to grow downwards towards the food. Use a complete lawn food, pulverised poultry manure or blood and bone (bonemeal). Don't use sulphate of ammonia, as it makes the soil acidic and kills valuable earthworms.

If you have a big tree growing in your lawn, the grass will need more fertiliser, as the tree will be constantly robbing nutrients from the ground around it. Never apply fertiliser to dry soil, as this can severely burn the grass. Feed your lawn immediately after rain or a good watering.

Hosing on fertiliser

Revive a dull lawn with some hose-on seaweed fertiliser.

1   Pour seaweed concentrate into a bottle that clips onto a hose fitting.

2   Following the manufacturer's instructions on appropriate application rates, hose the fertiliser onto your lawn.

Watering equipment

Lawn sprinklers range from sophisticated underground systems with pop-up heads to simple, fixed, single-head sprinklers. There are sprinklers with rotating heads — those that have a wide wave action — and travelling sprinklers with a tractor action. Your choice will be determined by the size of both your lawn and your wallet.

When you're using a sprinkler, keep checking that the water is soaking into the grass and not overspraying onto paths and driveways or simply running off and going to waste. You should also check the level of water penetration by digging into the soil half an hour or so after you have turned off the sprinkler to see how far it has soaked into the ground. Garden centres and large hardware stores keep a wide range of sprinklers so you can select the one that suits you best.

ROLLING

Many people think regular rolling will help to produce the perfect lawn, but this is not necessarily so. It's a good idea to roll freshly laid turf, especially if the area is large, as it ensures there are no air pockets between the turf sod and the soil, and also provides good contact so that growing roots may penetrate well into the ground.

As a general maintenance procedure, however, rolling your lawn can result in soil compaction and greatly reduced aeration of the soil, which in turn leads to poor root growth and potentially poor water penetration as well. Only high-quality turf grown on a well-formed, deep sand bed, such as a bowling or golf green, are suitable for rolling.

Lawn problems

Despite your best intentions and many hours of hard work, your lawn will suffer from some common problems.

AERATING COMPACTED LAWNS

In compacted or poorly aerated soils, root growth, and therefore grass growth, is poor. To improve conditions, you need to get air and water into the soil. Do this by using a coring machine, but only if you have sandy soil. In clay, it is better to push a garden fork into the ground and work it back and forth in rows about 10 cm (4 in) apart.

Then apply sand mixed with lime or dolomite and brush it into the holes. The lime, used at the rate of about 100 g per square metre (3½ oz per 3 square feet), opens the clay and improves aeration. Clay soils are best worked when slightly damp. If the soil is too wet you will create more problems, and if it is too dry it will be too hard to work.

Reshaping your lawn

If you need to reshape your garden beds and lawn because there are areas where grass is no longer thriving, or perhaps shrubs have outgrown their bed and need more room, do it in autumn so the lawn can grow back before winter. Use a hose or length of rope, a sprinkle of lime, or turf spray paint to experiment with new shapes. Once you have settled on a new shape, create a well-defined edge with a sharp spade.

Although replacing or installing edging is a suitable garden job for the cooler weather, do not do so after long periods of rain, as the ground may have become soggy and the edging may shift as it dries out. In addition, waterlogged turf will not tolerate wear and tear well.

Spiking or scarifying a lawn

If your lawn is growing on poorly drained or compacted soil, you'll need to make a series of puncture holes so the roots can breathe.

1   Press the tines of a hollow-tined spiker into the lawn to about 15 cm (6 in).

2   After you have spiked an area of lawn, remove the soil 'cores' and brush or rake small heaps of fine topsoil into the holes left by the hollow-tined spiker.

3   Alternatively, if you have a small garden, use a garden fork to make the holes.

THATCH

If the lawn feels soft and spongy to walk on, it's probably due to a layer of dead grass clippings or 'thatch' that has formed on the soil surface. If allowed to remain, this layer may harbour pests and diseases, as well as weed seeds, and can inhibit the penetration of water, air and fertiliser.

Bent, buffalo and kikuyu grasses are especially prone to thatching; you may need to dethatch bent and kikuyu each year with a scarifier or vertical mower. After dethatching, rake off the excess grass, then water and fertilise the lawn.

If you try to dethatch a buffalo lawn, you'll probably kill it. Instead, sweep or hose top-dressing mixed with poultry manure, or blood and bone (bonemeal) and hydrated or slaked lime into the thatched areas

SPARSE LAWNS

Lawns can become thin and sparse for a number of reasons.

▶   The grass has been mown too low. Constant low mowing weakens lawns severely. Warm-season grasses such as couch should be mown at 2–3 cm (¾–1¼ in), while buffalo and kikuyu grasses should not be cut at less than 4 cm (1½ in). Cool-season grasses are usually cut at 4–5 cm (1½–2 in), except for bent grass, which can be cut quite a lot lower.

▶   The wrong grass has been chosen for the site or the site conditions have changed — for example, tree growth has made the area too shady. Areas under trees can be dry and there is also a lot of root competition, both of which may also lead to poor water penetration. Use a commercial wetting agent on this area to ensure deep moisture penetration. If that doesn't work, put down another kind of grass in the problem area, or grow groundcovers instead.

▶   The area has been subjected to very heavy wear and tear so the soil has become hard and compacted. To remedy this, see 'Aerating compacted lawns' on page 219.

Earthworms
These beneficial creatures do a great job of aerating the soil, leaving little mounds on the surface. They are absolutely harmless, but if you are a lawn perfectionist and want to eradicate them, fertilise the area with sulphate of ammonia.

▶ The lawn has been killed by over-enthusiastic watering. A well-established home lawn should not need watering more often than once a week if it is done deeply, although in very hot, windy weather it may be necessary to water twice.

▶ The soil has become too acidic. This is most often caused by regular use of sulphate of ammonia and some other high-nitrogen fertilisers. Switch to organic fertilisers and give the lawn a dressing of lime or dolomite in winter.

Creating a path

If your lawn is the main route from one part of the garden to another, such as the vegetable plot, it may be worth thinking in advance about creating a pathway through it. The best form of path to choose for lawn is one of stepping stones sunk about 2.5 cm/1 in below the level of the grass. This will not only prevent the grass from wearing unattractively on your chosen route, but will also make mowing the lawn seamless.

MOSSES AND FUNGI

Cool weather encourages moss to grow in grass, lichens to cover flagging and fungi to emerge from rotting timbers.

▶ Providing the drainage is adequate, the warmer weather will kill off most mosses in your lawn, so why not relax and take the time to appreciate their beauty?

▶ If your paths are slippery with moss, apply a bit of bleach with a stiff-bristled brush; this method will remove the moss without giving your paving the 'brand new' look that results from water blasting.

▶ Some fungi and toadstools can be colourful in their own right. Other fungi work in a symbiotic relationship with plant roots, and can improve plant growth. Many lawn seeds now come with fungal spore added to the seed and starter fertiliser, as it aids germination rates and significantly affects the success of the turf.

Fairy rings

After rain you might find fairy rings popping up in your lawn. These are small to large circular areas of dead grass, often with mushrooms appearing in a mysterious ring pattern.

The soil under the dead grass is frequently packed with white thread-like fungal growth that kills the grass by depriving it of water and nutrients. The fungi start growing at one point, but gradually spread out into a circle so that the rings expand each year. Often the grass in the centre of the ring is green, as the fungi only do any damage where they're actively growing. Spread via the mushroom-like fruiting bodies, especially in warm and moist conditions, they are common in pastures and turfed areas, and can grow for many years if they're not treated.

The main treatment is to ensure adequate water penetration into the areas where the fungus is actively growing. To assist water penetration, use wetting agents and the hollow-tine forking or coring technique (see page 220) on the affected areas.

LAWN WEEDS

Most serious weed problems result from low mowing or poorly established lawns, the result of shade or the wrong grass type for the conditions. Deal with weeds in spring before they set seed over summer. Keeping weeds out of your grass used to mean hours of back-breaking hand-weeding, but modern treatments have made the 'bowling-green' effect attainable for the weekend gardener.

▶ The first step is to feed. Hungry grass is slow to repair damage caused by pets, insect attack and active children. Liquid 'weed and feed' hose-on products will give your lawn an instant pick-me-up and help control the majority of weeds.

▶ Use a small-pronged weeder to remove individual weeds by hand as soon as you see them. If that sounds too hard, cheat a little and use some 'lawn sand', which is simply 1 part dry sand mixed with 1 part sulphate of ammonia. Scatter this mixture over the weed-infested areas and within days weeds will bolt into growth before turning black and dying.

▶ For a heavy weed infestation, buy a selective herbicide, first reading the label to check it is suitable for your grass and your weeds.

▶ After weeding and fertilising your lawn, use a slow-release lawn food to provide a safe, sustained supply of nutrients over the rest of the growing season.

LAWN PESTS

▶ **Caterpillars** Grass-eating caterpillars feed on the leaves and may defoliate the lawn. They appear in late summer and autumn, and feed mostly at night and hide during the day. Spray these pests with a proprietary caterpillar killer or a lawn grub killer.

▶ **Leatherjacket or curl grubs** These fat, creamy white grubs are most destructive during summer and autumn. Lawns growing under stress and lawns that are mown too often and too severely are most affected. Birds feeding on a lawn can indicate their presence of the grubs, but other telltale signs are yellow patches on the lawn, caused by the grubs eating the grass roots. Spray the lawn with a lawn grub killer as directed on the pack.

▶ **Ants** These insects make nests in dry areas. If the lawn is badly disrupted by ant nests, treat it with a commercial wetting agent, followed by a deep watering. Ants themselves are not a threat to turf, only their nests.

BARE PATCHES

To fix disfiguring bare patches, especially at gateways and other entranceways, you can use either a hollow-tined roller or a strong fork to work lots of holes deep into the soil; this allows air and water to penetrate. You might also find aerating shoes at your local hardware store or garden centre. If areas of your lawn are subject to heavy use, aerate them several times a year. Whichever method you use, be sure to scatter coarse, dry sand over the surface before watering — this will flow into the holes to provide long-lasting drainage plugs.

Fungal leaf spot
This mostly occurs in areas with warm, humid summers. Whole areas of turf may appear yellowish, but close examination of the leaf blades shows brownish or reddish spots. Spray with a lawn fungicide and don't water for about 48 hours.

Repairing a lawn

Repair a damaged lawn by simply replacing a section of turf.

1 Using a spade, remove the damaged section of lawn. Cut an area the same size as the new piece of turf.

2 Lay the new section of turf down by hand, being very careful to butt it flush with the adjacent edges.

3 Tamp down the new turf well, and water it in thoroughly. Avoid walking on the area for a few days.

A spring makeover for your lawn

With the arrival of warm weather, your grass will have a surge of energy and make new growth, so spring is an ideal time to smother weeds and repair bare patches. Lightly fork over worn areas and mossy patches in the lawn, then give the whole area a vigorous raking over. An application of a 'weed and feed' product that clicks onto your hose will work wonders. Finally, sow some lawn seed or plant runners in any bare areas.

Groundcovers

Once the warm spring weather arrives, and if you've decided you don't need a putting green, consider replanting your lawn with an easier alternative — groundcovers.

Groundcovers are living carpets. They squeeze out the weeds, cover bare soil so that weed seeds can't find space to germinate and are less demanding than lawn in terms of water, fertiliser and labour. They provide seasonal interest, flowers and coloured foliage — all attributes that turf lacks. If you plant in spring, these carpet-like plants will be well established by summer.

In nature there is always something growing on the ground under trees and shrubs, except where there is very deep leaf litter or the light levels are very low (as on the floors of rainforests, which are clear of growth). In the garden, many groundcovers tolerate some shade, and they're especially useful on sloping ground where erosion is likely, or where mowing would be difficult or even dangerous.

Groundcovers for shade

- *Astilbe chinensis* 'Pumila'
- Barrenwort (*Epimedium sp.*)
- Bugle flower (*Ajuga reptans*)
- *Campanula poscharskyana*
- Catmint (*Nepeta hederaceae* 'Variegata')
- Dead nettle (*Lamium maculatum*)
- Ivy (*Hedera helix*)
- Lily of the valley (*Convallaria majalis*)
- Periwinkle (*Vinca minor*)
- Rock cress (*Arabis caucasica* 'Variegata')
- Wild ginger (*Asarum europaeum*)

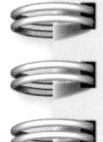

Groundcovers for sun

▶ African daisy (*Gazania* sp.)

▶ Creeping juniper (*Juniperus horizontalis*)

▶ Fleabane, babies' tears *Erigeron* sp.)

▶ *Grevillea* 'Sunkissed Waters'

▶ Lamb's ear (*Stachys byzantina*)

▶ Mint (*Mentha* sp.)

▶ Rose of Sharon (*Hypericum calycinum*)

▶ Snow in summer (*Cerastium tomentosum*)

▶ Star jasmine (*Trachelospermum jasminoides* 'Tricolour')

▶ Thyme (*Thymus* sp.)

CHOOSING GROUNDCOVERS

As with any other type of plant, it is important to choose the right groundcover for the aspect, climate, soil and space available in your garden.

▶ Some groundcovers can grow very vigorously, and can even become invasive, especially in moist, shady spots, while other mat-forming plants are more sedate and much easier to keep confined.

▶ Groundcovers come in a number of different forms, including running, trailing or mat-forming plants, or those with simple horizontal growth. Some climbing plants not usually thought of as groundcovers, such as ivy, can be used as such and, in fact, any low plant can serve this purpose.

▶ Before selecting a groundcover, mentally divide your garden into low-, mild- and high-traffic zones. Low-traffic areas, such as garden beds where weed seeds rather than trampling feet are likely to be a problem, can look great with the addition of rock cress (*Arabis* sp.), bergenia, bugle flower (*Ajuga reptans*), campanula, catmint, dianthus, Japanese windflower, lamb's ear, snow-in-summer and verbena. All will thrive, depending on the position.

▶ High-traffic zones, such as those where children play, call for tough plants. In these difficult areas only the toughest plants will survive. Choose from hardy selections such as fleabane or babies' tears (*Erigeron* sp.) or mini mondo grass.

Dealing with dogs!
If your dog urinates on the lawn, the grass can die in that spot and nasty brown patches appear. Saturate the affected patch with water for 5–10 minutes after the dog has urinated. If you're not quick enough and the grass dies, you might have to replace a patch of lawn, or overseed it (see 'Repairing a lawn' on page 223).

Lawn substitutes

For a green lawn look, try these great alternatives to grass.

- ▶ **Hot, dry areas** — Coprosma × kirkii, *creeping boobialla* (Myoporum parvifolium), *gazania, lippia* (Phyla nodiflora)
- ▶ **Under trees**— *bugle flower* (Ajuga reptans), *catmint* (Nepeta hederacea), *clivea, common yarrow* (Achillea millefolium), *mondo grass, spider plant* (Chlorophytum sp.), *turf lily* (Liriope sp.)
- ▶ **Sunny spot groundcovers** — *aurora daisy* (Arctotis sp.), *Canberra grass* (Scleranthus biflorus), Grevillea poorinda 'Royal Mantle', *veldt*
- ▶ **Shady spot groundcovers** — *isotoma, ivy, kidney weed* (Dichondra repens), *pratia, periwinkle* (Vinca minor)

PLANTING GROUNDCOVERS

Most groundcovers are long-term plantings, so it's worth putting some effort into good soil preparation and weeding. As there may be root competition for the new plantings it is a good idea to dig in some well-decayed manure or compost a few weeks before planting, but be careful not to build up the soil level under the canopies of existing trees more than a few centimetres or inches, and don't pile soil or mulch up around their trunks. Raising the soil level under trees can suffocate the surface roots and lead to the eventual death of the tree.

Weed eradication is most important, as it's very frustrating to find weeds coming up through the groundcover. Dig out or spot-spray with glyphosate the weeds you can see. Once they are dead, fork over the soil again, water it and wait for the next crop of weeds to emerge. If you do this two or three times before you plant the groundcover, you have a good chance of reducing the bank of weed seeds lying dormant in the ground. To eradicate perennial weeds such as onion weed and oxalis, which grow from bulbs, you'll need to make a determined effort.

EARLY CARE

The spacing of individual groundcovers at planting time will depend on how fast you need the cover and how large you expect each plant to grow. Most spreading groundcovers grow quite quickly, and it's not a good idea to overplant an area just to get an instant effect — the plants will have nowhere to grow.

You'll need to mulch areas of bare soil between plants while they are growing to help prevent further weed growth and also feed the plants and condition the soil. Most ground-covering plants growing under mature trees and shrubs will need regular feeding during the growing season due to the intense root competition. Regular, deep watering is also required, especially in the early stages when the roots will be concentrated at the surface and likely to dry out.

LATER MAINTENANCE

Once established, most groundcovers need little maintenance beyond shearing off spent flower stems or trimming to confine them to a specific area. If they grow too tall, shear them at the start of the growing season or after blooming. When weeds appear through the groundcover, pull them out promptly or paint them with herbicide, being careful not to get any of the chemical on the groundcover. Don't let weeds flower and set seed.

Plant an aromatic carpet

Low-growing, matting herbs release their delightful fragrance when crushed underfoot, and provide an unusual cover for many situations. Choose herbs that grow with stolons or runners so they will cover any bare patches that may develop. The mint family will grow where drainage is poor or there is dappled shade, otherwise most herbs like good drainage and plenty of sun.

- ▶ *A path of pennyroyal (Mentha pulegium)*
- ▶ *Carpeting patches of thyme between stepping stones*
- ▶ *Corsican mint as a groundcover in a fernery*
- ▶ *A herbal carpet in an area too small for a mower*
- ▶ *A cover of bugle flower where lawn will not tolerate shade*
- ▶ *A spectacular carpet of thyme on a sunny bank (there are many sorts to choose from — creeping thyme comes in pink, crimson and white-flowered varieties, and there are also golden, orange peel-scented and variegated leaf types)*
- ▶ *A fragrant chamomile footrest beneath the garden seat*

Growing a chamomile lawn

The fine, feathery, fragrant leaves and creeping habit of chamomile (*Anthemis nobilis*) make it a soft groundcover, suitable for being walked on occasionally, or sat on. Chamomile flowers in summer (the flowers are used to make chamomile tea), but if this does not suit your idea of lawn, you can mow it to remove the flowers on a very high setting. 'Treneague', a non-flowering variety, is the most suitable for lawn use, but this is often hard to obtain.

Chamomile is suitable for most climates, except the tropics, but in cold areas it becomes dormant in winter. This pretty herb prefers a sunny position and well-drained soil, and can be grown from seed sown in spring or by division of the roots of established plants.

1 Start by raking level the site for the lawn, firstly using a large rake to break down any large clods of earth, then a smaller rake with fine teeth to leave a smooth, even finish. Finally, remove any stones.

2 Use a garden line or string to mark the boundaries of the lawn and act as a planting guide for the position of the outer rows of plants.

3 Start by putting in the outer row of plants first, gently firming each plant into the soil to help them to establish quickly — loose planting often leads to drying out, which results in poor establishment.

4 Plants that have lots of stems and form clumps can be carefully divided into two sections to increase the number of plants and also help the lawn thicken up quickly.

5 If the plants have become long and straggly, clip over them with a pair of garden shears. They will need to be trimmed anyway and it is much easier to do this while they are still in the nursery tray. Also, clipping will make them branch from the base and spread along the soil.

6 Once all the plants are firmed into position, water the whole area with several cans of water, or use a hose.

Mondo grass

Perhaps the most popular ground-covering grass of all is Japanese mondo grass (Ophiopogon sp.). The common name is actually a misnomer, as this plant belongs to the lily family but has grassy foliage. It is fantastic en masse and can be used effectively as a turf substitute in the shade (especially the 'mini' cultivar), or as a border between beds and pathways. White, variegated, giant, dwarf and black cultivars make the long-lived mondo grass a very useful ornamental for foliage contrasts; however, mondo lawns and long borders can be expensive to put in. Buy the smallest pots you can, as mondo clumps up quickly once it's planted.

Container gardening

Containers make it possible for everyone to have a garden. Even if you have only a tiny suburban courtyard or a balcony, you can grow screening plants, sculptural plants as features and a range of salad vegetables. You'll just need to supply all the water and nutrients they require.

The right pot

Make sure the potting mix (potting compost) that you choose is suitable for the plants you want to grow, and of course choose waterproof containers for any water plants.

A container garden

Containers open up a whole world of possibilities to the gardener. Owners of small gardens — including rooftop gardens — can plant up pots that can be moved around as required to decorate every surface, including walls and steps.

You can grow almost anything in containers, from edible plants to water-loving ones. You can even grow trees, but obviously they will never reach the size they would in an unrestricted situation, simply because you would not be able to provide a container large enough for the full root span. Choosing slow-growing trees and shrubs will mean less work, and likewise, selecting drought-tolerant plants will cut down on the chore of summer watering in warmer areas.

Container materials

Your choice of container depends on the style of your garden as well as what you intend to grow.

PLASTIC POTS

These colourful pots are cheap, durable and light to move around; some even look convincingly like terracotta. As they are waterproof, they don't dry out as fast as porous containers, so the plants require less frequent watering and feeding. On the downside, they don't always look very good in your yard, especially if you have a wide mix of colours and styles. If you're using a lot of plastic pots, stick to one colour.

TIMBER CONTAINERS

Wooden pots usually look attractive, especially in rustic or natural-style gardens. Like plastic, they are waterproof and generally look best if you stick with the one style throughout the garden. The disadvantages of wood include its weight and the fact that it will eventually rot, although that does take a long time to happen. You'll need to raise them off the ground to minimise rotting on the bottom.

CERAMIC POTS

Ceramic pots include unglazed terracotta and glazed earthenware or stoneware. Terracotta pots, the traditional containers for plants, look good in most settings, while glazed pots are more decorative. Glazed pots and unglazed stoneware containers are waterproof, but terracotta pots are porous, so they can dry out fast and plants always require more frequent watering than waterproof pots. More frequent watering means more frequent feeding, as watering will wash nutrients out of the soil with every application. The disadvantages of ceramic pots include their fragility, weight and cost.

CONCRETE CONTAINERS

Concrete pots are heavy and best placed in their permanent position. Some are big enough to accommodate quite large trees, and when sold with a matching pedestal can make an impressive focal point in the garden. Weight and cost (especially the cost of the bigger, more decorative pots) are the main disadvantages of concrete.

Be creative

A workable planting scheme for a container garden requires a lot of forethought. The pots themselves will play a major role in the final appearance of the garden, so pay attention to container shape, texture and colour to ensure your chosen pots complement the textures, forms and colours of the plants. If you can create interesting contrasts or subtle harmonies, it will beautifully unite the display.

Look for plants with exciting forms — deeply coloured, interesting foliage, for example — and match these to plain or patterned containers in good-quality materials. You can also paint or decorate your containers to provide interest, but try to keep the patterns clean and simple.

Containers are wonderful for changing the mood or defining the style of a specific area of your garden.

▶ You could use metallic pots to achieve a minimalist look, or traditional wooden trugs to convey a cottage-garden atmosphere.

▶ Why not use one or two really large specimens in containers to create a stunning focal point? Try architectural plants, such as agaves and phormiums, or even a cactus or succulent if your climate is suitable.

▶ Use a simple flower or pot colour that coordinates with your garden furniture to enhance a seating area.

▶ Introduce some fragrant plants — such as fragrant nicotianas and lavenders and sweet scented-leaved pelargoniums — to an area of the garden where you like to relax.

▶ A display of the one type of plant, such as red-flowering gernaiums in terracotta pots all the same size, can look fantastic lined up on a plant stand.

Mossy effects

Many people like moss so much they will go to any lengths to get it to grow on pots and statuary. To speed up the softening effect of mosses and lichen on stonework or terracotta, smear on natural (plain) yoghurt or paint over with sour milk. You'll soon have a lovely culture of moss and mould. Use this method to make composite concrete look like stone.

Container size

▶ The size of pots and other containers varies from huge half-barrels to tiny pots that are specially made to hang from either walls or brackets.

▶ The imaginative gardener can adapt all kinds of household relics, from cast-off old metal colanders to bread bins (boxes) and even old boots.

▶ If you're planning to grow edible plants in containers, then the depth will be an important consideration, since plants that are eaten for their roots will need space in which to develop them.

▶ You can purchase some purpose-made containers for specific plants. For example, a strawberry planter is usually a terracotta container with a series of small planting pockets in the sides, which allows you to grow the maximum yield of strawberries in a relatively small space.

▶ Growing bags containing specially formulated potting mix (potting compost) for tomatoes and other nutrient-hungry plants are another option but, in a small garden where the container is clearly visible from the house, it might be more aesthetically pleasing to disguise these plastic bags with a wooden surround or something similar.

▶ If your garden is on a balcony or roof terrace, then weight is an important consideration. Take into account the weight of the container as well as its contents, which will be particularly heavy when wet. So if you plan to grow small trees or large shrubs on a balcony or roof terrace, you should consult a structural engineer for advice first.

▶ If you have very little room to spare in your garden, you can use hanging baskets or wall pots, suspending them on heavy-duty brackets or hooks and pulleys. Remember, however, that these containers tend to dry out extremely quickly due to the large exposed surface area, so they will require watering twice a day in very hot weather.

Trees and shrubs suitable for containers

Virtually any plant can be potted up in a container, as long as it's well looked after. Some plants may require root pruning every few years (which is, in effect, 'bonsaiing'), and some may need to have cores of the rootball removed each year. This can be an arduous task when heavy pots or moist potting mix (potting compost) is involved, and it's better to choose dwarf or smaller-growing specimens. Here are some examples.

- ▶ **Fruit trees** — 'Ballerina' apples, cumquat, 'Honey Murcott' mandarin, 'Nectazee' (a miniature nectarine), flying dragon rootstock on citrus or smaller growers such as 'Lisbon' and 'Meyer' lemon.

- ▶ **Screening trees**— dwarf lillypillies, small pittosporums ('Silver Pillar' and 'Tom Thumb'), smaller sasanqua camellias such as 'Mine-no-yuki' and 'Yuletide', yew

- ▶ **Flowering shrubs** — dwarf apricot oleander, dwarf duranta ('Blue Boy' or 'Towards 2000'), Elfin series daisies, 'Little Lianne' and 'Petite' sasanqua camellias, Japanese barberry, Weigela florida

Positioning pots

- ▶ You can use groups of pots for greater impact or to conceal an unattractive feature — pots of different shapes and sizes can look better when grouped together, and they're also easier to water.

- ▶ The arrangement and placement of plants is important in achieving an overall, pleasant effect. Pots should be uniform, all terracotta or all plastic, for example, not a mixture. Place them in some logical order, perhaps grouped around a feature plant in a large central pot.

- ▶ For added height, upturn an empty pot and use it as a pedestal for another.

- ▶ Raised pots look great when trailing plants are allowed to cascade from them — one beautiful, well-planted urn on its own can make a stunning focal point in your garden.

- ▶ For a classically formal look, position a matched pair of pots on either side of an entrance, pathway or stairway.

Container shape
Deep containers are ideal for growing large bulbs, perennials, shrubs and small trees, while wide, shallow containers are useful for small-growing plants, such as alpines, annuals, slow-growing succulents and many small herbs.

▶ Add interest and beauty to a pergola by festooning it with hanging baskets bursting with flower and foliage.

▶ When choosing plants, take into account the conditions in your garden. A sunny, exposed site may be perfect for a Tuscan theme with Italian lavender in terracotta troughs.

▶ Window boxes or troughs are the ideal shape for those long narrow spaces in smaller gardens.

▶ To add height, grow potted standard bougainvilleas, which flower for months and love basking in the sun, as do potted gerberas.

▶ For a damp and shady position, try planting begonias, dwarf arum lilies, ferns and impatiens.

Moving a heavy container

To move heavy containers around, you'll need a helper as well as a heavy-duty board and several dowels — lengths of narrow-gauge piping are ideal.

1 With the aid of your helper, slide the container onto the piece of board, having first used a length of piping or dowelling to raise the front end.

2 Slide a second piece of piping under the front end of the board, and roll the board with the container on it forward, placing a third piece of piping under the front end.

3 Pick up the first piece of piping as it emerges from the tail-end of the board, and insert it at the front. In this way, you can roll the board, with the heavy container on it, over level surfaces.

AVOIDING MISHAPS

Wind and weight are two important factors to consider when placing pots. Even quite heavy pots can be blown over by strong winds, especially if the plants they contain are large. If the result would be dangerous, don't put the pot in that spot — sooner or later a gale is a certainty. Hanging baskets are also severely affected by winds and should never be placed in exposed locations.

Pots or baskets are heavy — and they are doubly so when watered. Always satisfy yourself that your deck, pergola or balcony will hold the wetted weight of the pots or baskets you have in mind.

Choosing a potting mix

With container-grown plants, a good-quality potting mix (potting compost) is essential for success. Modern potting mixes are clean and weed- and disease-free, designed to be fast-draining yet moisture-retentive; because they are relatively lightweight, they make it easier to move pots from place to place.

There are specially formulated mixes for plants with specific needs, such as African violets, cacti and orchids, and also mixes for specific uses, such as hanging baskets or terracotta pots — these are more moisture-retentive to suit their particular purposes.

Preparing potting mix (potting compost)

To keep them in good condition, container-grown plants benefit from a good, loam-based potting mix combined with a measured amount of base fertiliser. It's easy to mix this up yourself.

1   Loam-based mixes consist of 7 parts sterilised loam, 3 parts medium-grade sphagnum moss peat, 2 parts grit or sharp sand, plus a base fertiliser. How much base?

2   Start by mixing the loam, peat and sand together until they form a uniform mixture. Then draw the resulting mix into a heap.

3   Sprinkle the base fertiliser over the heap and mix it in until there is no visible trace of the fertiliser.

Drainage

Good-sized drainage holes in pots are vital, as even the best potting mix (potting compost) won't drain if there is nowhere for the water to go. Avoid pots with drainage holes that seem too small for the volume of soil they will contain, unless you have the tools to drill more.

Never let pots stand in saucers of water. Small pots, in particular, easily become water-logged from below. Raise the pot on bricks, stones or pot feet, which are available from nurseries. Raising the pot allows excess water to run away freely, minimises water damage to the bottom of the pot and the surface on which it is standing, and deprives critters of somewhere to live.

Potting a plant

Always match the size of the pot to the size of the plants it will contain, bearing in mind that plants grow. If you're planting annuals from seedlings that are 5–6 cm (2–2½ in) tall but will soon grow into flowers 40 cm (16 in) tall, choose a pot suitable for the mature size, not the seedlings. But if you're planting a slower-growing shrub or tree, it's better to pot it up progressively each year or two than to plant it into a very large pot at the outset. Small plants in big pots cannot use all the food and water available.

Potting mixes (potting composts) contain little or no plant foods, so blend some into the mix at planting time. The amount varies with the size of the pot and the type of fertiliser but in all cases it's better to be stingy rather than generous, as too much fertiliser can kill plants. Not enough fertiliser just makes them grow slowly and is easily rectified. If you are unsure about this, read the directions on the fertiliser packet before buying. Choose a brand that explains how much to use in various sized pots. Slow-release fertilisers are a good choice for containers as long as you remember when to replenish them.

Pot plants so they are no deeper in the new potting mix than they were in the pot in which you bought them. To achieve this, partly fill the pot with potting mix, then sit the plant in it, adding or subtracting potting mix until the level is right. Unpot the plant and check that the roots are not spiralling around the base. If they are, gently tease them out. You can trim any that are overlong with sharp, very clean secateurs. Place the plant in the new pot and fill it with potting mix to within 2 cm (¾ in) of the rim. Gently firm the mix around the roots, but don't compact it or there will be insufficient aeration. Water the plant in well.

Rootball ratio

Try to choose the right pot for the plant and keep everything in proportion. The best container size for any plant is one that is roughly 5 cm (2 in) larger than the diameter of the rootball, and roughly 10 cm (4 in) deeper. After a year or so, depending on the speed of growth, you will need to repot the plant into a larger container. Planting a small plant in a much larger pot is not a time-saving solution, as plants do best in pots only slightly larger than their rootball. Check regularly that the roots are not growing through the base of the pot. If they are, it is time to repot.

Watering

Don't water potted plants according to a schedule. Instead, water when they need it. This will be much more often in summer than in winter, in sun than in shade, in porous than in waterproof pots, in smaller than in bigger pots, and in a windy than in a sheltered spot. To test whether water is needed, feel down into the top 3 cm (1¼ in) of soil. If it is quite moist, don't water, but if it feels just damp, go ahead. You'll soon get to know the watering needs of your different pots and won't have to feel the soil. Generally speaking, don't allow the potting mix (potting compost) to go completely dry, as it can then be quite difficult to re-wet.

Over time, potting mixes can become water repellent and no matter how much water you apply, most runs straight through to the bottom and the mix remains dry (although the surface looks wet). To test for this, water thoroughly and then, after the water has drained from the surface, scratch the soil in several places. If it is dry underneath, give it a good soak.

If you do allow a plant to dry out to the point of wilting, you can usually revive it by plunging the entire container into water. Hold it down so that the potting mix (potting compost) is beneath the water level, and keep it submerged until any air bubbles stop rising. Remove and allow to drain. The plant should then revive.

Fertilising

Only apply fertiliser during the growing season for that particular plant. Most plants grow more vigorously from spring to mid-autumn and do not need fertiliser from the end of summer until early spring, but they do need water. Some plants are dormant or at their least active during the hot months of the year and grow during autumn, winter and early spring. Feed these in autumn and in early winter.

Always apply fertiliser to moist potting mix (potting compost), never to dry, and always at the recommended rates — more fertiliser does not equal more growth; in fact, it makes the soil salty and toxic. Slow-release fertilisers can be very convenient, but you can also use complete plant food or soluble or liquid fertilisers. Its actually a good idea to alternate between types.

Remember, the more you water, the more fertiliser you will have to apply. The best way to give it is in frequent but very small doses — say, a quarter strength four times as often.

Fertiliser release rates
It's useful to know the rate your fertiliser will release into the soil. Release rates are as follows:
slow-release, 14–21 days; liquid feed, 5–7 days; quick-acting, 7–10 days; and foliar feed, 3–4 days.

Repotting

If the plant in question is already in a large enough pot, then scrape away about 3 cm (1¼ in) of potting mix from all around and replace the plant in its original container with fresh potting mix poured around the outside. This process is called repotting as it does not involve a bigger pot.

Potting on

Plants that have outgrown their containers should be potted on (or potted up), which is best done either in early spring or early autumn.

▶ Remove the plant from the pot and examine the roots. If you don't water it for a few days beforehand, then the soil will shrink and it will be much easier to extract it. If you see much more white (roots) than black (soil), or roots protruding strongly from drainage holes, then it's definitely time to pot on.

▶ Tease out any compacted or spiralling roots, and trim any that are overlong and looking unhealthy.

▶ Replant into fresh potting mix (potting compost), in a pot that is one size bigger than the existing pot.

▶ Water in well and place the plant in a bright but shady and sheltered spot for a week so it can recover before you move it to its new or original location.

Supporting smaller container plants

Supports benefit not only potted climbers but also some weak-stemmed annuals and perennials. Perennials such as daisies and pelargoniums will benefit from some form of ring staking and the plants will eventually bush out, disguising the ring support. Other useful staking devices are twiggy bits of brushwood inserted around the perimeter of a container, or metal-linked stakes that fit together to provide a containing girdle for your plants.

Edible container plants

Some edibles are easier to grow in containers than others. Avoid cauliflower, celery, corn, parsnip, pea and swede (rutabaga). Among the easiest are the many beans, beetroot, carrot, cucumber, lettuce, potato, radish, spring onion (green onion), silverbeet (Swiss chard), tomato and zucchini (courgette).

Capsicum (pepper), chilli and eggplant (aubergine) are not difficult but require warmer temperatures and more sun in order to ripen. Blueberries, raspberries and strawberries are among the easiest edibles to grow in a container. Tree fruit such as 'multigraft' apple trees, which have two or three varieties on one dwarf rootstock, are ideal.

THE YEAR-ROUND EDIBLE CONTAINER GARDEN

SUMMER	AUTUMN	WINTER	SPRING
Beetroot (beet), capsicum (pepper), carrots, chillies, cucumber, eggplant (aubergine), French beans, lettuce, potatoes, raspberries, runner beans, silverbeet (Swiss chard) strawberries, tomatoes, zucchini (courgette)	Apples, carrots, blackberries, raspberries (autumn-fruiting), runner beans	Lamb's lettuce	Radish, spring onions (green onions)

Hanging baskets

Every home, no matter how big or small, has a transition zone, the space that connects the inside of the house to the outside. Whether it's a porch, veranda or a large pergola-covered entertaining area, this area can be the most exciting and enjoyable of all. Choose annuals filled with seasonal colour or a mass planting of mixed seedlings, pendulous plants and even a small shrub or two.

In recent years many improvements have been made to moisture-retaining products, potting mixes (potting composts) and fertilisers, making growing plants in baskets a much easier pastime. Water crystals act like a reservoir in the soil by holding water in the basket. Potting mixes now use premium-quality ingredients, while controlled, slow-release fertiliser means plants need only be fed once every 9 months, which is usually sufficient for the life of the display. There is even a product that, when watered onto the soil, draws the moisture down into the mix.

Top-quality potting mixes contain all three of these products — slow-release fertiliser, water-storing crystals and wetting agents.

There is also a new product for lining the inside of the basket — sheep wool waste. In the old days, bark was removed from trees under license and used for lining the insides of hanging baskets. The new liners are environmentally friendly and recycle an excellent product.

Baskets are very decorative in courtyards and balconies but they dry out quickly, particularly in hot, windy weather. As a rule, the bigger the basket, the less often you'll have

Wick watering

Next time you're away, use a wick watering system to keep your pot plants moist. Simply wrap a cotton wick around the rootball, leaving a length of wick at the bottom of the plant. Feed this through one of the drainage holes in a plastic pot, then place the plant in the pot. Finally, place the other end of the wick in a small container of water.

to water and the more scope there will be in plant selection, so choose something at least 30 cm (1 ft) wide or larger.

Planting a hanging basket

1   Place the basket upright in the top of a large empty plant pot. This will hold the basket in position while you fill it. Line the lower half of the basket with a layer of sphagnum moss.

2   Press the moss layer firmly against the wire mesh of the basket, before adding potting mix (potting compost) to the same level as the moss lining. Add water-retaining granules (follow the manufacturer's instructions).

3   Insert the first layer of plants into the basket by passing the roots of the plants through the mesh around the sides of the basket, and resting them on the potting mix, with the tops of the plants hanging down the outside of the basket.

4   Line the top half of the basket with a layer of sphagnum moss before adding potting mix, but make sure you leave sufficient space for planting. Insert the second layer of plants into the basket.

5   Position the largest plants in the centre of the basket, but angle them slightly outwards, towards the rim of the basket.

6   Add smaller plants around the edge of the basket, before topping up the potting mix so that it is almost level with the rim, but leave room for watering. Hang the basket in its desired position and water thoroughly.

Window boxes

One way to create window box plantings is to plan displays that will look attractive at different times of the year. In spring, small bulbs are ideal — crocus and dwarf daffodils, combined with early primulas; in summer, try dwarf cosmos or dwarf wall-flowers with miniature lavenders and thymes; in early autumn, dwarf chrysanthemums can replace the wallflowers; and in winter replant the window box with heathers and hardy cyclamen.

Problems

Pests, diseases and weeds will always present a challenge to the gardener, but there are many organic techniques and treatments that will help you combat every kind of problem. Understanding how to maintain the health of your garden's ecosystem is the first step.

Healthy plants deter problems

The first principle to note is that the healthier a plant is, the more it will resist pest and disease attack. Insect pests are attracted to the weakest, most stressed plants in a crop. Improving soil structure and fertility with organic matter results in healthier soil, which in turn results in strong, healthy crops — and minimal crop damage. Organic gardening techniques also produce plants that grow steadily rather than rapidly, as is the case with chemical fertilisers, so plants do not become soft and sappy and prone to attack.

GARDEN HYGIENE

Many diseases and plant pests can be eliminated from the garden simply by practising good garden hygiene and dealing with problems as they arise.

- ▶ Compost garden waste. If material is infected, put it in the centre of the compost, where the high temperatures will kill spores. Infected prunings, however, should be burned, if possible.

- ▶ A thorough clean-up at the end of summer or early in autumn can do much to prevent pests and diseases in the next growing season. Digging the garden over at this stage not only aerates the soil but can also expose the overwintering larvae of various pests.

- ▶ Don't leave any vegetables on the ground. If possible, burn any vegetables that have become mummified.

- ▶ After pruning deciduous trees, check for the presence of borer and destroy any you find by poking a wire into their holes. Use a wire brush to remove any loose bark, which often shelters overwintering pests.

Being green

If you're making the effort to minimise exposure to chemicals inside your home, it makes sense to extend the same care to your outdoor areas. Reducing the use of harsh chemicals to control insects and other pests is better for you and your family as well as for the environment. You may need to experiment with alternative methods, and some of them may need more frequent application than strong chemical pesticides, but the rewards are a healthy, safe garden for your family and a welcoming environment for all the local wildlife.

CHOOSE YOUR PLANTS WISELY

With some forethought, you can create a garden that automatically needs less chemical assistance. For instance, some plants are bred for resistance to attack by particular insects or to a disease. Ask the staff at your local garden centre when buying plants and seeds, and do some research of your own.

▶ Lawns are big users of water and also chemicals such as herbicides and fertilisers, which tend to leach nutrients off the lawn during rain, potentially polluting water systems. You could decide to reduce your lawn area or forget it entirely.

▶ Some plants — including chrysanthemums and pyrethrum daisies, and herbs such as chives, garlic and nasturtiums — help repel bugs. Many gardening experts recommend companion planting to reduce pests — for instance, planting nasturtiums among tomatoes and brassicas (the cabbage family) is said to protect against whitefly. It's certainly worth trying (see also page 245).

▶ Planting groundcovers rather than leaving soil bare not only reduces moisture loss but also leaves less room for weeds to grow, reducing the temptation to use herbicides in the garden.

▶ Choose plants that are best suited to your soil and local conditions rather than struggling on with unsuitable plants, which are more likely to surrender to fungal or bacterial disease or pest infestation.

BENEFICIAL INSECTS AND ANIMALS

To prevent pests getting out of control, try to attract a natural army of parasites and predators. Many pests have natural enemies that can keep them in check, but if you use insecticides, particularly broad-spectrum ones, you run the risk of killing off these helpers too. Beneficial garden insects include ladybird beetles, wasps, assassin bugs, predatory mites, stick insects, praying mantises and lacewings. Also encourage other wildlife, such as birds, frogs, lizards and spiders.

It may be a simple matter of one plant shading another, or modifying the humidity. One plant's roots might aerate the soil, or help drain excess water. And some plants can protect others as much as themselves by virtue of defense mechanisms such as thorns and stinging hairs, or by producing compounds that are poisonous to insect pests. Other plants offer benefits to their neighbours by attracting or housing desirable insect predators, or by exuding odours that attract insect pollinators.

GOOD AND BAD COMPANIONS

GOOD COMPANIONS	BAD COMPANIONS
Basil with apricots, asparagus, beans, fuchsia, grapes and tomatoes	Apples with potatoes
Beans with potatoes and sweet corn	Beans with garlic
Chives with carrots, cucumbers and tomatoes	Cabbages with strawberries
Cucumbers with potatoes	Gladioli with beans, peas and strawberries
French marigolds (*Tagetes* sp.) with beans, potatoes, roses and tomatoes	Sunflowers with any vegetable but squash
Horseradish with potatoes	Wormwood with almost everything
Hyssop with cabbages and grapes	
Leeks with celery	
Lettuce with carrots, onions and strawberries	
Melons with sweet corn	
Mint with cabbages and other brassicas and peas	
Nasturtiums with apple trees, cucumbers, squash, and zucchinis (courgettes)	
Onions with carrots, kohlrabi and turnips	
Peas with carrots	

Reduce nematodes with marigolds

Nematodes (eelworms) cause reduced growth, low yields and wilting in a variety of vegetable crops. The surface of infected plant roots appear to have tiny gall-like growths (gardeners often mistakenly attribute these effects to drought or poor soil fertility). However, nature has produced a powerful nematicide, a biomolecule produced to some degree in the roots of all species of marigolds (Tagetes sp.). The dwarf French marigold (Tagetes patula) is particularly useful as barrier plantings around garden beds. If the brilliant golden or orange flowers don't go with your garden colour scheme, simply shear off their heads.

Weed control

Weeds are not only unsightly but also take space, light, water and food from your plants. They can also harbour pests and diseases. Your garden will never be free of weeds, but they're easier to control if you do 'a little weeding often'.

MANUAL CONTROL METHODS

▶ **Hand-pulling** Hand-weeding is preferable for those small spaces in the garden. Use a garden fork and trowel to remove the whole of the root system. Always hand-weed when the ground is moist.

▶ **Hoeing** A Dutch hoe is a useful tool with a long handle and flat blade. The blade cuts off weeds just below the surface of the soil so the tops die off and provide mulch for the garden. A sharp hoe is one of the best cultivators for small gardens. Early and frequent hoeing will control most weeds in flowerbeds and vegetable gardens.

▶ **Chipping** A chipper — a thin, narrow blade on a long pole — works with a slicing action and you don't have to bend down to use it. It is a fast way to remove weeds in lawns, paving, walkways, fence lines and garden beds.

MULCHING

Mulching is an excellent way to keep your garden weed-free. When applied thickly, mulch will smother and kill most weed seedlings; any that do manage to poke through can easily be cut down. Should you pull a large weed from the mulch, make sure you re-cover any exposed soil.

Shoo fly!
Place fly-deterrent plants such as basil, bay, chamomile, lavender, lemon verbena, mint, rosemary, sweet wood-ruff and thyme at exterior doorways and on verandas and patios.

Weed fertiliser

Here's a handy way to use your dug-up weeds — replace nitrogen in the garden by making liquid fertiliser from them.

1   Fill a plastic garbage bin almost to the top with weeds.
2   Cover the weeds with water and replace the lid.
3   In warm weather it will take a few weeks for the weeds to break down. Dilute the fertiliser 10:1 with water, then pour it directly onto the garden.

GROUNDCOVERS

As all weeds need light to live, an easy way to suppress them is to cover them with thickly foliaged, evergreen plants. Small shrubs that are densely leafy to the ground are ideal. Plant them so that when they are mature, they completely cover the soil. Any weeds that germinate underneath will struggle to live in the very low light. A few may survive but, as long as the shrubs are taller than the weeds, you won't see them and the weeds definitely won't thrive.

Solarisation

This technique, which involves stretching a sheet of clear or black plastic over soil that has first been stripped of weeds and then dug over, will totally clear a weed-infested area. It traps heat from the sun and raises the soil temperature by several degrees, thereby killing weed seeds, roots and bulbs in the ground. It will also eradicate soil nematodes (eelworms) and some diseases, such as verticillium wilt.

Solarisation only works during hot, dry weather when temperatures are above 25°C (75°F). First, water the soil deeply, then cover the area with plastic sheeting. Seal the edges of the plastic so that the entire soil surface is covered. For maximum effect, try to keep the plastic on for at least 4 weeks — and hope for continuous hot, sunny weather. As soon as you remove the plastic, you can plant directly into the treated soil.

WEED MATS

Woven weed mats are made of a plastic mesh, which is similar to shade cloth. They are very effective at controlling weeds while still allowing air and water to penetrate to the soil and root zone. The weed mat can be worked around existing plants but is most effective when spread over an unplanted area. You can set new plants in the ground through holes cut in the weed mat. The mat can then be hidden with a topping of organic mulch.

USING HERBICIDES

Before deciding to use a herbicide in your garden, it's important to identify the weed you want to kill and also to make sure that the chosen herbicide will kill it.

Most herbicides that are sold for home-garden use are based on the chemical glyphosate, which is absorbed through the leaves and then circulated through the sap so the entire plant dies. A glyphosate herbicide is most effective when applied during the active growing season of the plant. As it is a non-selective chemical, take care not to let it touch your wanted plants. Either spray it on or apply it directly to the weed by dabbing or painting.

When it is used according to directions, glyphosate is a relatively safe garden chemical, for both humans and the environment. Remember, it will kill or damage anything it touches. If you are spraying, do so on a still day to avoid spray drift.

There are also selective herbicides that kill only certain types of weeds. These were developed for use on lawns in order to kill the weeds without damaging the grass. Some are quite toxic so, for general use around the garden, it's better to carefully apply glyphosate; however, glyphosate may not kill some woody weeds.

Act fast!
On cultivated land you'll inevitably find a fresh crop of annual weeds when warmth and rain combine to encourage weed seeds to germinate. Remove weeds promptly, before they start to flower and set seed.

A pinch of salt
You can effectively kill dandelions and plantain weeds by simply dropping a pinch of salt onto them.

Removing weeds with tap roots

Many of the most troublesome lawn weeds are those with a rosette or spreading habit and a long tap root. If you spot them early, remove them with a sharp knife.

1   Insert the tip of the blade into the soil at a steep angle, about 5 cm (2 in) away from the centre of the weed.

2   Push the blade into the soil towards the weed to a depth of about 15 cm (6 in). Try not to cut through the root or it will regrow.

3   To remove the weed and root, lever the blade upwards. If the soil is soft, rest the base of the blade on a block of wood to stop it sinking.

4   Collect the weeds and dispose of them in the garbage bin.

Dealing with perennial weeds

Established perennial weeds can be particularly difficult to eradicate, as even the smallest piece of root has the capacity to develop into a new plant. Use a garden fork to systematically work over an area and gently ease the roots out, making sure that they are not broken. Wear gloves (especially for prickly weeds such as thistles), and pull the weeds out of the soil with as much of their root as possible. When you have finished weeding, carefully dispose of them. Remember, never add perennial weeds to the compost heap.

Dealing with garden pests

The most important step in pest control is to check your plants thoroughly and frequently, and try to combat any infestation fast, before it has time to catch hold. Some insects will damage only one plant, while others will quickly destroy a whole crop. However, it's generally not in nature's interest to destroy the host plant, so most problems with predators can be treated as annoyances rather than catastrophes.

Finally, decide whether to treat problems organically, which is safer for the environment, or use non-organic, chemical solutions.

BARRIERS

The relatively recent development of finely woven, transparent cloths has made it much easier to protect vegetables and fruit trees. These admit water and maximum light and air while excluding insect pests. Floating row covers are ideal for the vegetable garden.

Other relatively newly developed barriers are sticky, non-drying glues that trap insects migrating up the stem or trunk. The glue is placed on a paper collar around the base of the plant. A simple non-sticky collar, made from a cardboard cup with the base cut out, and placed around the base of a seedling, is sufficient to protect it from damage by the cutworm.

In some areas, carrot fly is a real problem. But the female needs to hover low over the crop in order to detect the odour of the carrots. Erecting a simple, temporary barrier fence of hessian (burlap) around the row will force the female to hover too high to detect the scent.

Attract birds to eat pests

One of the gardener's small joys is witnessing a honey-eating bird drawing nectar from a flower, or a flock of fin busily extracting insect pests from an old lemon tree.

Birds need gardens, and gardens need birds for the control of insect pests. Birds are essential in helping to keep the balance of nature. They can deal with at least half your insect problems, but if you use chemicals they may eat the poisoned insects and die. Birds that eat sprayed insects and survive tend to lay infertile eggs. If you must spray, always use the least toxic chemical available for the job.

TRAP PLANTS

Some plants are particularly attractive to pests — because of their colour, smell or taste — and thereby protect other plants from attack. Bright yellow nasturtiums lure aphids away from cabbages, while zinnias have long been used to attract Japanese beetles. Dill is traditionally used to attract green tomato caterpillar. In themselves, trap plants are not sufficient protection for your garden, but they do contribute towards maintaining healthy crops.

Beer bait for snails
Beer in a shallow saucer makes an effective trap for snails. Set it up in the evening and empty it out in the morning.

Fruit fly trap

Try this trap for fruit flies. Make a funnel entrance by cutting a plastic 2 litre (70 fl oz) bottle in half, then place the top half inside the bottom, with the neck pointing downwards into the rest of the bottle. Choose from various baits — yeast, yeast extracts, beer or citrus skin — then hang it in a tree or among plants.

CHEMICAL CONTROLS

You may have an infestation of a pest that simply does not respond to preventative measures or natural remedies, but you don't have to resort to highly toxic chemicals. Other relatively low-risk options include the following.

▶ Derris is a broad-spectrum insecticide generally used to protect against caterpillars and beetles and many other crawling insect pests. It is moderately toxic and will also kill ladybird beetles, lacewings and other beneficial insects. It is also very toxic to fish and pigs.

Earwig trap
Place a hollow piece of drinking straw or a piece of sponge among the earwigs' flower of choice (dahlias or chrysanthemums, for example). Examine the traps each morning and blow any prisoners into boiling water.

▶ Pyrethrin, from the pyrethrum daisy, is a broad-spectrum insecticide that is also toxic to fish and cats.

▶ *Bacillus thuringiensis* (BT) is a bacterial preparation that is toxic to caterpillars but not to other organisms, although it may sometimes kill some butterfly larvae.

▶ Methoprene and hydropene are insect-growth regulators that keep insects in the juvenile, non-breeding stage. There is no known effect on humans. They are considered an ideal alternative to most other pesticides, as they act only on target organisms.

▶ White oils and other petroleum and vegetable oils work very well in controlling the target pests by suffocating them. It is worth trying these on aphids, azalea lace bugs, caterpillars, mealy bugs, sawflies, scale, spider mites and whiteflies. They are relatively safe for other organisms and humans, although they may kill some beneficial insects if you spray them directly.

▶ Sulphur is toxic to mites, powdery mildews and rust, but has low toxicity for humans and animals; however, it may be toxic to some beneficial insects when it is sprayed directly onto them, and it may damage some sulphur-sensitive plants.

NATURAL PEST SPRAYS

With a few basic ingredients you can make a range of non-toxic, economical and effective pest-control solutions to use in the garden. Less toxic methods may need more frequent application — for instance, controlling aphids with soap or garlic sprays may necessitate spraying every 3 days. You may also need to exercise a little more care during the application process — for example, spraying the underside of azalea leaves if they are being attacked by azalea lace bug.

You can make this all-purpose garden insecticide and use it for aphids, azalea leaf bug, leafhoppers, mites and white fly.

Soft soap insecticide

56 g (2 oz) soft soap (from chemists)
4.5 litres (158 fl oz) hot water

1 Dissolve the soft soap in the hot water, then allow it to cool.

2 Pour it into a spray bottle and spray it directly onto plants.

Safe use of pesticides and herbicides

▶ *Always read the label carefully, don't take any shortcuts, and follow the manufacturer's instructions exactly.*

▶ *Choose the early morning of a cool, calm day when no rain is expected.*

▶ *Wear a long-sleeved shirt, long trousers, rubber gloves, goggles and any other protective clothing indicated on the label.*

▶ *Mix concentrated liquids outside or in a well-ventilated place, and avoid breathing in the fumes.*

▶ *Mix only as much spray as you need, measuring accurately. Overdosing does not give a better result and can even be damaging.*

▶ *Don't leave any spills or chemicals around the house or garden while you are spraying. If you do spill the concentrate or the solution on yourself, wash it off immediately with lots of water.*

▶ *Keep both people and pets well out of the way while you are spraying and until the spray has dried. Many pesticides kill fish, so cover any ponds containing them.*

▶ *Never smoke or eat while using garden chemicals.*

▶ *Do not spray in confined places, such as greenhouses, for any prolonged period. If this is essential, make sure you wear a breathing apparatus that is approved for the job.*

▶ *Wash your hands and face immediately after using chemicals.*

▶ *Wash out all spray equipment thoroughly when you have finished but don't tip the waste water down the drain. Instead, decant it into an empty plastic drink container, and check with your local government authority on its safe disposal — some councils run special depots for poisonous items.*

▶ *Store all chemicals in their original containers, preferably in a locked cupboard, and always well out of the reach of children.*

Cat and dog deterrent
Sprinkle chilli and pepper around the garden as an effective deterrent to cats and dogs, which don't like the smell.

COMMON GARDEN PESTS

PEST	SYMPTOM	CONTROL
Aphids	Commonly green, aphids may also be pink, black or grey. All suck sap and feed in large groups, usually on new shoot tips and buds but sometimes on leaves and roots. They cause new shoots to die, distort flowers and can spread plant diseases. They tunnel and leave a mass of sawdust and oozing gum from the wound	There are many natural predators of aphids and gardeners can easily squash clusters of the pests by hand or squirt them away with a strong jet of water. Soapy water mixed with white oil is a non-toxic control and the pyrethrum- or fatty-acid based sprays, which are more effective, are among the safest to use
Borers	Borers are caterpillars that attack shrubs and trees, entering at points of injury. They tunnel and leave a mass of sawdust and oozing gum from the wound. Branches or whole trees may be ring-barked. Borers often attack old, weakened or damaged trees	Scrape away webbing and damaged bark and probe into tunnels with a piece of thin wire. If this fails to bring out the pest, squirt in a few drops of kerosene or methylated spirits (denatured alcohol). Putty the holes to prevent the entry of water, which could lead to more problems
Cabbage white butterflies	These green caterpillars have a faint yellow stripe down their back and sides. The white butterflies have three or four black spots on the tips of their wings	Spray with carbaryl or with *Bacillus thuringiensis* or BT (a disease that affects only caterpillars), or use a contact powder such as derris or cabbage dust
Fruit flies	Fruit flies attack fruits and vegetables, laying eggs into the fruit as it ripens, which then hatch into maggots. When mature, the maggots drop to the ground and emerge as adult flies. Attacks start in spring and become worse through summer. Control is essential	Collect fruit as it falls and seal it in a plastic bag and leave it in the sun. Then dispose of it in the garbage bin. Don't leave fruit on the ground for more than 3 days, and never bury it. Spray fortnightly from fruit set. Splash baits and traps only warn you that the fly is present — they are not a control in themselves
Leaf miners	The larvae of moths, flies, wasps and beetles tunnel inside the leaves of the plants, leaving narrow, twisted trails	If damage is minor, remove the infected leaves and trash them. If spraying, use a systemic or penetrant spray such as dimethoate. A weak solution of white oil may help combat citrus leaf miner
Mealy bugs	These small, sap-sucking insects, which are covered in wax threads, cluster on the undersides of leaves, in leaf joints and crevices, and on roots. They cause wilting on young shoots and attack a range of plants, especially cactus, ferns, palms, succulents, as well as many trees and shrubs	Spray with a systemic insecticide such as omethoate or immerse potted plants in a maldison solution. Ladybirds, wasps and small birds are natural predators of mealy bugs, but as the pests secrete themselves in crevices and beneath the soil, chemical control is usually necessary

PEST	SYMPTOM	CONTROL
Mites	Mites attack a variety of plants, and are often a serious pest of indoor and greenhouse plants. Most adults are not visible to the unaided eye. Their attacks are worst during hot, dry periods when the pest sucks the sap from the leaves	Mites have several predators, including ladybird beetles, but the most effective is another mite — the predatory mite. These can be bought and released onto affected plants, but once released, toxic sprays will kill the predators. Miticides are available but are not always effective
Nematodes (eelworms)	Microscopic, worm-like nematodes live in the soil and attack roots and bulbs. Some feed on stems and leaves, resulting in bead-like swellings or galls on roots, rot in bulbs, distortions on stems, and brown, dry leaves. Affected plants may also exhibit leaf yellowing and stunted growth	Root nematodes thrive in light, sandy soils, and are discouraged by high levels of organic matter in the soil. Growing marigolds (*Tagetes* sp.) can clear an area of nematodes, which are repelled by an exudate from the plant. In the worst cases, treat soil with a nematicide and in vegetable gardens practise crop rotation
Sawflies	Similar to caterpillars, sawfly larvae feed on plant foliage. They cluster on branches by day and spread out at night to feed. When disturbed, they eject a sticky yellow fluid	Large birds feed on the larvae and should keep populations down. Otherwise, remove infested twigs and squash the sawflies underfoot. If spraying is necessary, use maldison
Scale	Scale are small bumps on leaves, branches and stems. They suck sap, hiding beneath a protective shield or mealy or waxy secretions. Severe scale can cause weakening and death. Sooty mould may grow on the secretion and affect the vigour of the plant	Small numbers can be washed off with a brush and soapy water. Spray larger infestations with white oil or combinations of white oil and maldison until all the insects have been killed
Snails and slugs	Most active during spring and autumn after rain, snail and slug numbers can build up fast if not controlled. They feed, mostly at night, by rasping the surface from foliage, leaving a silvery trail of mucus behind	Clean up hiding places such as under the rims of pots, under bricks and in the folds of leaves close to the ground. Collect on dewy mornings and drop into salty water. Encircle with a band of sawdust or coarse sand. Snail baits are effective but attractive and poisonous to dogs, so scatter thinly; never pile it in heaps

PEST	SYMPTOM	CONTROL
Thrips	Thrips are tiny insects that grow to about 1 mm ($\frac{1}{32}$ in). They cause a silver streaking or blasted appearance on leaves and flowers. They attack vegetables and ornamentals and are most often seen during hot, dry conditions. The eggs of most thrips are laid within the plant tissues and the nymphs and adults shelter within partly opened blossoms	Thrips are often hard to control as they are protected inside flowers or under leaves for most of their lives. Maldison and dimethoate control thrips. After a 10-day interval a second application of the chemical is recommended
Whiteflies	These sap-sucking, tiny white flies infest the undersides of foliage, causing yellowing and wilting. Sooty mould will also grow on the honeydew they secrete. When disturbed, they rise in clouds, but they quickly resettle. They attack many plants and may be a big problem in greenhouses, especially on ferns and orchids	The parasitic wasp *Encarsia formosa* often keeps the numbers of whiteflies down. If spraying is necessary, use white oil or dimethoate at fortnightly intervals. Commercial, non-poisonous, sticky, whitefly traps are available

Plant diseases and nutrient deficiencies

Plant diseases can be caused by a variety of things, such as bacteria, fungi and viruses, and can be spread by insects and by spores floating through the air, in the soil or in garden debris. Using secateurs, pruning knives and other gardening tools can also spread diseases from one plant to another. Some non-pathogenic diseases may be due to environmental conditions, nutritional deficiencies, chemical injuries and the incorrect use of herbicides or fertilisers.

REMOVE DISEASED PLANTS QUICKLY

Viral diseases are mainly spread by sap-sucking insects. As soon as you detect a virus-infected plant, remove it and add it to an activated compost heap or, if possible, burn any diseased plant material.

COMMON PLANT DISEASES

DISEASE	SYMPTOM	CONTROL
Black spot	This fungal disease affects a number of different plants, notably roses, but also apples, pears, plums and quinces. Usually worst when humidity is high or in tropical and subtropical areas, it causes dark spots on the leaves, which wither and fall prematurely. Extensive defoliation can kill a young plant	Collect all fallen leaves. Cut off and destroy infected leaves. Spraying may also be necessary. A number of fungicides, such as captan, copper oxychloride and mancozeb, control black spot. Ensure good air circulation by not overcrowding plants
Collar rot of citrus (*Phytophthora citrophthora*)	Collar rot usually occurs on the trunk, close to ground level, causing flaky bark and rotting wood. First you may notice gum followed by damp, soft bark. Later this bark may become dry and flake off. Badly affected trees fail to produce new growth and will die. Lemons are most susceptible, but all citrus trees can be affected	Treat by cutting away damaged bark to expose healthy bark and clean wood. Paint with a paste of copper oxychloride to cover the wound
Downy mildews	These mildews are a group of fungi that attack a wide range of vegetables, fruits and ornamentals. Small, yellow, pale green or brownish spots appear on leaves and cause portions of the leaf to dry out and die. In humid conditions, greyish downy patches develop on the undersides of the leaves under each spot	Do not overcrowd plants. Avoid overhead watering. Remove and burn affected leaves. Spray with a fungal spray such as zineb, wetting the undersides too. If plants are regularly infected, your climate is probably too humid for them
Powdery mildews	The powdery mildews are a group of fungi that coat leaves, young shoots, flowers and fruits with a conspicuous white or pale grey, ash-like film. It occurs on many plants, including vegetables and ornamentals. Powdery mildew is more prevalent in warm, humid weather and spreads rapidly via the wind from plant to plant	Where possible, grow mildew-resistant varieties. Remove and destroy affected foliage. Avoid overcrowding and overhead watering. At first sign of infection, spray with wettable sulphur or coat with sulphur dust at regular intervals

Chilli and soap insecticide
You'll need: chillies, soap, grater, sharp knife, chopping board and a spray bottle. Grate the soap (or use soap flakes), then add it to a spray bottle nearly full of water. Add 8 chopped chillies to the bottle. Shake, then spray onto any plant.

DISEASE	SYMPTOM	CONTROL
Root rots	Root rot is caused by fungal diseases. One of the most serious is *Phytophthora cinnamomi*. In hot weather a healthy plant may wilt and die within days. Armillaria root rot spreads through the soil by flat, black cords that resemble shoelaces. Infected trees lose vigour, leaves yellow and branches die back from the tips. Clusters of honey- or gold-coloured toadstools appear at the base of dead trees or from roots remaining in the ground	Remove dead plants, including their roots. Drench the soil with Fongarid or Ridomil; early application can save mildly affected plants. In future, grow plant tolerant species
Rose canker	Dark reddish lesions and cracking bark on rose canes are symptoms of rose canker. They are caused by a fungus that enters through pruning cuts or wounds. Cankers can encircle stems and cut off the flow of nutrients and water to growth further up	Prune off and burn diseased canes. Canker can be spread from plant to plant by infected secateurs. Make a neat slanting cut to just above a good outward-facing bud and disinfect secateurs often
Rusts	Rusts are recognised as small yellow or orange patches or spots, which appear mainly on the upper surfaces of leaves. On the underside, powdery, raised pustules appear under each spot. This disease can cause leaf fall and seriously weaken plants. Most rusts attack a specific plant or a small group of related plants and will not transfer from one host to another, but there are varieties for a broad range of plants	As a preventative measure, it is best to grow rust-resistant varieties of plants whenever possible. As different rusts affect a great many plants, the treatment often differs. Spraying with zineb, sulphur or oxycarboxin is effective against most rust fungi. Clear away fallen leaves to prevent a carry-over of the disease
Sooty mould	This dark fungal growth forms on the sticky secretions (honeydew) produced by sap-sucking insects. It causes black mould to appear on leaves and stems but doesn't harm plants directly. Occasionally sooty mould will appear on shrubs growing under trees or palms infested with pests as their sugary secretions have fallen onto the leaves below	If you remove the primary infection, such as the aphids, scale or psyllids, the sooty mould will disappear. Hose the plant with a strong spray to assist in the clean-up

Index

Page numbers in **bold** print refer to main entries

watering, **237**, 240
window boxes, 234, **240**
converting measurements, **70–1**
cooked meat, preparing, 73
cookies, freezing, 67, 68
cooking fat stains, 92
cooktops, saving energy, 11
cookware *see* grill pans; pots and pans
cooling, saving energy, 12
copper, cleaning, **46**
pans, 39
taps, 35
coppicing, 175
coral jewellery, 124
cordons, 206
corduroy, laundering, 83
Corian surfaces, cleaning
benchtops, 32
sinks, 35
coriander, 244
corks, recycling, 13
cot death, **137**
cots, buying, 136
cottage cheese, freezing, 67
cottage gardens, 181
cotton
ironing, 100
laundering, 84
courtyards, clearing, 169
cow manure, 154
crayon, removing
from carpets, 25
from fabric, 92
from timber floors, 22
from walls, 28
cream
freezing, 67
refrigerating, 65, 69
crop rotation, **203**
cross-contamination, 73
crystal, cleaning, 40
cup measures, converting, 70, **71**
cupboards, child safety, 134, 135
cured meat, refrigerating, 65
curl grubs, 223
curtains
cleaning, **31**
as dust traps, 18
laundering, **96**
cutlery, cleaning, 40
cuttings, **161–3**, 183
cylinder mowers, 216

D

dairy products
freezing, 68
refrigerating, 65, 69
damp
preventing, **20**

walls, 108
dandelions, 249
darning, 119
decks, 177
defrosting freezer, 11
denim, laundering, 84
deodorising
bathroom bins, 51
garbage bins, **37**
shoes, 125
derris, 251
de-scaling
ceramic surfaces, 50
coffee pots, 41
kettle, 42
taps, 51
detergents
dishwashers, 11
laundry, 9
disbudding roses, 194
dishcloths, refreshing, 37
dishwashers
cleaning, 43
saving energy, 11
dishwashing, **37–41**
dishwashing liquid, recipe for, **38**
disinfectant, recipe for, 34
division (plant propagation), **160**, 182
dogs
allergies to, **58**
deterrent, 253
in the garden, 226
urine stains, 59
doonas, cleaning, **19**, **96**
doors
fire safety, 128
maintenance, **113**
rattling, 113
weather strips, 12
double-digging soil, **144–5**
downy mildews, 257
drainage, soil, **144–6**
container gardening, **235**
lawns, **213**
drains
preventing blockages, **107**
unblocking, recipes for, **36**
drawers
child safety, 134
refreshing, 118
dried fruit stains, 92
dried goods, storage, **63**
drill sowing, 159–60
drilling safety, 133
drip-dry fabrics, laundering, 84
driveway, **178**
drought-tolerant plants
grasses, 214
vegetables, **205**
dry-cleaning

doonas and eiderdowns, 96
home kits, 121
reducing costs, 9
dryers, 9, 97, **99**
drying
laundry, **97–9**
shoes, 125
dual-flush toilet, 8
dust
as compost, 147
removing, **18–19**
dust mites, **18–20**, 255
duvets, cleaning, **19**, 96
DVDs, storage and cleaning, 54
dyeing, 119
dyes
natural dyes, 72
removing from ceramic surfaces, 50
testing fabrics for colourfastness, 80
dylan, laundering, 84

E

earthenware, cleaning, 39
earthing up, 206
earthworms, 6, 142, **148–9**, 220
edging lawns, **216–17**
eelworms, **247**, 255
egg cartons, recycling, 13
egg stains, removing from carpets, 25
eggs, refrigerating, 69
eiderdowns, cleaning, **96**
elastinane fibres, laundering, 84
electrical jobs, **105–6**
electrical outlets in sheds, 105
electrical safety, **132**
electrolytic cleaners, **48**
emergency phone numbers, 128, **131**
enamel pans
burnt, 38
cleaning, 39
whitener for, 38
enamel sinks, cleaning, 35
energy saving, **6–13**
air-conditioning, **12**
appliances, **10–11**
garden, 6–7
heating, **12–13**
laundry, **9**
lighting, **11–12**
espalier, 175, 206
essential oils, **60**
eucalyptus oil, 60
evergreens
growing, 182
pruning, 174
exhaust (extractor) fans, 9

Published in 2012 by Murdoch Books Pty Limited

Murdoch Books Australia
Pier 8/9
23 Hickson Road
Millers Point NSW 2000
Phone: +61 (0) 2 8220 2000
Fax: +61 (0) 2 8220 2558
www.murdochbooks.com.au
info@murdochbooks.com.au

Murdoch Books UK Limited
Erico House, 6th Floor
93–99 Upper Richmond Road
Putney, London SW15 2TG
Phone: +44 (0) 20 8785 5995
Fax: +44 (0) 20 8785 5985
www.murdochbooks.co.uk
info@murdochbooks.co.uk

For Corporate Orders & Custom Publishing contact Noel Hammond,
National Business Development Manager Murdoch Books Australia

Creative Director: Deb Brash
Designer: Debra Billson
Project Manager: Kit Carstairs
Editor: Sarah Baker
Production: Joan Beal

National Library of Australia Cataloguing-in-Publication Data
The Home Book
ISBN 9781742665900
Dwellings—Maintenance and repair—Amateurs' manuals.
Dwellings—Remodeling—Amateurs' manuals.
Outdoor living spaces—Decoration—Amateurs' manuals.
Do-it-yourself work.
Dewey Number 643.7

A catalogue record for this book is available from the British Library.

Printed by 1010 Printing International Limited, China.

Readers of this book must ensure that any work or project undertaken complies with
local legislative and approval requirements relevant to their particular circumstances.
Furthermore, this work is necessarily of a general nature and cannot be a substitute for
appropriate professional advice.